HELEN OF TROY AND HER
SHAMELESS PHANTOM

A volume in the series

MYTH AND POETICS

edited by GREGORY NAGY

A list of titles appears at the end of the book.

HELEN OF TROY AND HER SHAMELESS PHANTOM

Norman Austin

CORNELL UNIVERSITY PRESS

ITHACA AND LONDON

First published 1994 by Cornell University Press.

Printed in the United States of America

⊗The paper in this book meets the minimum requirements
of the American National Standard for Information Sciences—
Permanence of Paper for Printed Library Materials, ANSI Z39.48-1984.

Library of Congress Cataloging-in-Publication Data

Austin, Norman.
    Helen of Troy and her shameless phantom / Norman Austin.
        p.   cm. — (Myth and poetics)
    Includes bibliographical references and index.
    ISBN 0-8014-2955-2 (alk. paper)
    1. Greek literature—History and criticism.   2. Helen of Troy (Greek mythology) in literature.   3. Trojan War in literature.   I. Title.   II. Series.
PA3015.R5H372   1994
880.9'351—dc20   93-42418

To My Brothers
Stephen, Paul, Alvyn, and Gordon

πάντα τοι καλά, τοῖσίν
τ' αἰσχρὰ μὴ μέμεικται.

All things are beautiful that are not mixed with disgrace.
—Simonides, fragment 542.39–40 PMG

Contents

Illustrations

Foreword

GREGORY NAGY

Helen of Troy and Her Shameless Phantom, by Norman Austin, is an exquisite point of contact for myth and poetics. And there are two kinds of myth here, two kinds of poetics. On one side, we see Helen of Troy herself, whose story of shameless beauty and betrayal was widely known and accepted by ancient Hellenes as a centerpiece of their primary epic tradition, the *Iliad* and *Odyssey* of Homer. Myth merges here with poetics. On the other side, however, we see—or we think we see—Helen the *Eidōlon* or "Phantom," whose story is that there was no such story. What kind of poetics, then, can we expect to merge with this anti-myth?

The story of Helen the Phantom, like that of Helen of Troy, was widely known by Hellenes, but its mythical authority was by no means universally accepted. Made famous by the *Palinode* or "Recantation" of the lyric poet Stesichorus, the myth behind this story was local—not pan-Hellenic like the myth of Helen that became universalized by the epic poet Homer. The "truth" of this local myth, held to be sacred in various Dorian cultural enclaves, was that Helen, a sort of nature goddess, never in fact left home. Rejecting the pan-Hellenic myth, which insists that Helen shamefully left for Troy with her lover Paris, this myth that we see taking shape in the poetics of Stesichorus' *Palinode* reacts by making Helen of Troy a fleeting image, an *Eidōlon*.

There is another myth that accompanies, like some background musical instrument, the rejectionist poetics of Stesichorus: once upon a time, this lyric poet had sung a different tune, which accords with what the epic poet Homer sang, that Helen did indeed leave for Troy. As punishment, Stesichorus had been struck blind by the outraged goddess Helen. Once the lyric poet sings his recantation, however, he regains his vision. The implicit contrast here between ancient Greek lyric and epic poetry is striking: unlike the lyric poet Stesichorus, the epic poet Homer never recants—and he stays blind forever.

Helen's problem, both for her and for those who sing about her, is that the mythical concept of a nature goddess, whose explicit role requires her to be perpetually transferred from one mortal lover in one place to another mortal lover in another, becomes vulnerable *as a concept* once it gets exposed to narrative traditions belonging to Hellenic cultures that do not even have a cult of Helen as goddess. What is in one culture a sacred *logos* about the *enlèvement* of a goddess, with cataclysmic consequences for the cosmos, can become in another Hellenic culture the scandalous tale about the seduction of a heroine, with disastrous consequences for the political future. The Homeric tradition is synthetic enough to blend both the sacral and the desacralized dimensions of Helen, but in the end it is the image of the profane Helen that prevails. The Stesichorean tradition is also synthetic enough to accept the presence of Helen at Troy, but it insists that the profane Helen is just that, a mere image.

Norman Austin's book captures the complexities of this dual Helen, starting with the conflicting epic and lyric versions of Homer and Stesichorus and tracing the far-reaching consequences of these versions through the poetics of Sappho and the history of Herodotus all the way to the celebrated "Palinode to Eros" by Socrates in Plato's *Phaedrus* and the ultimately revisionist tragedy of Euripides' *Helen*. What Austin says about the latter drama can justly be applied to his own book: it is "a sympathetic treatment of the woman who because of her beauty was fated to be both one with, and separate from, her value as a sign."

Acknowledgments

A book is a long-term project, which owes perhaps as much to the helpers along the way as to the author. This one is no exception, and I take pleasure in thanking those whose encouragement has aided in bringing it to completion.

First, I am grateful for invitations from the Community Lecture Series in Tucson, the 1990 Congress of the International Comparative Literature Association in Tokyo, and the Freshman Seminar at Bard College in 1992 to lecture on aspects of the Helen myth, which provided the occasion for developing the groundwork of this book.

My thanks are due to the University of Arizona for a grant enabling me to study the Oxyrhynchus Papyri in the Bodleian Library, Oxford; to the staff at the Bodleian and the Ashmolean Museum for their assistance in my research; and to the Bodleian Library, the Museum of Fine Arts in Boston, and the Kunsthistorisches Museum in Vienna for permission to reproduce photographs of papyri or vase paintings in their collections.

It gives me pleasure to acknowledge here W. E. H. Cockle, Revel Coles, and P. J. Parsons, who generously shared with me their expertise in papyrological matters. Long will I remember what I learned from these philologists, and my understanding of Sappho *Ode* 16 LP (= P. Oxy. 1231) has been immeasurably improved by discussions with them. They are not to be held responsible for my conclusions regarding Sappho *Ode* 16 LP, but I trust that my treatment of the papyrus will reflect something of their exactitude in the study of the ancient classical texts.

Four friends—Charles Davis, William Mullen, Gregory Nagy, and Bella Zweig—deserve special thanks: Charles Davis, for his patience in listening to my musings on the themes in this book over many months; William Mullen, for his invitation to present the ideas in Chapter 2 to the Freshman Seminar at Bard College, and for taking the time to examine P. Oxy. 1231 with me at the Bodleian Library; Gregory Nagy, for his careful and encouraging reading of the manuscript at various stages in its progress; and Bella Zweig, for sharing with me her unpublished paper on Euripides' *Helen*.

I would be seriously remiss if I omitted from my acknowledgments the staff at the Plaza International Café in Tucson. Chefs, servers, managers—a number of persons at the café contributed significantly to this project, and I take this opportunity to thank them all for their friendly words, for the fiesta of balloons that appeared on one occasion at my hospital bed, and for the cup of coffee that miraculously never ran dry.

HELEN OF TROY AND HER
SHAMELESS PHANTOM

Introduction

On us the gods have set an evil destiny,
That we should be a singer's theme
For generations to come.

—Iliad 6.357–58

So Helen, reflecting on her destiny, understands that her function is not primarily, or even secondarily, to be a woman but to be first and foremost a story. Helen speaks here with two voices. One is her own, the voice of a woman who perceives herself cast as a character and a theme in a drama authored by the gods. The other voice is Homer's, or, more accurately, it is the voice of the epic tradition speaking through the *Iliad*, the tradition beholding itself in and through Helen, and reflecting on its godlike power to create icons and endow them with a life to rival the immortality of the gods. But both voices converge on one unhappy truth. Whether we view the Trojan War through Helen's eyes or through the eyes of the tradition, it is the same story, in which Helen was and remains the major scandal. In her every appearance in the *Iliad*, Helen shows herself conscious of the scandal of her behavior at Troy, and the scandal that she would become in the songs of the epic bards. Thanks to the immortalizing power of epic, Helen would be forever remembered, but in her case shame would be her distinction.

Helen's scandal may be softened in the *Odyssey*—it seems to be almost a thing of the past—but it is never entirely erased. At

I

almost the end of the poem Penelope, in apologizing to Odysseus for her extreme caution in recognizing him, invokes Helen's evil reputation in her own defense (23.218–21): "Not even Argive Helen herself, born of Zeus, would have joined with a foreign man in the bed of love, had she known that the warlike sons of the Achaeans would bring her back to her fatherland." The Trojan War is barely over, but already Helen is encoded in the epic tradition as the woman who was doubly disgraced, first by entering a foreigner's bed, and then when she was forcibly removed from the foreigner's bed and returned to her lawful place in her husband's bed. With so much disgrace to hold before her, Penelope would need to exercise so much the more discretion, lest she be remembered by the epic singers as a second Helen.

Such was the portrait of Helen as it was transmitted through the tradition that culminated in the Homeric poems—the woman who disgraced herself and betrayed her family and people. In the post-Homeric literary tradition Helen is again and again reviled, whether as the treacherous wife or as the libertine who preferred pleasure to honor. Even Sappho, when she thinks of Helen (*Ode* 16 LP), thinks not of the Helen worshiped as a goddess at Sparta but of Homer's Helen, the shameful woman canonized in the epic tradition.

But in the archaic period, when lyric poetry was emerging as a personal reflection on the traditional myths, a curious countermovement arose to rescue Helen's name from the disrepute that had accrued to it from the epic tradition. Stesichorus, the sixth-century poet from Sicily, is the first in our literary record to give voice to this revision of the Helen myth. Sappho, Stesichorus' contemporary, though exonerating Helen on the grounds that beauty and the desire for beauty are absolutes that override all other ethical and social considerations, makes no effort to revise Homer's myth. While Sappho simply accepts the Homeric tradition, Stesichorus proposes a radical revision: Helen herself had never sailed to Troy but had been impersonated there by a ghost or eidolon. Thus at a single stroke Helen would be removed from Troy, the ambiguities would disappear from her character, and the scandal would be erased once and for all.

Our primary source for the story of this revision is Plato, who refers to it in two passages. In the *Phaedrus* (243a–b), Socrates, admitting that he has just slandered Eros by speaking in favor of the lover masquerading as a nonlover, offers to expiate his transgression by performing an ancient form of purification. This purge, he claims, Stesichorus knew, though Homer did not. Stesichorus, as Socrates tells the story, was deprived of his sight for his slander (*kategoria*) of Helen. He did not remain in ignorance, however, as Homer did, Socrates continues, but being "musical" (*mousikos*), he understood the cause of his blindness and composed "the so-called *Palinode*" (that is, his "song re-sung," his re-cantation), whereupon his sight was restored.

Socrates quotes three verses, which have generally been taken to be the prelude to the *Palinode*. These verses give us the first term that is essential for the revision, that Helen never sailed to Troy. We can glean the second essential term from a passage in the *Republic* (586c), where Plato likens the pursuit of false pleasures to the Trojan War as Stesichorus interpreted it, in which the Greeks and the Trojans fought for Helen's eidolon, in ignorance of the truth. The Trojan War, thus revised, became a war not for a woman but for her ghost, shadow, or image—the various meanings contained in the Greek word *eidolon*.

The *Palinode* stands as the first instance in our literary record of a Greek poet attempting a deliberate and wholesale revision of a myth canonized in the epic tradition. Greek myths abounded in variants, and the story that Stesichorus told, of Helen replaced by a ghost of herself at Troy, may have been such a variant, perhaps promulgated by the devotees of Helen's shrine at Therapne in Sparta, where Helen continued to be worshiped as a goddess into the historical period. But whatever his source, Stesichorus presented his version of the Helen myth not as a variant but as a thorough repudiation of the Homeric story. Without Helen at Troy, the *Iliad* and the *Odyssey* would fall to pieces. We can scarcely even imagine an *Iliad* in which the Helen at Troy was only a ghost. The *Odyssey* too would have to be retold. Young Telemachus would listen spellbound as Menelaus described a ten-year war fought for a ghost, and Helen would be a fund of amusing anecdotes about her solitary life in Sparta while her husband made a fool of himself chasing her ghost across the sea. No other revision of a traditional myth presented such a fundamental challenge to the Homeric authority.[1] No other character in Greek myth was ever so radically revised. The only comparable case is the revision proposed by Hesiod in fragment 23a MW, where he explains that Iphimede (= Iphigeneia) had not died at Aulis, because Artemis had spirited her away to become "Artemis of the Road," while substituting an eidolon for her at Aulis. But this revision, while curiously similar to, and perhaps even contemporary with, the *Palinode*, would not have the far-reaching effects on the story that would be required by Helen's eidolon.[2]

The motifs expressed in the anecdote of the *Palinode*, as Socrates tells it, show that honor and shame are the driving forces of this revisionist plot, as they were of the Homeric plot.[3] First, the Helen of this story is not a woman but has been elevated to unambiguous godhood. With Helen now a goddess, we have the motif common in myth of a man insulting the goddess, wittingly or unwittingly, and the goddess taking her immediate and ruthless revenge. A period of alienation then follows between the man and the goddess, but finally a reconciliation is effected. Included in the anecdote is

1. A point well made by Bassi (1993, 60).

2. See West 1985, 130–35, for the suggestion that two eidola in Homer (of Aeneas in the *Iliad*, of Herakles in the *Odyssey*), the eidolon of Helen in Stesichorus, and the eidolon of Iphigeneia in Hesiod may be poetic motifs all introduced into literature at about the same period.

3. Bassi (1993, 52–53) questions whether a moral motive can be imputed to the *Palinode*, and even whether the *Palinode* exonerated Helen. In my view the ethical problem that Helen presented was precisely the issue that led Stesichorus to compose his *Palinode*, though we today can read other, sexual motives at work in the *Palinode*, masked as ethical concerns. I am in full agreement, however, with Bassi's argument that the *Palinode* was unsuccessful in its intention, since Helen's "dyadic presence only reiterates the difficulty of controlling female behavior (especially as it is figured in the female body as the object of sexual desire)" (53).

yet another mythological motif, that of the poet or prophet blinded
for his blasphemy but purged of his errors and restored to sight
after he humbles himself before the angry deity.[4] While our discussion of the motives of the *Palinode* can be only speculative, since so
little of the poem remains, we are on firmer ground when consid-
ering Socrates' (or Plato's) motives. Decency and shame are certainly uppermost in the mind of Socrates when he tells the story of
the *Palinode*. His language is full of religious significance; for him
the story of the *Palinode* is a parable that tells of blasphemy with
regard to sacred matters (*mythologia*), punishment, repentance, and
rehabilitation.[5] Socrates concludes the parable by applying it to
himself: he offers to make amends to Eros, the god whom he has
just blasphemed, by composing his palinode with his head bared,
"and not veiled in shame, as before." The common elements that
link Helen, Stesichorus, and Socrates in this passage in the *Phaedrus*
are Eros, and the shame and punishment that are so integral to the
erotic experience. Socrates, who strongly rejected any scandals
imputed whether to gods or heroes in the traditional myths, here
gives his approval to Stesichorus as a mythmaker to whom it had
been revealed how to erase the scandal from one of the significant
icons of the Greek mythical tradition. Socrates, imitating the refor-
mist poet, would compose a palinode in his turn to erase the scandal that he had falsely imputed to the great deity Eros.

Stesichorus' *Palinode* marks a significant moment in the history
of thought in ancient Greece. For the first time the implicit plot of
the *Iliad* was laid bare, and it was plainly articulated that the Trojan
War was a war fought not for a woman but for a woman's image.
Unfortunately nothing more of the *Palinode* has survived beyond
the three verses quoted by Socrates. The *Palinode* became a celebrated topic while the poem itself slipped into oblivion. A Helen
story that removed Helen from Troy, while making for a memor-

---

4. This motif, of the blinding of the poet and the restoration of his sight, has
received much attention in recent years; see Bassi 1993, 54, for a brief discussion of
the scholarship.

5. The nature of Socrates' recantation in the *Phaedrus* has itself become a topic of
major interest recently; see Svenbro 1988, 222–38; Bassi 1993, 67, for an interesting discussion and references to previous scholarship.

able anecdote, could not prevail against the story that had been canonized in the Homeric tradition. Helen was pleased with the poet's revision, so we may infer from the fact that Stesichorus was cured of his blindness, but her pleasure and her powerful intervention in composing the new plot could not erase the old plot that the Greeks had inherited from the Homeric tradition.[6]

Stesichorus proposed a reading of the Helen myth which, like many progressive ideas, was both of its time and ahead of its time. If Stesichorus was the first poet to read the Trojan War explicitly as a war over an image, the general question of images was a topic much in the air in the cities of archaic Greece. Xenophanes, the Ionian philosopher whom tradition curiously links to the brother of Stesichorus, was propounding the more general theory that all the gods of traditional myth were but images composed by the human mind, self-made and self-reflecting icons that humans then venerate as their gods.

But timely as the *Palinode* was, it was still too modernist even for its modernist age. On one hand, as a simple repudiation of the Homeric myth, it was doomed to failure, since the ghost of Helen could never replace "Helen of Troy." On the other hand, from another angle the *Palinode* was a remarkable elucidation of the *Iliad*. That Plato would twice refer to the *Palinode* suggests that he found it philosophically interesting. The whole of Socrates' life could be read as a palinode in its own way, since Socrates, like Stesichorus, dedicated himself to erasing the blemishes falsely attributed to the gods and to clarifying the distinction between the name and the person, Being and the semblance of Being. But if Socrates found the *Palinode* a satisfying or challenging reading of the Trojan War, it was no doubt difficult for most of his contemporaries to see its premise as anything more than an exercise in ingenuity. However

6. On the problem of a revisionist text competing against the authorized text, see Bassi 1993, 51: "Texts that overtly deny other texts . . . are ambivalently situated within the tradition they inhabit and help to define." See also p. 58: in purporting to negate the Homeric Helen, the *Palinode* in effect "creates another Helen (or, more precisely, a look-alike Helen) to take the place of the old and, in doing so, finances its own subversion."

serious his intentions in composing the *Palinode* as a replacement for the Homeric story of the Trojan War, Stesichorus succeeded only in adding a curious marginal note to the canonical text.

Yet, in dichotomizing the Homeric Helen neatly into her real and her imaginary forms, Stesichorus had made explicit the oscillation around Helen's name both in Homer and in the post-Homeric literary tradition. Thus though the story of the phantom Helen could never enjoy anything more than a codependent existence, as a curious addendum to the Homeric myth, it continued to exercise its own shadowy influence on the Helen myth and to develop in the course of time an interesting history of its own.

Herodotus makes no reference to the eidolon story, but, like Stesichorus, he too claims to have discovered the true account of the Trojan War, and his version, too, flatly contradicts the Homeric story in one important respect, namely, Helen. His truth does not rely on poetic inspiration, as in the case of Stesichorus; he claims to have learned it in Egypt, from priests at the pharaoh's shrine in Memphis. In this Egyptian story, so Herodotus claims, Paris had indeed abducted Helen from Sparta, but he was blown off course en route to Troy and was forced to make a landing in Egypt. There the pharaoh, discovering Paris' crime, detained Helen and sent Paris on his way despoiled of his prize. The Greeks, unaware that Helen was not at Troy but was being held in Egypt, waged their war against Troy and discovered the truth only after they had sacked the city.

This Helen story attributed to Egyptian priests is certainly at odds with the revision that Stesichorus had proposed, insofar as we can infer the gist of the *Palinode* from Plato's two brief allusions. A story that had Helen being carried off by Paris, even if only as far as Egypt, would hardly deserve to be called a song resung.[7] Yet though the two stories suggest two different revisions, perhaps created to serve quite different ends, we cannot but suspect that Her-

---

7. Cf. Bassi (1993, 56–57), who accepts the very late testimony of P. Oxy. 2506 (= Stesichorus, frag. 193 PMG), which asserts that Stesichorus had included in his *Palinode* a story of Helen removed from Sparta to Egypt.

odotus arrived in Memphis already knowing an eccentric version
of the Trojan War, in which Helen had never reached Troy. The
true story of the Trojan War had become a topic of speculative
debate. While the phantom Helen might be inappropriate in the
Egyptian story, Herodotus and Stesichorus are closer than they
might seem at first glance, since Stesichorus imputes the Trojan
War to a false image, and Herodotus imputes it to a misperception.
And on one point at least Stesichorus and Herodotus are in full
agreement, that the true story requires Helen to be absent from the
scene.

After Stesichorus, Helen's eidolon first reappears explicitly in
Euripides. In several of his plays Euripides presents the traditional
Helen, the woman of infamy. In the *Trojan Women*, in addition to
portraying the faults traditionally ascribed to her—infidelity and
promiscuity—Euripides has made Helen into a sophist of the
cheapest sort. Yet this infamous Helen is curiously shadowed by
the phantom that Stesichorus had introduced into the myth. In
Euripides' *Orestes*, where Helen is painted in the most pejorative
light, it unexpectedly transpires that Orestes, thinking to kill
Helen, kills instead only her simulacrum, which Apollo had substituted for Helen at the last minute (lines 1629–42). Helen herself
Apollo spirited into the Ether so that she might share in her brothers' function as the protector of sailors. Why Euripides would
begin the play with the disgraced Helen of the epic tradition and
then in the final act revise the very ground of the play by removing
this Helen into the Ether or why he would confuse the strategy of
the *Palinode* by introducing the eidolon into the plot only after
Helen had done her damage at Troy are puzzles I have not attempted to solve in this work.

But then, at the very end of his career, Euripides made a complete volte-face and composed his own palinode to the Helen
whom he had so often vilified in his earlier career. In 412/411
B.C.E. he produced his *Helen*, a play in which he takes up the theme
of the eidolon, to dramatize two confrontations—the one in the
mind of Menelaus between the true Helen and her fickle double,

and the other between Helen herself and the image of her for which the Greeks and Trojans fought at Troy. Since Stesichorus' *Palinode* has disappeared, Euripides' *Helen* is the only surviving treatment of the phantom-Helen theme from antiquity. It is also the only attempt by an ancient poet to enter imaginatively into the problems that the *Palinode* had unwittingly introduced into the myth by splitting Helen into her self and her image. Specifically, Euripides' *Helen* is a valiant, albeit flawed, attempt to reconcile two Helens— the Helen of the *Iliad* and the Helen of the *Palinode*.

The most interesting aspect of the play is that Euripides has made Helen the protagonist, a woman compelled to confront her own ontological ambiguity, represented by the eidolon that impersonated her at Troy and wielded so much more power than Helen could ever hope to wield, though the eidolon was but a ghost, while Helen was the daughter of Zeus. Helen's ontological ambiguity was a theme worthy of the intellectual ambitions of fifth-century Greece. Across the Greek world the disjunction between essence and phenomena was the chief topic of conversation among the philosophers and mathematicians, and one of the principal themes of Athenian tragedy. What plot more topical in late fifth-century Athens than the story of a woman divided into her real and her imaginary selves? What figure of traditional myth offered greater scope for tragedy than a Helen who was innocent in her very being confronting the damage done to herself, to Greece, and to Troy by the confusions wrought by her image and in her name?

Yet, as a tragedy, Euripides' *Helen* could be judged a failure. Modern commentators generally read it as a comedy or at best a tragicomedy. The impediment to a tragic treatment was that a Helen who was truly innocent on all counts could scarcely stand as a persuasive protagonist on the tragic stage. Inevitably, a story of the Trojan War in which Helen was excused from the plot but happily reunited with her husband after the plot was over would easily slide into a romantic comedy. Yet Euripides' *Helen* remains significant not only as a document to the intellectual currents of late fifth-century Athens but as a sympathetic treatment of the woman who because of her beauty was fated to be both one with and separate from her value as sign. If the problematic relations between the real and the imaginary Helens resisted a satisfactory solution, Euripides at least perceived something of their tragic consequences on both the personal and the collective level.

The *Palinode* may have failed to redeem Helen's honor, but its introduction of the eidolon into the Helen story succeeded at least in revealing the ontological ambiguity that is the basis of the Homeric portrait of Helen.[8] In the *Iliad* Helen is a woman—a woman of superlative beauty but a woman nevertheless. Yet she is privileged above all other women. Her privilege is hinted at in the recurrent formula for Helen, "the daughter of Zeus," and it is spelled out more plainly in book 3, when Aphrodite threatens to withdraw her special favor if Helen persists in her insubordination. But the full nature of Helen's privilege is not revealed until the *Odyssey*, where we find first that Helen suffered no harm at all after the fall of Troy for her complicity, real or imagined, in the war, and then that Menelaus will be exempt from death and transferred to the Islands of the Blest as his privilege for being Helen's husband. Taken together, the *Iliad* and the *Odyssey* represent a complicated Helen who is both a woman at the mercy of human desires and constraints, and someone more than human, a daughter of Zeus who escapes human constraints altogether, including the nemesis that attends on transgressions of the ethical codes.

The *Palinode*'s project, to remove the dishonor from the traditional story by ascribing all Helen's ambiguity to her simulacrum, far from resolving Helen's ambivalences, had the unwitting effect of making Helen into a ghost of her own ghost, the negative of a negative.[9] All that could be said of this revised Helen was that she

8. For the extensive implications of this eidolon, as a mimetic, second Helen, see Zeitlin 1981, 203; Bassi 1993, 62–64.

9. On this point, cf. Wohl (1993, 34), who, borrowing the suggestion made by Loraux vis-à-vis Pandora, writes of Helen as "la femme: une copie de soi-même" ("woman: a copy of herself"). Cf. Zeitlin 1981, 202: "For as fictive *eidolon*, Stesichorus' Helen acquires the capacity to impersonate herself." Cf. also Bassi 1993, 64 n. 28: "The Palinode is clearly drawing upon a tradition which figures women

was not that troublesome ghost who had caused the grief at Troy.
If it was asked what this Helen had done while her ghost played at
Troy, the answer was "nothing," since the only reason for this
Helen's being was to be not–Helen of Troy.

To pursue this confusion further, as it is manifested in the Helen
myth, I have borrowed Jacques Lacan's figure, which I used also in
my *Meaning and Being in Myth*, of two overlapping circles, one of
which Lacan labels "Meaning/the Signifier," and the other "Be-
ing/the Subject."[10] For "Meaning" we might prefer to substitute
the term "Significance." The overlap of the circles Lacan marks as
an eclipse, in fact a double eclipse, since each circle eclipses the
other: Meaning (Significance) eclipses Being, as Being eclipses
Meaning. Language, the system of interlocking codes that determine our place and value in the social structure, can be at most only
a map, but a map is only an approximate topographical diagram.
Thus the Signifier, while purporting to enclose all value and significance within its domain, must inevitably point to something beyond itself, which in Lacan's diagram is the Subject. But the Subject is to be found only in the circle of Being. When we look there,
however, the Subject is not to be found, since the only indications
and clues that the Subject exists are to be found in the circle of the
Signifier, which is excluded from Being. In *Meaning and Being in
Myth* I cited the biblical account of the Tower of Babel as the
ancient parable that illustrates the paradox.[11]

The idea that in our language-dominated human culture Meaning and Being, though mutually exclusive terms, require each other for their existence is at the heart of the *Iliad*. It is almost incomprehensible to Achilles to have Being without significance. He may
ponder the intrinsic value of life deprived of honor when he is
excluded from the battlefield, but the call to achieve significance is

---

as imitations and substitutes and therefore as objects of incomplete and elusive
reference." We should note that already in the *Odyssey*, Helen is "mistress of
mimesis," as Zeitlin puts it (204).
10. Lacan 1978, 211.
11. Austin 1990, 20.

far more numinous than life without significance to a young warrior educated, as Achilles was, to be always "the best." As the *Iliad*
unfolds, Achilles grows to comprehend the tragedy that he can
achieve his significance (in Homer, his *kleos aphthiton*, "imperishable glory") only by sacrificing his very being. Yet, in sacrificing
his being for honor, Achilles discovers that he has also irreparably
damaged his honor. To be transformed into an imperishable theme
in epic song is the best compromise that Achilles can hope for as his
prize for sacrificing both his honor and his life.

In Helen's case the terms are reversed. She enjoys an amazing
degree of freedom from the constraints that bind other humans.
She is not inhibited by the social code, nor will she suffer any serious retribution for her transgressions of that code, including the
final retribution, death. This is to graze the very border of Being.
But the price for this privilege is that Helen must forgo honor.
Helen is "terribly like the deathless goddesses," the old men mur-
mur when they see her at the city wall. From their perspective she
enjoys the privileges that are available only to those who dwell in
the circle of Being, where Meaning neither inhibits action nor
imposes serious consequences.

Of course the case is more complex. Helen is strangely both a
goddess and a human at the same time and therefore occupies both
circles, of Meaning and Being. A woman who has no reason to fear
either nemesis or death is not a human but a god. Yet this same
person is very much a human in her function as an object of contention among men, as other women are, a prisoner to the social
order. As a goddess Helen transcends shame, yet as a woman she is
acutely conscious of her function, to be the icon of shame. To
the old men gazing on Helen at the city walls, Helen is all but the
Subject itself. But alas, for all her prerogatives, Helen is not the
Subject but a signifier, one of the most numinous perhaps but still
only a signifier, of the Subject.

This book does not pretend to be an exhaustive treatment of the
whole Helen myth in ancient Greek art and literature but focuses
more narrowly on the eidolon theme, since the eidolon, whether

taken as a revision or as an intriguing interpretation of the traditional myth, is an uncanny expression of the ambivalences contin-
uously at work in the construction of the Helen myth. Even so, I
have omitted the two treatments of theme in the postclassical
period—in Lycophron's *Alexandra* and in the *Trojan Oration* of Dio
Chrysostom—except for brief allusions. These two treatments,
the one from the Hellenistic period and the other from the Greco-
Roman period, are both Alexandrian in their outlook (their authors
resided in, or were familiar with, Alexandria), and as such they are
interesting footnotes to the history of the *Palinode* of Stesichorus,
though the emotional force that generated the *Palinode* was by their
time largely spent.

To keep to the eidolon theme, I have omitted any consideration
of Aeschylus' representation of Helen in the *Agamemnon*, or her
portrait in the lyric poets, except for Sappho and Stesichorus. Similarly, though Euripides represents Helen in several of his plays and
employs the eidolon as a dramatic device in two, I have restricted
my discussion to the *Helen*, where Helen's ghost is, if not the
protagonist, certainly the principal metaphor of the play. In the
fifth century we find Helen's rehabilitation emerging also as an
oratorical theme, but I have excluded the encomia of Helen composed by the two Attic orators Gorgias and Isocrates, since theirs
was a different strategy. They accepted the traditional Helen as
Homer had represented her, but then presented her case as if they
were her counsel defending her in a court of law. These encomia
have been interpreted as bravura legal performances, demonstrating the orators' skill at making the worse cause appear the better,
but a full discussion of this method of rehabilitating Helen deserves
separate treatment.

Initially, I had thought to trace Helen's eidolon from its first
reported appearance in Stesichorus down to the modern period, to
compare the ancient treatments of the theme with the treatment in
both Marlowe's and Goethe's *Faust*, then in the 1926 opera by
Richard Strauss and Hugo von Hofmannsthal, *Die ägyptische
Helena*, and finally in H.D.'s *Helen in Egypt*, published in 1960. But

the complexity of the theme convinced me that the modern poets should be examined separately, since they bring considerations peculiar to their own times.

To do justice to Goethe's use of Helen's eidolon in *Faust*, we would need to consider at some length Helen's role in the poem, whether as woman, ghost, or idol. We would then need to set this theme within the broader framework of the relations between idealism and realism in late eighteenth-century philosophy, and the relations between Hellas and classicism as it was being defined in Goethe's mind. To appreciate what Strauss and Hofmannsthal brought to the theme in *Die ägyptische Helena*, we would need to speak first of Goethe's towering influence on German lyric, and then of the modernist movement of the late nineteenth and twentieth centuries, so strongly influenced by symbolism and psychoanalysis. H.D.'s *Helen in Egypt* is sui generis, being the first instance since Sappho in which a woman poet undertakes to give us her reading of the Helen myth. Here Helen has become a hieroglyph, but at the same time she is the priestess of the hieroglyph, who must read its meanings both for herself and for others. But H.D.'s complex reading of the ancient Helen myth, in which she struggles to find the unifying hieroglyph that will represent the multitudinous Helen portraits of antiquity, deserves more than to be an addendum to the present work.

The concerns that the modern poets bring to the theme can certainly be found in the ancient treatments. Realism and idealism, the Signifier and the Subject, the woman and the woman-as-sign—these themes, which seem peculiarly modern, can all be traced in ancient Greek thought as early as Homer. What separates the Greek treatments from the modern uses of the theme is the simple problem of Hellenic honor. From Homer to Euripides, wherever Helen's name is introduced into the discourse, honor is the issue, whether it be her honor or the honor of Hellas or, more often, both. If Helen had brought disgrace on herself by preferring Paris to Menelaus, this was also a disgrace for Hellas. True, Paris paid dearly for his transgression, and Helen was recovered from the foreigner's bed and set back in her lawful marriage bed, yet questions remained that reflected unfavorably on Greek womanhood, but even more on Greek manhood. If Hellas, "the fatherland," as the Greeks called it, had recovered its manhood by wiping Troy from the face of the earth, it was still a question whether Menelaus had been something less than a man to allow Paris or Helen, or the two of them together, to nullify his marriage bed. Was there not also something womanish about the flower of Hellas hurling itself to a precipitous death on foreign soil for a woman of dubious virtue? Helen might be the very paragon of beauty, but was it manly to be so seduced by beauty?

In Homer we can see the code of honor shaping Helen's role in two distinct ways. In the *Iliad* it determines her function, to be the sign for which men fight, while in the *Odyssey* it dictates that in the end Helen's transgressions will be forgiven and Helen will be elevated to godhood. If it were possible to distinguish in Homer between the primary text ("Homer") and the secondary texts (post-Homeric "emendations"), we might be tempted to argue that Helen's apotheosis, which is implied, though not explicitly stated, in the *Odyssey*, is the first major revision of the Iliadic Helen, since it is the element needed to erase the dishonor that still adheres to the story when the *Iliad* closes.

The Homeric poems omit any reference to Helen's earthly father, Tyndareus; instead, she is invariably "the daughter of Zeus." This omission may be a calculated strategy on the part of the epic tradition to play down the promiscuity that figures in the Helen myth. By excluding Tyndareus from the text, the epic quietly disengages itself from some of the greater embarrassments of the Helen myth, which the name of Tyndareus invariably invokes. Other poets lose no chance to remark that Tyndareus was singularly unfortunate, cursed even, to be the father of singularly promiscuous daughters—Helen and Klytaimestra being the two most memorable. With Tyndareus excluded, the question of Helen's promiscuity was not eliminated, but it was somewhat muted, thus easing the way for Helen's later apotheosis. If Helen was the daughter not of a human father but of Zeus, her promiscuity could be viewed in a more favorable light. Her eventual apotheosis would be the inevitable conclusion of the tale, since that would mean her return to her rightful place, as the obedient daughter of the celestial father. If, after the fall of Troy, Helen was reinstated first as the lawful wife of Menelaus, and then as the obedient daughter of Zeus, the blood spilled at Troy in the name of Hellenic honor would be redeemed.

But even apotheosis was inadequate to settle the issue. Helen's shame was not to be canceled by simply removing her husband to the Islands of the Blest. Stesichorus proposed the more radical solution, to erase Helen of Troy from the story altogether and replace her with the goddess who had never lapsed from her pristine purity.[12] Yet the curious and contradictory history that his *Palinode* engendered reveals that even removing Helen from Troy did not so much settle the issue as generate new questions.

The confusion that arises when Helen's honor or shame is the issue has left uncanny traces of itself in several manuscripts, some of them primary literary works and others commentaries of late antiquity that allude to the *Palinode*. One of the most remarkable instances where textual confusion mirrors the confusion in the story is to be found in the final strophe of the Great Mother ode in Euripides' *Helen*. I address this passage at greater length in Chapter 6, on Euripides. Suffice here to say that the two Helens, the real and the imaginary, which the whole purpose of the *Helen* is to keep

---

12. Bassi (1993, 53) observes that the *Palinode* did not achieve its objective: Helen "is not chastened." I would distinguish here between the overt and the covert motives, however speculative our discussion must remain. The two can be described in terms of the two contradictory meanings in our English verb "to chasten." The explicit, public motive of the *Palinode* was surely to redeem the honor of Hellas by making Helen chaste again, to remake the woman of shame into the immaculate, virginal goddess. This motive can be traced very clearly through Euripides' *Helen*. It would be realized by the simple strategy of removing Helen from Troy; as the story was erased, the shame would disappear with it. But if the covert motive of the *Palinode* was to chasten Helen—that is, to discipline the woman who had disgraced Hellas by her behavior at Troy—this motive was doomed to failure for all the reasons that Bassi discusses.

separate, have fallen into confusion, and the text has followed suit. The *Helen* is Euripides' palinode to Helen, ironic perhaps but a palinode nevertheless, which adopts the strategy proposed by Stesichorus, to render the real Helen guiltless and ascribe all guilt and shame to her ghost. But here, in the final strophe of the Great Mother ode, as the play moves to its finale, we encounter some gibberish to the effect that Helen, though she had never set foot in Troy or betrayed her husband's bed, was guilty of an offense against the Great Mother. What could her offense have been?

Someone, whether Euripides himself or, as I would prefer to think, an interpolator, recognized that a blameless Helen was an oxymoron. An offense must have been committed, not by the flimsy ghost but by Helen herself, if Helen was to be a persuasive protagonist on the tragic stage. The strophe does its best to strike a compromise. Those who needed crime and punishment in their story could be satisfied that Helen had indeed committed an offense, and punishment indeed had been exacted. Those who balked at the idea of Helen's guilt and punishment could be relieved that she was not so much punished as reprimanded, but then forgiven, and welcomed back into the radiant circle of the Great Mother. With the patriarchy and the matriarchy yoked here in uneasy alliance, we should not be surprised if the strophe caves in and leaves us treading the empty air.

To set the revisionist myth within its context, I have begun this work with a discussion of the locus classicus for the traditional Helen portrait—the third book of the *Iliad*, where Helen's disgrace is definitively articulated. I have followed this discussion with a chapter on Sappho's *Ode* 16 LP, where Helen is named, though Sappho does not belong among those who thought it necessary to revise the traditional Helen story. I have included a discussion of Sappho's Helen for several reasons.

First, if *Ode* 16 is in fact an ode of Sappho's, as we have good reason to believe, it is one of the earliest commentaries on Homer which have survived from ancient Greece. In invoking Helen as the judge of the beauty contest that stands as the central metaphor of

the poem, Sappho takes us directly back to the *Iliad*, and specifically to book 3, where Helen is at the center of the conflict between
beauty and ugliness, honor and shame. Although Sappho makes
no explicit reference to the question of Helen's shame and passes
no judgment on Helen's choice of Paris over Menelaus, even to allude
to the infamous triangle—Menelaus, Helen, Paris—is to raise questions of honor and shame. In my view the argument of Sappho's
Ode 16 derives its emotional force from the field of shame, which
was invariably activated by the merest reference to Helen of Troy.

An archaic Greek poet's reading of the *Iliad* is intrinsically interesting, and even more interesting when the poet is Sappho, and her
topic is the memorable Helen of the *Iliad*. But my final reason for
including Sappho's "Anaktoria" ode is that the papyrus fragment
on which the ode appears offers another illustration of the uncanny
way in which ancient texts dissolve when Helen's name is
broached. In this case there is no question of an interpolation or of
editors garbling the text. The culprit is time itself, which has torn
the papyrus exactly where Helen's name appears, leaving even her
name incomplete and adrift, surrounded by empty spaces on either
side. The reconstructions of the sentence attempted by modern
scholars give remarkable testimony to the ambivalence that continues to affect attitudes toward Helen even in the modern period,
when the topic is either her beauty or her behavior. The two readings proposed of the ragged sentence, which hinge on the problematics involved in such simple Greek terms as *ariston* (the best)
and *kalliston* (the most beautiful), remind us that even today the
question of Helen's guilt or shame has not been laid to rest.

After my discussion of Sappho, I consider Helen as she is represented in the *Odyssey*. While this Helen is certainly the same person
that we see in the *Iliad*, the *Odyssey* shifts the emphasis so as to
suggest that the process of revision that later led Stesichorus to
invoke the eidolon had already begun. The Helen of the *Iliad* is
already something of a ghost, since she understands herself to be
simply a persona in a parable authored by the gods, but her ghostly
aspects are given greater prominence in the *Odyssey*. Living in

absolute domestic rectitude, Helen seems already to dwell in a realm that is beyond our world and closer to the world of the gods. Sparta, as portrayed in the *Odyssey*, bears resemblances to the underworld, as scholars have remarked, and Helen bears resemblances to Persephone.[13] The drug (*pharmakon nēpenthes*) that Helen drops into the wine at Sparta has the power to purge the past of all its negative emotions—shame, guilt, fear, hatred.

But, even more important, when Menelaus informs Telemachus that his reward for being Helen's husband is that he will be transported to the Islands of the Blest, the result is to insinuate into the world of the epic an escape from human destiny that is never hinted at in the *Iliad*. The *Iliad* removes the obviously divine aspects from Helen's character, leaving only subliminal aspects, as in her formula "the daughter of Zeus," but the *Odyssey* seems to reverse the process and reinvests Helen with the divinity that would no doubt be dramatically inappropriate in the context of the *Iliad*. At the same time, however, the *Odyssey* gives us the domesticated Helen, as a foil to the undomesticated Helen of the *Iliad*. Her magical powers are still at her beck and call, but they have been tamed. No longer threatening either to her husband or to the Greeks, they can even be turned to benevolent ends, the most benevolent being the gift of immortality that Menelaus will enjoy for being Helen's husband.

In the ensuing chapters, on Stesichorus, Herodotus, and Euripides, I focus specifically on the revisionism of the archaic and classical periods, when the eidolon was introduced into the Helen myth. Since Herodotus does not allude to the eidolon, however, it would be more accurate to say that although the eidolon was an important element in the ancient revision of the Helen myth, the most significant element was simply the removal of Helen from the story.

To trace a single theme through the literature of several centuries is to risk doing injustice to the individual authors, particularly

13. See Anderson 1958.

when the authors are of the stature of those treated in the present work, and to the large body of scholarship on those authors. The story of the Trojan War which Herodotus attributes to Egyptian priests, for example, raises questions regarding his use (or invention) of foreign sources and his attitude toward myth, history, and religion. Similarly, Euripides' use of the eidolon theme in his *Helen* invites us to ponder the portrait of Helen in his various plays. That portrait in turn is part of a larger context, which includes his attitudes not only toward myth and religion, as in the case of Herodotus, but more particularly toward women. Or again, to understand Helen's place in the Homeric poems requires a full discussion of each poem taken as a whole. But to keep within certain bounds, I have restricted my discussion to what seemed most germane either to the specific question of Helen's shame or to the vagaries of the eidolon theme as it appears and disappears in antiquity.

I should note here, however, three essays that appeared in *Arethusa* 26 (1993) after this book was substantially complete—Ann Suter's contribution on Paris and Dionysus, Victoria J. Wohl's on sexual ideology in the *Odyssey*, and Karen Bassi's on the *Palinode* of Stesichorus. All three are germane, and I regret that I have not been able to refer to them as fully as they deserve. In particular, I acknowledge the significance of Bassi's study of the *Palinode*. Bassi and I may disagree on particulars as to what was or was not included in the *Palinode*, but these points will probably always remain conjectural. On essentials we are in agreement, regarding both the paternalistic attitude toward Helen embodied in the *Palinode* and the reasons why such a revision could not expect to supplant the traditional Homeric story. I trust that this work will support Bassi's arguments by providing a larger context of the problematic history of the eidolon from its first brief references in Plato and Isocrates to the confused discussions of the topic in the commentaries of late antiquity. Helen's eidolon was a lively topic in antiquity, and the several artistic and poetic treatments of the theme in this century indicate that it is as alive today as it was two thousand years ago.

PART I

THE TRADITIONAL HELEN

CHAPTER I

The Helen of the *Iliad*

Helen of Troy is no doubt the most famous woman in European history after the Virgin Mary, and certainly the most fascinating. The story reverberates through the ages, and mysterious Helen is still a poet's theme, appearing most recently in Derek Walcott's *Omeros*. Such long-enduring fame raises the inevitable question, Was there a real Helen of Troy? Put another way, Was Helen no more than a story?

Time was when the Trojan War was taken to be no more than a story, richly embroidered by folk imagination, but archaeology has taught us caution. Troy has been uncovered, several Troys in fact, layer upon layer, and Mycenae too. Treasures enough have been found in both citadels to make King Agamemnon and King Priam at least plausible historical figures. But Helen? Here scholars balk. Modernists, we smile at the fables of the ancients, and when they talk of thrones and diadems we see economics.

Perhaps a devastating war was fought in the late Bronze Age between the Myceneans and the Trojans for economic motives. No one, reading Agamemnon's majestic offer of goods and property, including his own daughter, to Achilles in *Iliad* 9, could miss the economics of the Trojan War. Homer's Greeks and Trojans loved their commodities with a passion and required ever new territory, it seems, to preserve and enlarge their treasuries. The new technology, which required ore and mines, and shipping lanes to those mines, had the whole Mediterranean in thrall.

But above economics Homer places a more seductive cause—the quest for beauty. Beauty is among the greatest, if not the greatest, of all the archetypes in Homer's pantheon. Whoever possessed beauty in Homeric society would possess the world, so high was the value placed on beauty. Aphrodite may be wounded by a mere man (in *Iliad* 5) or abused by Hera and Athena for her soft, womanish ways, but we should not be misled by such temporary insults to her dignity. Hers was the power to undo even the political arrangements of Olympus (as in *Iliad* 14, when Hera borrows Aphrodite's charms to divert the will of Zeus). Beauty in the *Iliad*, as in Plato's cosmology, is the Subject to which every signifier turns, like the compass point to its magnetic pole.[1]

On one side Homer places the other commodities for which men fight—horses, bronze, chariots, breastplates, greaves, silver, gold, slaves male and female. But Helen belongs in an economic category of her own. If we take the Helen tradition as a whole, we see that Helen, though often captured, is not, never was, and never will be a slave. Of all the women in the *Iliad*, Helen alone escapes the slavery in store for the others—Chryseis, Briseis, Andromache, Hecuba, the seven beautiful and gifted women of Lesbos whom Agamemnon gives to Achilles in book 19—the list is almost endless. Helen is conspicuously different.

To heighten the difference even further, Helen, with nothing more to lose but her reputation, will be responsible, or held responsible at least, for the slavery that befalls the other women. They will be reduced to the level of commodities "through" or "because of" Helen, while Helen herself remains a free woman. Homer's formula for Helen, "the daughter of Zeus," reminds us that Helen transcends economic categories. Like Aphrodite,

---

1. For the place of beauty in the archaic pantheon, cf. Hesiod (*Theogony* 120), who calls Eros "the most beautiful [*kallistos*] among the deathless gods." Cf. also Isocrates *Encomium on Helen* 54: Helen "possessed the greatest share of beauty [*kallos*], which of *things that exist* is the most venerated, most honored, and most godly." "Things that exist" (*ta onta*) was, in Isocrates' day, the conventional philosophical term for Being itself. Beauty for Isocrates is next to Being, if not Being itself.

Helen's Olympian archetype, Helen transcends categories altogether. Beauty writes its own laws. Helen, like Aphrodite, may be wounded but never bought, sold, or killed.

Could Homer's uncouth pirates have waged war for beauty? We smile at the romanticism. The tribal imagination spins complex social history, which today is generally read as the politics of acquisition and dominance, into romance—the "Rape of Helen," the "Judgment of Paris," the "House of Atreus," the "Trojan War." The Homerist, asked to sift through the romance for "the real Helen," responds with the scholar's shrug. The archaeologist, on one hand, will settle for nothing less than material proof, and no spade has yet uncovered Helen's sandal.[2] On the other hand, the literary critic needs no facts. No historical documents or artifacts will ever diminish Homer's Helen or improve her. What has art to do with history? Beauty is truth; that is all we need to know.

But while Homerists of whatever stripe may dismiss the real Helen as irrelevant, whether for history or for literature, the story goes on, retold from generation to generation, and curious listeners continue to ask, "Was there ever a real Helen?" The question may be naive, yet in its innocence it shows a surer instinct for Homer's art than the scholar who brackets the question to attend to questions of graver import. The question is, in fact, central to Homer's *Iliad*, and we can still hear its echo in the *Odyssey*. Whoever asks the question is Homer's true reader, responding to the enigma that Homer himself named "Helen, daughter of Zeus."

When we ponder "the real Helen," we venture beyond the simple historical question that might be asked of Homer's other characters.[3] We have no difficulty imagining an overbearing, truculent king like Agamemnon, a garrulous old soldier like Nestor, a

2. "Helen's Sandal" was a shrine in Sparta where the sandal that Helen lost in her flight from Sparta was venerated; see Roscher, 1: 1950. But apparently at Iapygia in southern Italy there was another shrine where other sandals of Helen's were venerated: cf. the story told by Lycophron (*Alexandra* 852–55) of Menelaus dedicating a krater, his shield, and Helen's fur-lined slippers at Iapygia when he was roaming the Mediterranean in search of the lost Helen after the fall of Troy.

3. A point made by Bassi (1993, 60).

vain, young hotspur of the royal house like Paris. But Helen stands
on another ontological plane. Was she goddess or human? Was she
seduced by Paris or raped? Was she a libertine or the victim of
society? Helen will never die for her honor, as Achilles will, and a
host of others, including Agamemnon, Patroklos, and Hector.
Helen will lose neither life nor honor; instead, she will be given,
according to the syntax peculiar to the Homeric epic, immortality
in return for having no honor to lose. That is to be her sign for
eternity: to be the woman with no shame.

Disgraced in life, Helen is spared punishment, and even death,
which is the common fate of all other women, whether virtuous or
not. Instead, Helen is fated to spend eternity in a state of grace, or
as close to grace as human impersonations of the gods can reach. In
the version given to us in the *Odyssey* (4.561–69), Menelaus will be
transported to the Islands of the Blest, where we may infer that he
and Helen will be united for all eternity, though other stories outside the epic suggested that if Menelaus were rewarded with a place
in Elysium, Helen herself would be advanced even higher, to
the very skies. Yet other stories arose, which told of Helen and
Achilles as lovers after death, two eidola—icons, images, shadows
—consummating their secret, spiritual union on Leuke, the island
in the Black Sea where Achilles was honored in cult after his
death.[4] Even in death Helen's state was undecided—whether she

---

4. Pausanias 3.19.11. The distinction between local cult traditions and the tradition of the epic, which Nagy emphasizes (1979, 1990b), is extremely significant in
any treatment of Helen in ancient myth. While alluding to, or echoing, the cults of
the various Greek heroes included in the Trojan expedition, the Homeric poems
lay a trail of their own. In the tradition outside the Homeric texts the major heroes
of the Trojan expedition have passed through the mortal state to a quasi-divine
state. Many were thought to have reached islands somewhere far at sea (whether in
the Black Sea in the far northeast, or in the Atlantic in the far west), where they
became the tutelary spirits of their respective islands. These were collectively the
Islands of the Blest. "Blest" here refers to the hero whose cult was maintained on
the island. As the daimon of the island, the hero was blest himself with the
perquisites of the gods (i.e., the devotion of his worshipers) and blessed his devotees in return for their devotion. Some heroes—Diomedes, for example—were
claimed as the local daimon of several separate locations. The distribution of the
hero cults throughout the Mediterranean suggests that on the historical level the

remained with her husband or rejoined her brothers, the Dioskouroi, or found true love with Achilles. Neither Homer's
Greeks nor his Trojans knew what to make of Helen, who was as
hated as she was privileged, and Helen herself was as perplexed as
they.

Achilles and Helen—the two occupy a position of supreme privilege in Homer's world, she as the daughter of Zeus, and he as the
son of Thetis. She is the fairest of the Achaeans, and he the best.
But the terms are synonyms in Homer's shame culture: the best is
the fairest; the fairest, the best.[5] Achilles is the most beautiful and
the best in the masculine form; Helen, the most beautiful and best
in a woman's form.

But privilege in myth is double-edged. Seen by their peers,
Helen and Achilles stand on the pinnacle of good fortune, their
being bordering Being itself, to borrow Parmenides' eloquent
phrase.[6] But seen through Homer's eyes, the gap between their

---

cults on the various islands probably represent traditions that the Myceneans carried with them in the diaspora after the fall of Mycenae. The hero cult on the island
was testimony to the islanders' descent from the true Myceneans.

Homer's heroes, however, have no such consolation to look forward to. After
death the best that they can expect is to fade into ghosts or eidola, mere images or
shadows of themselves, perpetuated by bardic memory. Of Homer's heroes, only
Menelaus reaches the state granted to the heroes in the religious cults, to escape
death and reach the closest approximation to Being in the Elysian Fields, as his
compensation for being the husband of Helen. Homer's other heroes must hope
to find their immortality through their *kleos*—their fame as it was transmitted
through the epic tradition.

5. For *kallistos* and *aristos* as synonymous in Homer, see *Iliad* 3.124, where Iris
takes the form of Laodike, who "of the daughters of Priam was best in physical
form" (*eidos aristē*); cf. also Alcaeus 42.11 LP, where Thetis is "best of the Nereids."
For one extended conversation in antiquity regarding the good, the beautiful, and
the ugly, see Simonides, frag. 542 PMG, and Plato's commentary on the poem at
Protagoras 339a–346d. See Dodds 1951, 26 n.109, on *kalon* and *aiskhron* as significant
terms in the shame culture of ancient Greece; also Adkins 1960, 154–58; 185–89;
Cairns 1993. For the supreme significance of *aristos* (the best) in the *Iliad*, see Nagy
1979. To call ancient Greece an "honor," rather than a "shame," culture would be
more in alignment with its own orientation.

6. Frag. 348. 4–5 KR: "For all is full of Being. Wherefore the all adheres. And
Being borders Being [*eon gar eonti pelazei*]." Even Parmenides, while denying the
possibility of an interval between Being and Being, must compose a second section

being and the full, extravagant being of the gods, slight as it is, is the focus for the deepest existential anxiety. Born of the archetypes (the gods), they are not themselves the archetypes but only their icons in human form. Heroes can only approximate the gods, though this they do heroically, so heroically in Helen's case that she is destined to enjoy a paradise that is a simulacrum of Olympus itself.

As if to mark their privilege in his own way, Homer makes Helen and Achilles his two surrogates, seers and poets. Far removed in time from the plains of Troy, relying on hearsay ("the Muses"), Homer stations Achilles as his one seer in the Greek camp, and Helen, his other, in the bedroom at the heart of the Trojan affair. Placing the two at the vortex of the storm, Homer forthwith removes them to the periphery. Achilles, "the best of the Achaeans"—as athlete, horseman, and warrior—is banished by his pride, which is his internalized representation of the code of honor, from the arena where a hero's honor is established.[7] Idled at the ships, Achilles is a hollow shell with perhaps potential, but no actual, significance. Helen is banished too, but to her own room, secluded not only from the men but from the grieving wives and widows, to hide her shame. Whether compassionate or not, how could Helen join the other women in their mourning, being herself the cause of their grief, at least in their eyes? Both Helen and Achilles, situated exactly where mortality grazes immortality, are thus marginalized and made to observe the action from the spectator's seat. Sequestered, each learns to sublimate life into art, as they watch their own being drained from them to render them into icons for posterity. To diagram honor and shame in their culture,

---

of his poem to explain the *apparent* space between the two. In myth, the heroes illuminate that same *apparent* space, as a zone of intense friction between quotidian being and Being, where signifiers shade into what they signify, which is Being itself.

7. *aristos Akhaiōn* (best of the Achaeans) is a regular formula in the *Iliad*; for its significance see Nagy 1979, esp. chap. 2.

Achilles would serve as the icon of glory, and Helen as the icon of shame.[8]

Whatever Achilles' existential doubts when he is banished from the field of glory, Helen perhaps plumbs the ontological abyss more deeply when she wonders (to Hector, at *Iliad* 6.357–58) whether the gods designed her life with Paris specifically that she and Paris might be a theme for singers, by which she means a byword for generations to come. Achilles, watching his brief life unravel, may come to perceive that he will one day be no more than a story, but such a realization is far from his mind when he is rampant in the heat of success. Irony comes late to Achilles, but Helen was born to it. Achilles never hazards the possibility that the sole reason for his life was that he should figure in someone else's story. Until the death of Patroklos transformed his story into the "Death of Patroklos," Achilles could still live in the illusion that the story was his own to shape as he chose, whether gloriously or ingloriously. Helen is allowed no such illusions, certainly not at least after *Iliad* 3. Only Helen is compelled to read her own life as a ghost story. Only she must, consistently and from the beginning, learn to convert (or subvert) the stuff of her daily life into her function as the glyph for "shame/shamelessness" in the storybook of the tribe.

Helen first appears on the European stage in Homer's *Iliad* 3, when Iris takes us from the battlefield directly into Helen's private room. The rupture between Achilles and Agamemnon in book 1 has been glossed over. The two armies have marched forth, ready for war again. Menelaus, sighting Paris in the Trojan lines, beauti-

8. See Dodds (1951), who applies to classical Greek thought the distinction drawn by anthropologists between shame and guilt cultures. But no hard line can be drawn between the two. Some cultures may be more shame-oriented, and others more guilt-oriented; but probably both guilt and shame are to be found to some degree in every culture. My view is that literacy contributes significantly to increasing guilt and devaluing shame, since it moves the locus of judgment from the public arena to the private screen of the individual reader. Readers learn to internalize what in nonliterate cultures is played out on the highly public stage. For the enormous influence of literacy in reshaping thought and culture, see Havelock 1963; Ong 1982; Svenbro 1988.

ful in his leopard skin, rejoices like a lion sighting his prey. But Paris, who is, as the *Iliad* presents him, short on substance, on first sight of Menelaus shrinks back into the Trojan ranks. But then stung, for the moment at least, by Hector's insults to his manhood, Paris strikes a noble attitude to recoup his (and Hector's) honor. He calls for a truce and offers to settle the issue of the war in a duel between himself and Menelaus.

Heralds are dispatched to the city and to the ships to fetch the sacrificial animals to secure the covenant. While some race to fetch old king Priam from his palace to witness the covenant, Iris, normally the messenger of the gods but acting this time without waiting for her instructions, takes the opportunity to fly to Helen's rooms, to lure her out to the city walls.[9] At once we are in the forest of ambiguity.

Why is Helen needed at the city walls? To witness the duel that will decide her status once and for all, between Menelaus and Paris, whatever we may call them—her two lovers, her two husbands, her husband and her lover, her past and her present husband. But why should Helen witness the duel? We, the audience, will be fascinated, of course, but we are not Helen. The question is more pointed if we have read ahead and know the true, but ignominious, conclusion of the duel—Helen and Paris in bed, at the end of book 3.

Will one duel between two spearsmen, however noble, really settle the issue that a protracted war between two great armies has only exacerbated? "You will be declared the beloved wife of the victor," Iris explains to Helen (3.138). But Iris is naive. She does not know the mind of Zeus, or of Homer, as we do. Menelaus will win the duel, by default; Aphrodite will steal her darling from the field of shame and put him to bed, where Helen will comfort him for his lack of manhood on the battlefield. On the field the duel will end in Paris' disgrace, but then, in the bedroom, we will witness the true end and function of the duel, when Helen capitu-

9. Cf. Edwards 1987, 192: "Iris is really the messenger of the poet." See his pp. 191–97 for many apt remarks on the ensuing scenes in book 3.

lates and joins Paris in his disgrace.[10] Outside the bedroom Pandaros will objectify the disgrace in a more public way by shooting an arrow that tears the truce to pieces. The war will resume, and everything will be as it was before the duel. Helen's status remains as it was—undecided—except that for the moment she is to be found in Paris' bed, which signifies the disgrace that attends upon undecidedness.

Why is Helen really needed at the city gates? The answer is obvious. If Helen is required as witness to the covenant between the Greeks and Trojans, the plot requires also that she be witnessed. She may observe, but more important she must be observed. Her function is to be proudly displayed by the Trojans from the tower, and gazed at by the tormented Greeks, as the prize worthy of such a contest. As Deianeira watches Herakles wrestling with Achelous, with herself as the prize, Helen's part in the story is to stand witness to her own value as the prize in a contest of such heroic dimensions. But the two cases are not symmetrical. At least Herakles had the blood of Zeus in his veins; Helen's prize is Paris, whom his brother Hector calls a travesty of manhood (and Paris cheerfully agrees, at 3.39–66).

Far from witnessing the decision to clarify her status, Helen is asked to witness instead that her status cannot be decided. Behind the human contests are ranged three contestants on Olympus—Hera and Athena on one side, and Aphrodite on the other. Helen, so close to godhood herself, must function as Aphrodite's sign, and Aphrodite's favors are not bound by the normal social contracts. Like all signs, Helen must be equivocal. The greater the sign, the more equivocal its meanings: that is in the nature of the sign. Men cannot agree on her meaning, even when they stage a contest secured by oaths sworn in the presence of the upper and nether gods, because Aphrodite, the archetype of which Helen is the human copy, is not to be netted in human signifiers.

10. Slatkin (1991, 43 n.30) observes that while Aphrodite's beneficiaries (Paris and Aeneas) "escape destruction and survive the *Iliad*, their individual heroism, from an epic standpoint, has been permanently compromised."

To add to the complications, Helen must be both woman-as-sign and woman, person and impersonation, at the same time. Without the woman herself, who would want the woman-as-sign? What use is the icon if the god will not dwell therein? Were Helen an icon empty of substance, the sign would lose all value. In the story spun for her by the gods, Helen must be both the object of desire and its subject, the source of desire and its goal. To fulfill this function she must not only appear equivocal; she must also equivocate, if she is to appear credible.

For a clearer vision of Helen as the Subject we could turn to the local cult of Helen at Sparta. Herodotus tells a lovely story of this Helen, the goddess, beautifying an ugly child, who grew up to become the mother of the Spartan king Demaratos.[11] Of the stories told of Demaratos, two were particularly remarkable. One concerned the marriage of his parents; the other, the peculiar fortunes of his mother, who was a living witness to Helen's power to beautify the ugly.

The first story tells of the parents of Demaratos and the clouded circumstances of his birth. Ariston, one of the kings of Sparta, was still without heirs after two marriages. He then took a fancy (an erotic itch, in Herodotus) for the woman who was considered the most beautiful of Spartan women. She, however, was already married, and to Ariston's good friend Agetos. Undaunted, Ariston conceived a clever plan. He persuaded his friend to make an agreement of exchange, no doubt in token of their friendship, in which each would hand over to the other that one thing, whatever it might be, which his friend desired. The agreement was secured under oath. We already know the end of the story. The trusting Agetos lost his wife, notwithstanding his protests that she had not been included in the agreement. Ariston promptly divorced his barren second wife and took as his wife the woman who was remembered as the most beautiful of Spartan women. The gods were kind, and Ariston's third wife, the anonymous beauty, now

11. 6.61.

the queen, produced an heir at last, whom the people called Demaratos (Prayed for by the People), since Ariston was a much-loved king.

This story is the *Iliad* repeated in compact, local form: two men, friends, compete for the most beautiful woman, who is already married to one of them. A friendship is betrayed, a marriage is annulled, the woman is exchanged.[12] To make the story truly Iliadic, the man who wins the "most beautiful" woman (*kallistē*) is himself named "the best" (Ariston), though his means are foul. "The best," here as in the *Iliad*, is immediately problematic. Ariston's behavior—deceit, trickery, abuse of friendship (the typical gifts of Aphrodite)—comports poorly with his name. But where the libido is concerned (or where there are dynastic considerations), liberties are allowed.

Herodotus plays out the problematics of the story at some length. The marriage of the best man and the most beautiful woman should have produced the best of heirs. And so it did. Demaratos, welcomed at his birth, would grow up to become the king. But no story in Herodotus is complete without its blind curve. Given his heritage, we could surmise that Demaratos would have an equivocal history. When Ariston was brought the news of his son's birth, as he was seated in council with the ephors, he counted the months on his fingers and concluded that Agetos might be the father. Ariston refused to acknowledge the child as his legitimate son. In years to come, when Demaratos, "prayed for by the people" but disinherited by his own father, grew to be exactly the son Ariston had prayed for, Ariston regretted his early suspicions. But by then it was too late; the damage had been done. As in the *Iliad*, winning the most beautiful woman does not guarantee a man happiness.[13]

---

12. See Boedeker 1987, 188–89, for the pattern of the Helen myth in the story of Demaratos.

13. As we might have predicted, neither Ariston nor Agetos was, it turned out, the father of Demaratos. The true father was the stable boy; see Herodotus 1.68. When Demaratos pleaded with his mother to tell him the true story of his birth,

The second plot concerns the mother of Demaratos, whose story is even more striking than his. Though known in her maturity as the most beautiful of Spartan women, the mother of Demaratos had been born the ugliest of babies. Her nurse, sympathetic to the distress of her parents at having a baby so ill formed (for they were prosperous people, Herodotus adds), made it her daily practice to take the baby to Helen's shrine at Therapne, a suburb of Sparta, across the Eurotas River. She would carry the baby heavily swathed, being under strict instructions from the parents to let no one see their disgrace. Her practice was to place the baby at the foot of the cult statue (the agalma—Helen's idol), and beseech the goddess to change the baby's "misshapenness" (dusmorphia).

One day, as she was leaving the shrine with the unsightly child heavily shawled against prying eyes, the nurse encountered a woman who inquired about the bundle in the nurse's arms. At length the nurse confessed it was a baby, but she would not show it; that was strictly forbidden. The strange woman persisted, the nurse's opposition melted (as whose would not?), the parents' prudish injunction was forgotten, and the ugly baby was exposed to the stranger's view. The stranger (Helen, of course, in a cameo appearance) then stroked the baby's head and said she would become "the most beautiful" (kallistē) of Spartan women. From that day, Herodotus concludes, the baby's appearance changed for the better.

This story points on the literal level to the idol of Helen—her agalma—in her shrine, but the beauty of the story is Helen, who is not the idol but the source of all beauty, Beauty herself, far transcending her idol, yet deigning to inhabit it on occasion, taking on

---

she explained that the story of the "stable boy" (onophorbos, "donkey boy") as his father was pure gossip. His real father was the cult hero Astrabakos (He of the Mule Saddle). Astrabakos, she further explained, had visited her in disguise, as gods are wont to do, taking on the form of her husband, the king Ariston. The *Iliad* comes full circle: the most beautiful woman "chooses" not the best of men but the likeness of the best, who turns out to be either the donkey boy (in the local gossip) or (in his mother's version) the god of the stable. Nagy (1990b, 335–36) discusses the mule theme, as it was used by Demaratos' opponents to disparage his pedigree. See Burkert 1965 for more on the strange hero Astrabakos.

human form and playing the visitor at her own temple, when a devotee reaches her heart. When gods deign to visit their shrines, we expect miracles. The ugly is changed into the beautiful, and another girl becomes Helen's latest idol and idolater.

Centuries after Herodotus, Pausanias, our guide to the shrines and monuments of ancient Sparta, tells the same story in an abbreviated version, leaving out the first plot (the contest between the two men for the most beautiful woman), and concentrating on the second plot (Helen as the source of beauty). Helen's miraculous power to beautify the ugly was no doubt more germane to his tour of the Spartan temples and shrines.[14]

In paring down the tale to a bare summary, Pausanias diagrams the mythologem even more sharply. Herodotus, in love with the particular, gives us the myth. But myth and mythologem together reveal how deeply mythopoeic thinking permeated ancient Greece into the historical period. The terms of the mythologem are *kalos* (beautiful), with its superlative, *kallistos* (most beautiful); *agathos* (good), with its superlative *aristos* (best); and, at the other end of the scale a single term, *aiskhros* (cause for reproach, disgraceful, ugly) and its superlative, *aiskhistos* (most disgraceful, the ugliest).

The axis of the mythologem is shame, over which Helen presides, being herself the signifier of beauty and therefore delineating, while transcending, shame. At one pole is the cluster of synonyms for the good and the beautiful, and at the other pole a single term will suffice as the common antonym, disgrace and the ugly being synonymous. In the shame or, more correctly, the honor culture of archaic Greece, the beautiful was good, and ugliness a disgrace. To quote Isocrates: "Of the things that lack beauty we will find not one that is loved and cherished [*agapōmenon*], but all are despised except those that partake of this form [namely, Beauty.]"[15]

Putting the two stories together, as told by the two authors, we

14. Pausanias 3.7.7.
15. *Encomium on Helen* 54.

have a single story that is dominated from beginning to end by
Helen's awesome and equivocal power. Through Helen's intervention the ugliest of babies became the most beautiful of women; the
disgrace of her infancy was transformed into her undying glory.
Thus transformed, she was in time married to the best of men
(Ariston), though the circumstances of the marriage bring her
again into disrepute. Her son, who would not have been born had
she not been beautified by Helen in her infancy, is then disinherited
by his father for—ironically—his questionable paternity. The boy,
who was "prayed for by the people," is the shadow that haunts the
woman's fame, the signifier of a beauty won at the cost of honor,
as it is in the *Iliad*. The final touch of shame is added when Demaratos learns that his father was the donkey boy, but even this
disgrace is turned to glory, since "donkey boy" here is a code for a
god in disguise.

Helen, by virtue of her beauty, transcends both ugliness and
disgrace. Hers is the power to transform disgrace into the beautiful;
yet she is also the woman who brings men into disgrace. The
Helen of our *Iliad* seems to recognize the chilling aspects of such
equivocal power, when she uses terms and formulas to represent
herself as someone in whose presence people shiver, with cold
Stygian fear.[16] Stories of this power may be charming when told
by Herodotus, though even in Herodotus Helen's power is far
from benign. But in the *Iliad* the force that transforms the ugly into
the beautiful is death. Once in the field of the signifiers, where men
fight for their meaning, there is no access to the luxury of Being,
where signifiers dissolve into the Subject, except through death.

Lured to witness the spectacle from the city tower, Helen will
discover (as if she did not already know) that of spectacles she is the
spectacle.[17] The duel between Menelaus and Paris is inconsequen-

16. See Clader 1976, 41–62, on Helen's character as revealed through epic diction.
Note the words of reproach that Helen uses of herself, and Clader's discussion,
pp. 18ff., of those epithets and phrases that allude to Helen's "hateful; i.e. deadly"
nature (*stugeros*; cf. Styx, the ice-cold river that puts even gods into a coma).
17. For Helen as spectacle, cf. Hesiod *Catalogue of Women*, frag. 204.58–63 MW,

tial, except for the image of Paris prancing on the field in his leopard skin and then snatched from death by the sweetly smiling Aphrodite. But who would forget the following scene in the bedroom, where the libido is declared victorious over honor?

Helen will not be declared the legitimate wife of the man who wins the duel by honorable means. Instead, after witnessing her lover's disgrace on the battlefield, which is also her disgrace, she will be returned, to her own greater shame, to the bed of the man without shame. Aphrodite, Helen's Olympian protector, knows nothing of shame cultures.[18] Her birth preceded the age of shame, though as shame cultures developed the mythic mind would fabricate stories to compress Aphrodite into the confines of the developing social codes. Eros, in Hesiod's cosmology, is self-generated, one of the four prime elements or principles.[19] The libido precedes all stories. Helen, to impersonate such a goddess, must learn to dispense with shame.

Helen, alone in her room, weaving her silent record of the war that rages all around her, is an unforgettable image. On the loom is her crimson tapestry, on which she weaves (or embroiders?) the "many contests that the horse-taming Trojans and the bronze-chitoned Achaeans were suffering for her sake in deadly war" (3.125–28). The image, where Homer's art is at once most simple and most profoundly suggestive, has justly prompted much dis-

---

where the poet describes Idomeneus coming in person from Crete to Helen's bride contest "so that he might see Argive Helen for himself and not only hear from others the *mythos* that had already spread throughout the land."

18. Cf. the point made by Slatkin (1991, 43 n.30), that Aphrodite's effect is to compromise those whom she protects.

19. *Theogony* 120. At 173ff. Hesiod recounts the myth of the castration of Ouranos as, in effect, a second explanation for the origin of desire. In this version Aphrodite was born of the severed genitals (i.e., the semen), and the Erinyes (spirits of revenge) sprouted from the spilled blood. The primal, undifferentiated libido here divides into two, with sex and life on one side, and shame, guilt, and death on the other. The goddess has been revised into polar opposites—into the chthonic Furies on one hand, and the smiling daughter of the celestial father on the other. See also Bergren 1989 on Aphrodite's primeval power to tame gods, humans, and animals, which is tamed in turn by Zeus.

cussion.[20] It calls to mind the later scene, in book 9, when Agamemnon's ambassadors come upon Achilles at his (or rather, Andromache's) lyre, singing "the famous deeds of men." Lyre and
loom, singer and weaver—Achilles and Helen are two impersonations of the poet, transmuting nature into art, Being into Meaning.[21]

For Achilles, "men's deeds of valor" (*klea andrōn*) are his paideia,
both his childhood education into manhood and his adult ideal.
Achilles' songs of valor console him for his occluded glory, but
they are also an incantation of the victor's crown, which Athena
promises him in book 1. His glory eclipsed for the moment,
Achilles will yet assimilate himself to the mighty heroes of earlier
generations, like his father Peleus or his great ancestor Aiakos.

Achilles is at one remove from the center of his song, since the
glory, fame, or radiance that men win (their *kleos*) can be won only
in the field of action, in contest with other men. Achilles is excluded from the contest, but Helen is inevitably at the center. Her
tapestry tells of men's valor too, but the deeds she commemorates
are those waged for her sake, or in her name. The figures of her
tapestry are not of the past, as we assume Achilles' heroes are.
They are the very men fighting to the death on the fields below the
city walls. Her theme is the Trojan War and its subject (or object),
Helen.

Homer calls the tableaux on Helen's tapestry *aethloi* (contests),
rather than using a more specifically military term. *Aethloi*, as
Linda L. Clader notes, are "contests for a prize."[22] Such contests in

20. On the associations in ancient Greek between weaving and poetic composition, with good references to the scholarship on the subject, see Clader 1976, 7;
Bergren 1979; 1983, 79. On Helen's tapestry, see also Kennedy 1986.
21. On Helen as poet, see Clader (1976, 8), who calls Helen "both author and
subject of her work." Cf. also Bergren 1983, 79: Helen "is both the object of the
war and the creator of its emblem." On Achilles as the singer in *Iliad* 9, see
Whitman 1958, 193. See also Murnaghan 1987, 152, on the poets or surrogate
poets in the Homeric poems (e.g., Helen and Achilles), who are all in some way
"disqualified from heroic action."
22. 1976, 7. See also her discussion of Helen as the prize of the Trojan War,
through whom the heroes win their fame (*kleos*), and therefore symbolic immortality.

archaic Greek tradition lead in two directions: to athletic contests, on the one hand, like the celebrated Olympian Games; and to bride competitions, on the other, where heroes gathered as a woman's suitors and competed for the woman-as-prize. Athletic contests were held for a variety of reasons besides bride competition (to honor the death of a local hero, for example). But Greek myth curiously preserves several stories of women won through bride competition—Thetis, Hippodameia, Deianeira, Penelope, the fifty daughters of Danaos, and, of course, Helen. Even Herakles, wrestling Thanatos (Death) to retrieve Alkestis from the dead, is a variant on the same theme.

Bride competitions continued into historical times, if we are to believe Herodotus, who tells us of Kleisthenes, tyrant of Sikyon, announcing a public competition for the hand of his daughter, Agariste (Best Woman by Far), wishing, as Herodotus says, to discover "the best" man (*aristos*) in Greece for his son-in-law.[23] A certain Hippokleides, an Athenian distinguished for his wealth and looks, was one of the two finalists, having acquitted himself with honor both in the gymnasium and at the table. On the final night the suitors competed in contests of music and after-dinner oratory. Hippokleides, alas, under the convivial effects of the drink, disgraced himself by dancing upside down on the dinner table, waving his legs in the air and exposing what should not be exposed (what in Greek were called *ta aiskhra*, "the disgraceful parts"), and certainly not to the prospective father-in-law. Hippokleides lost the competition—all honors garnered in a full year of competitions were turned to shame by a single indiscretion—but he was too far gone to care. Megakles, the other Athenian contestant, was declared the winner. From his marriage to Agariste was born the celebrated Kleisthenes, and feckless Hippokleides drops from view.

The *Iliad* is bride competition told in epic fullness. Helen weaves on her tapestry all such bride competitions, recording her own as the common paradigm shared by all other women. But Helen's

23. 6.126–29. Note also Herodotus' explicit statement that Agariste's suitors were "the best in looks and birth."

bride contest is significantly different from all other contests in that the competition in her case is perpetually renewed and perpetually undecided. Helen's tapestry, indeed Helen herself, if she is to be true to her own story, must portray indecisiveness. If to win Helen is, as Clader notes, to win immortality, the nature of this immortality and how it is to be granted remain mysterious.[24] Helen's privilege is to signify for men that zone where quotidian being borders Being itself, where all meanings are in perpetual dispute, and misinterpretation is death.

The Helen myth is a story of bride competition repeated again and again.[25] In her childhood she was seized by Theseus, from whom she was rescued by her brothers, the Dioskouroi (the "sons of Zeus" rescuing "the daughter of Zeus"). When Helen reached marriageable age, her (human) father, Tyndareus, held the contest in Sparta, where the heroes gathered from all over Greece to compete as her suitors. Here, oddly, the winner was the man who did not, in fact, compete. Agamemnon acted on behalf of his brother Menelaus, while Menelaus stayed at home. Being already married to Helen's sister Klytaimestra, and therefore hors de combat, Agamemnon acted as the proper go-between, cementing the diplomatic (and military) alliance between the two great Mycenean houses, the house of Atreus and the house of Tyndareus.[26]

Now, despite all the oaths sworn by the contestants to honor the marriage of Menelaus and Helen, the contest for the bride has been reopened. It is no longer a rivalry between the Greek tribal chief-

24. Clader 1976, 11–12.
25. On the Trojan War as Helen's bride competition, see Clader 1976, and cf. Bergren (1983, 82), who perceptively notes that Helen "is the female forever abducted but never finally captured." In a similar way the contest between Penelope's suitors and Odysseus in the *Odyssey* replays the original competition for Penelope. For curious stories of Penelope's original courtship, see Pausanias 3.12.1–2, 4; 13.6.
26. See Hesiod, frags. 196ff. MW, for the list of Helen's suitors. Even the contest between Menelaus and Paris, as Greek versus Trojan, repeats itself in the *Iliad* at 13.516, when Deiphobos hurls his spear at Idomeneus. The scholiast (= Ibycus, frag. 297 PMG) explains that Deiphobos and Idomeneus were deadly enemies, as rivals for Helen's love.

tains but has become an issue between Greece and its allies on one side, and Troy and its allies on the other. A local conflict has been globalized, since the contestants are not simply the Greeks and the Trojans; they have become signifiers warring in the field of Meaning for the Subject, which, alas, is never to be found in the field of Meaning but only in the arcane recesses of Being.

Helen, Homer's eyewitness at the center of the action, becalmed except when she is needed for her public function as the spectacle, becomes, like Homer, a weaver of stories.[27] She has special gifts for this part, being uniquely both Greek and Trojan. Helen's stereoscopic vision will serve Homer well, as it serves Priam on the city walls. Yet such privilege, to be the poet's poet, only marks Helen's impotence. Her tapestry is a woman's composition, woven in solitude and privacy—who would ever visit Helen's rooms, except Paris and her own slaves? The woman's view is not solicited in the contests that Helen represents in her tableaux. Helen may, indeed must, observe, but she must keep her silence. One day, perhaps, assuming the war ends and peace returns, Helen's tapestry may hang in a king's halls to entertain the king and his barons. But perhaps not. Perhaps it was never intended for men's perusal, or for women's perusal either, since Helen was even more alienated from women than from men.

Helen, always compliant to any tug on her emotions, hurries from her seclusion to witness the contest for her significance. Now her contradictions will be blazoned forth for all to see. Excluded from the decision-making process, except as the prize, Helen is a participant all the same, being intimately related, through the marriage bed, to both contestants. Iris, painting the stirring scene of the armies marshaled on the field, and Helen's two husbands at the center, prepared to duel to the death, had aroused in Helen a

27. For Helen as weaver and storyteller, and the associative links between woven fabric, poetry, and intelligence (*mētis*), see Bergren 1983, 73; Zeitlin 1981, 203–6. Extrapolating from these links, Bergren reads the marriage of Zeus and the goddess Mētis (Cunning Intelligence) as a story told to explain "the semiotic power assigned to the female and its (re)appropriation by the male."

"sweet yearning for her former husband, her city, and her parents" (3.139–40).

But Helen's sweet yearning, though a sufficient motive to draw Helen from her room, is beside the point. Helen's first function is to be the sign that will guarantee either happiness or immortality or both. Her second is, by witnessing the contest, to ratify it in her unique and mysterious way, to validate herself, and therefore her value as sign. Her personal investment is not germane to such mathematics. It must be occluded in favor of Helen's meaning, which others will decide. Helen must be the dispassionate spectator.

Yet, such is Helen's paradox, a dispassionate Helen would lose all value. If Helen is to impersonate Aphrodite, she must play a woman of unbridled passion, since unbridled passion is precisely Aphrodite's nature, or the play would have no meaning. If Helen is to be the object of men's desire, the equation will not compute without Helen's libido included. Who would Helen be without her libido?

At the Scaean Gates, Helen, in the role reversal characteristic of her, finds herself, once outside her own private space, not the spectator but the protagonist on the most public of all stages, with the old men of the city, buzzing like cicadas, as her tragic chorus. So much we should have inferred when Iris captivated Helen's emotions and drew her to the public stage. Why else was Helen posted to the city gates if not to be seen? Helen's voyeurism, to which Iris appeals in erotic excitement, is a thin disguise. We are the voyeurs. When Iris calls Helen "dear bride" (*numpha*, at 3.130), the formula is for our benefit as much as it is for Helen's. We are the audience impatient to witness the duel for a bride whose beauty overrides shame.

The status of the city elders is ambiguous, as if everything to do with Helen falls into indeterminacy. They are no longer the strong warriors of the city but the speakers (*agorētai*, "those who speak in the assembly"). Like Helen, they are removed from the field of action where men determine significance. Seeing Helen, the elders, though past the age of indiscretion themselves, can allow for the hormonal storm that would precipitate war among the younger men for such an emblem: "for she looks terribly like the deathless goddesses"; but even so, they say, "let her sail home in the ships so that she may not be left here as a woe to us and our children hereafter" (3.156–60).

The old men's response to Helen epitomizes her ambiguity. "It is no disgrace that the Greeks and the Trojans suffer long evils for such a woman," they say, using the word *nemesis*, the strongest term in Homer's shame culture for "blame."[28] The Trojan War is no cause for shame on either side. More pointedly, there is no cause for blame, and no reason to fear retribution, when the object is Helen, who awes the beholder into believing himself a witness to a god's epiphany. There is neither shame nor blame when men war for the hidden Subject to which all signs refer. But the elders of Troy could not be more mistaken, thinking their war over Helen was free of nemesis. Helen is nemesis.[29]

The old men are good speakers, Homer adds (at 3.150–52),

---

28. LSJ defines *nemesis* as "distribution of what is due; but in usage always retribution, esp. righteous anger." In the same entry *aidōs* is distinguished as subjective (shame), and *nemesis* as objective (retribution). I would refine the distinction, to call nemesis the fear that attends the violation of shame taboos, projected as retribution, whether human or divine. On nemesis in the *Iliad*, see Redfield (1975, 113–16), who notes that nemesis is represented as an excited condition. He cites *Iliad* 8.198–200, where Hera, experiencing nemesis, shakes on her throne, "and great Olympus trembled"; and 15.101–3, where Hera grins through her teeth, but her face is not smiling.

29. Cf. the connection between Helen and nemesis at Hesiod, frag. 197.8 MW, where Helen's courtship "aroused the nemesis of the gods." See also frag. 204.82 MW, where Tyndareus exacts the oath from Helen's suitors that they would exact vengeance on any man who, "putting aside nemesis and *aidōs*," would take Helen by force. On the frequent association of nemesis and Helen in Greek art, see Ghali-Kahil (1955, 1: 59–60), who discerns two possible influences here. On the literary side, the *Cypria* gives us the story of Helen as the offspring of Zeus and Nemesis (see *Cypria* 7 Allen); and significant on the religious side was the cult of Nemesis at Rhamnous in Attica, where she was worshiped as "The Rhamnousian [Goddess]." We can trace the confluence of these two sources in the epithet Rhamnousian, which the Alexandrian poet Callimachus used of Helen (*Hymn to Artemis* 232).

"like the cicadas in the leaves, which pour forth their lily voices."
Dry husks they may be, the elders, with all passion and substance
transmuted into voice, but it is still the liquid, fragrant voice of
experience.[30] Theirs is the guiding voice of the city. But, alas, like
cicadas, old men are no more than voice. Wisdom will not prevail
over youthful ambition in this contest. Helen will one day be returned to Greece, but not through old men's diplomacy. Face-to-
face with Helen's compelling significance, the elders have only
words, but words too fail. Helen, transcending words, is truly
terrible. When old men's words fail, the contest will be returned to
the young warriors, who can still believe that trial by arms can
reach a meaning where words cannot.

Priam breaks in on the elders' murmuring to call Helen to his
side, and Helen, chameleonlike, reverses herself again, from spectacle to spectator (3.161–63): "Come, dear child, and sit here by
me so you may see your former husband, your people, and your
friends."

Dear child? A moment earlier Helen was a virtual goddess; before that she was a bride; now she is an old man's child. It is a
formula, of course; by convention Helen has become Priam's
daughter, as he has become her father. But around Helen even
mundane formulas resonate. Has Priam, the eldest of the elders,
fallen under Helen's spell that he would, as if inadvertently, from
sheer custom, address Helen as he might address Andromache or
any other of his daughters–in–law but Helen?

Priam interrupts his own train of thought, as if to gloss his
indiscreet show of affection (3.164–65): "To me, you are not the
cause. The gods I hold responsible, who have roused this long,
grievous war against us from the Achaeans." The Trojan elders
give a general absolution to both sides, Greek and Trojan, for the
war. But specifically they absolve the men on the field, the warriors on both sides, for consenting to go to their death when the

---

30. On the men's "lily voices" and the comparison with the cicadas' sound, see
Stanford 1969. On voices as liquid, see Svenbro (1988, 101 n.39), with his citations
from Pindar's odes.

prize is of such daimonic significance. Priam, however, standing in for Helen's father, reverses the equation and absolves Helen. And rightly so. She is, in fact, but a child in the social order, to be passed from one supervisory male to another as the rules dictate. Priam's counselors would do without the sign altogether, given its cost. But Priam is not of their persuasion. Bewitched by both the woman and the war, he calls Helen to witness the great spectacle of men fighting to their death to calibrate the cost of beauty.

They make an odd couple, Priam and Helen, so like and unlike father and daughter. Helpless to influence the action (Priam disqualified by age, Helen by her sex), both are cast as spectators, though the spectacle in this case is their lives. They chat like father and daughter, as if war were in the far distance. Priam asks his daughter-in-law to identify the enemy (Helen's onetime family and people), much as if they were at an entertainment, the rivalry between a woman's two clans, her biological family and her in-laws, formalized into an afternoon's athletic contest. Helen, decorous in all her functions, lends Priam her eyes, as a daughter would, and gracefully submits to being his military aide.[31]

But Helen is more than a military scout. Depending on the point of view, she is either a hostage or a wanton fugitive from the Greek side. In either case she is a captive. The point is made, however graciously. The plot is transparent: the hostage sits in the commander's box, where she is seen to chat amicably with him, while her ransom is being arranged on the field below. Helen obliges, and as if this were a holiday at the races, the hostage turns her knowledge to her captor's use.

But Helen, serving as Priam's eyes, is never allowed to forget that she is the real spectacle (3.173–76): "Would that death had come on me," she replies to Priam's graceful invitation, "before I followed your son hither, leaving my own room, my people, my child, and my friends of my youth. But that was not to be, and I

31. On the power of Helen's eyes, cf. Stesichorus, frag. 201 PMG, where he is reported as saying that the men who advanced toward her to stone her "at the sight of Helen dropped their stones to the ground."

waste away in grief." But Helen's shame is her private affair, irrelevant both to the contest on the field below for the fairest and
the best, and to her function as the woman with no shame. As the
daughter of Nemesis (as she is represented, for example, in the
Cypria), Helen must be completely dispassionate.[32]

Putting her own investment aside, Helen obediently reads off
the roll call of the enemy—friends in her eyes, though enemies in
Priam's—as if she were reading the program notes to an aged
father with failing eyesight.[33] Her grief and shame pass unnoticed.

32. On the goddess Nemesis, see Roscher, 3: 117–66, s.v. "Nemesis"; and 1: esp.
1930–31, s.v. "Helena II." On Nemesis as goddess of vegetation, and Helen's
connection with both Nemesis and vegetation, see Cook 1925, 3: 1015; Clader
1976, 73. Worth noting also is Stesichorus, frag. 223 PMG, where Helen and
Klytaimestra are the punishment visited on their father, Tyndareus, by Aphrodite,
when he sacrificed to the other gods but omitted her from his devotions. Aphrodite in her anger punished him by making both his daughters promiscuous.
    Farnell (1921, 324) finds no "true mythic tradition" in the story of Helen's birth
given by the poet of the *Cypria*, who makes her the daughter of Nemesis. He
considers the story "studied and didactic," an extrapolation from Helen's role in
epic as the daughter of "divine wrath." In my view, however, the story as told in
the *Cypria* of the mating of Nemesis (Apportionment) and Zeus has the ring of a
genuine, archaic cosmogony dating from the mythopoeic age, rather than of a
fiction invented by a sophisticated reader of the *Iliad* to explain Helen's role and
behavior in the epic. According to further details supplied by later authors, Nemesis, resisting Zeus by changing from one form into another, finally changed herself
into a goose (a fish in Athenaeus 8.334c), whereupon Zeus did likewise (or chose
the swan form), and thus they consummated their love. From their union Nemesis
gave birth to an egg (the cosmic egg), from which in turn Helen emerged; that is,
Beauty herself. The stories told of Zeus pursuing Leda and Nemesis are remarkably similar, suggesting that both were cognates of an older archetype. In one
story, which explicitly connects Leda and Nemesis, Nemesis is given as Helen's
true mother, but she gave Helen to Leda to raise, and Helen was thus mistaken for
Leda's daughter. See Lindsay 1974, chap. 12, "Nemesis," for a sympathetic discussion of Nemesis as Helen's mother.
33. Clader (1976, 9) notes the oddity of Helen as the reader of the roll call: "It is
striking that a woman should be the poet of a catalogue of this sort. Traditionally,
such a scene should be dominated by a member of the opposing side, who could
provide information about his former comrades on the basis of his own material
experience." Clader concludes that Helen's "catalogue of the troops" represents
her own bride competition, when all the Greek heroes gathered at Sparta as her
suitors: "The *Teichoscopeia*, then, is a reminder that the Trojan War is a second
contest for the possession of Argive Helen" (10). Clader suggests further that the
absence of Menelaus and Achilles from Helen's roll call of the Achaean heroes at

Priam's gaze is fixed on the majesty of Agamemnon and the magnificence of the bronze-chitoned Achaeans.

Concluding her roll call of the Achaean heroes—its subtext being the list of her own suitors, with Priam standing in for her father—Helen, overtly the prize but implicitly the judge, since beauty sets the rules, discovers an absence that, but for her keener sight, would have been overlooked. Our attention, like Priam's, is drawn to the warriors on the field; if we had noticed an absence, it would have been the absence of Achilles. But Helen, scanning the field, finds her brothers, the Dioskouroi, nowhere to be seen. We would expect to find them, now that our attention has been drawn to them, in the front lines, defending their family honor as Agamemnon defends his brother's honor. If Achilles, Ajax, and Odysseus were prepared to fight for Helen to the death, what motivation could have kept Helen's own brothers from the field?

Greek myth and tradition credited the Twin Riders, Castor and Pollux, with miraculous rescues both on land and at sea. In cult they were known as *sōtēres* (saviors). They had rescued Helen when she was captured by Theseus. Where were they now? They were, after all, "the sons of Zeus" (*dios kouroi*), and Helen, their sister, was "the daughter of Zeus."[34] Why did they not race to their

---

Troy may reflect her original bride contest, where the same two heroes were notably absent. On the Teichoscopeia as a traditional catalogue of warriors shaped to its present position, with Helen being its focal point, see Edwards 1980, 102–3. See also his discussion of Helen and Paris (1987, 149–58, 191–97). We should also note that the duel in *Iliad* 3 replays, on the field of battle, the original offense, when Paris violated the code of honor and abducted Helen from her lawful husband. The contest is restaged, and once again honor loses to the libido. On honor and shame in the *Iliad*, see also Schein 1984, 168ff.

34. On the Dioskouroi as heavenly saviors, see Alcaeus, frag. B2 LP, and Page (1955, 265–68), who lists the other major testimony from ancient literature on the subject; also Cook 1925, 2: 431–40, in connection with other divine twins, and 1003–19, "Dioskouroi and Helene in Folk-Tales." Farnell, (1921, 175–228) discusses the wide distribution of their cult through Greece, but particularly in western Greece (Sicily and Magna Graecia), where the Doric presence was strong. In frag. adespota 1027(c) PMG, they are addressed as *kallistoi sōtēres* (most beautiful saviors); in Euripides' *Helen*, the Chorus invokes them as "the saviors of Helen" (line 1500), which, in the *Iliad*, they conspicuously are not.

sister's rescue, as they had in the past? Helen assumes the worst: her brothers, kinsmen and dauntless warriors though they be, did not dare show themselves on the battlefield for shame (3.326–42). Her assumption is incorrect, but that is less important than Helen's reminder that the spectacle to which she has been so gracefully invited, by Iris first on the divine plane, and then by Priam on the human plane, is the spectacle of her own shame, or lack of it.[35]

Helen's shame deepens when Aphrodite herself, with Paris freshly bathed and perfumed and safely to bed, sallies forth to lure Helen to her next assignment. Playing the familiar old crone of romance, tugging at Helen's sleeve, Aphrodite is all breathless lubricity, coaxing Helen into Paris' bed. Iris was lubricious too,

35. For Helen's shame in the epic tradition, cf. Hesiod, frag. 176 MW: "Helen disgraced the bed of Menelaus." See Redfield 1975, 113ff. If we can accept the Dioskouroi as cognate forms of the Twin Riders of the Vedic tradition, as Clader (1976, 48–53) argues, her suggestion that Helen's twin brothers have been replaced in the epic tradition by the two Atreidai, Agamemnon and Menelaus, and are thus rendered superfluous to the plot is attractive. Farnell (1921, 175–228) is not sympathetic to the theory that the Dioskouroi represent the Greek version of the Twin Riders, but see Nagy 1990b, 93 n.46, for further references, and 255–56. The prominence of the twin element in the Helen myth, both in Homer and outside the Homeric texts, suggests an enigma that is not easily explained as a "fiction" invented by the poet of the *Iliad*, which would then have to be imported into a large number of Helen's non-Iliadic myths. Rather, this element alone suggests that the Iliadic Helen is a portrait shaped by the epic but drawn from a much wider Helen tradition. Among the double or twin elements are Helen's two brothers absent from Troy; the two sons of Atreus warring to recover her from the two sons of Priam; Theseus and Peirithoos associated in the story of Helen's childhood rape, with the two Dioskouroi as her saviors; her two brothers' twinned destiny: the two alternating between life and death, and each alternating with the other; the two sisters born from the same egg; and the two mothers. In art, Helen is frequently represented as flanked by two men; see Roscher, 1: 1969. Cook (1925, 2: 447ff.), in discussing the twin theme in myth, notes that in some instances one of the twins is effeminate. We hear the echo of this distinction in Homer, in both the sons of Atreus and the sons of Priam. In each case the one brother is a mighty warrior, while the masculinity of the other is deeply problematic; then the problematic males must define their masculinity vis-à-vis Helen. Cf. the comic version of the Helen story in Petronius *Satyricon* 59.11–12, which has Diomedes and Ganymede as Helen's two brothers (the warrior and the effete).

though she veiled her voyeurism under the rubric of "contests"—who does not want to see a contest, especially a contest for love? And what bride would not want to witness her own bridal competition? But now the libido is undisguised. Rescued and restored, Paris awaits Helen in full sexual arousal.

Helen's contempt for Aphrodite is magnificent, but useless, when Aphrodite abandons her crone persona and, revealing her true being, threatens to withdraw her love if Helen disobeys (at 3.414–17): "I may come to hate you as greatly as now I love you." Love? Words take on manifold meanings where Helen is concerned. Helen may continue to enjoy Aphrodite's charisma, provided she subsume her personal being within her broader public function, which, in her case, is to expose all social convention as so much flotsam in the tide of the libido. Helen will survive, as Aphrodite's favorites do, provided she accept Aphrodite's terms, that her honor be compromised.[36]

Commanded by Aphrodite to forgo her shame, Helen displaces onto Paris the anger that she is forbidden to direct toward Aphrodite, who, as a god, is taboo. But Paris is no more accessible as a target than Aphrodite. He is all sexual arousal, and Helen's sarcasm has no effect, unless perhaps to stimulate his erotic imagination. Helen's sarcasm is an arrow that reaches only its archer, since only she knows shame: "Would that I had married a man who knew the meaning of nemesis and shame," Helen will later say to Hector (6.350–51). But Paris is impervious to shame.[37] On the contrary, Paris revels in his luxury, possessing the queen of the world, while Helen must both live with her shame and accept her function as the spectacle of shamelessness. Shame may govern families and order

36. Boedeker (1974, 34) notes that Helen's reluctance to join Paris "recalls the motif of shame which in epic poetry is frequently attributed to characters under the influence of sexual desire." See also p. 35: "Aphrodite is represented as an effeminate and debasing love goddess."

37. Cf. Redfield 1975, 114: "Paris accepts himself as he is; he did not make himself he says, and he cannot be otherwise. For the poet of the *Iliad* such an attitude is fundamentally unheroic—because it is unsocialized."

cities, but it is an empty word in Aphrodite's cosmology. What better illustration of the extravagance of the libido than the sight of Helen, for whom grown men die, playing the fairy godmother, indulging the sexual fantasies of a boy who has never outgrown infantile narcissism?

CHAPTER 2

Sappho's Helen and the
Problem of the Text

Sappho and Stesichorus, two of the canonical nine lyric poets
of archaic Greece, give us portraits of Helen that must count as
among the earliest of the commentaries on Homer which have
survived from the post-Homeric period. In both cases the portrait
is fragmentary, on account of the sorry state of the surviving texts,
yet enough has been preserved for us to see that the two poets'
attitudes toward Helen proceeded in opposite directions.

Stesichorus, from Doric Sicily, at first accepted the Homeric
Helen, but then he recanted, perhaps reacting with pro-Spartan
sympathies to the shame in the story. Coming to understand the
truth, as Plato tells the story, Stesichorus rejected the Homeric
Helen altogether and attempted, we infer, to replace her with the
Helen who was worshiped at the shrine in Therapne—not the
woman but the goddess, who had never left Sparta, never sailed to
Troy, and certainly never betrayed her people. But Sappho, from
Lesbos, off the coast of the Troad, was an Aeolic Greek, and Aeolic
roots went deep in the epic tradition. Lesbos figures prominently
in the *Iliad*: the epic credits the island's capture to Achilles himself,
thus celebrating him as the first to stake Hellenic claims to Lesbos,
and the seven beautiful women from Lesbos are an important item
in the compensations that Agamemnon offers to Achilles in book
9. It was not perhaps as easy for an Aeolic poet as it might have
been for a Doric poet from western Greece to imagine the Trojan

War with Helen removed from the plot. Besides, Sappho, a devotee of Aphrodite's as Helen was, found Helen's behavior less offensive than it seemed to Stesichorus. She did not, as far as we can tell, feel the same compulsion that Stesichorus felt to revise the Trojan War in such a way as to redeem Helen's reputation and restore her from the fallen woman into the peerless goddess. She accepted Helen as Homer had presented her, though she gave herself permission to read the myth in her own way.

Helen appears in Sappho's "Anaktoria" ode as Sappho's mythological *paradeigma*, the model she presents to support her argument that beauty is not an absolute value but a subjective judgment driven by desire.[1] Unfortunately, the papyrus is most damaged exactly where Helen enters the text (fig. 1). The ode begins fairly securely, assuming it is the beginning:

> Some men say the cavalry is the fairest sight
> On the black earth; others say the rank and file
> Soldiers; and others, the fleet. But I say it is
> Whatever a person desires.   4
>
> Very easy it is to make this intelligible to anyone.   5
> . . .   Hele[na the] man . . .

Here, alas, the accidents of time have torn the sentence to pieces, leaving Helen's name adrift like an island marooned in the open sea. Even her name is not certain, though we can infer it with a fair degree of confidence—Helena (Helen, in the nominative case). This reconstruction gives us the necessary subject of the sentence. The object of the sentence is also secure—*andra* (man)—but unfortunately the verb is uncertain. A. S. Hunt, the first editor of the papyrus, assumed that *andra* was a reference to Paris, but E. Lobel,

---

1. *Ode* 16 LP. For the original transcription see P. Oxy. 1231 and 2166(a)2. See also Voigt 1971 (= *Ode* 16), with its copious notes; Page 1955, 52; and Theander 1934, on the major problems of the text. For further discussions of the poem, see Hampe 1951; Ghali-Kahil 1955, 1: 36–37; Koniaris 1967; Stigers 1981; Winkler 1981, 71–73; Burnett 1983; duBois 1984.

Figure 1. Papyrus fragments P.Oxy. 1231 and 2166 (a) 2, Bodleian Library, Oxford, MS. Gr. class. c. 76/1 (P) = Sappho, *Ode* 16, lines 1–22 Lobel and Page. (Courtesy, The Bodleian Library, Oxford.)

in adding to the papyrus two minute pieces that had been attributed to another papyrus, altered the reading and made Menelaus the reference of *andra*.[2]

The sentence continues in impressionistic detail, given the gaps in the text. With Lobel's additions to the papyrus, the sentence has been reconstructed to read "Helen, deserting her husband, sailed to Troy, giving no thought to her child or her dear parents, but . . . led her astray." By whom Helen was led astray is another point left to be inferred, and scholars generally assume a reference here to Aphrodite (or Eros). With the Helen sentence completed, Sappho shifts our attention to her friend Anaktoria, "whose graceful walk and bright glance" Sappho professes to prefer to all "the chariots of Lydia."

To return to Helen, the following may be taken as a fairly literal translation of the problematic sentence, based on the actual evidence of the three papyri fragments that have been pieced together to produce the sentence:

for she, far sur [passing?	6
Beauty of humankind, Hele [na,] man	7
b]est	8
Deserting, sailed to Troy . . .	9
Daughter and dear parents	10
forgotten . . . led her astray,	11
	12
for flexible . . .	13
and lightly . . . etc.	14

In spite of the lacunae, the gist of at least the first half of the sentence is clear. "The fairest sight" (*kalliston*), Sappho has just

2. In his 1925 edition of Sappho's poems, Lobel followed Hunt's original transcription, but the 1955 edition of Sappho and Alcaeus (LP), edited by Lobel and Page, has incorporated the fragments from P. Oxy. 2166(a)2 and gives the reconstruction of the text that has since become canonical.

argued, is never anything other than the expression of a person's private erotic leanings. As proof of her proposition, Sappho points to Helen—the archetype of a person who in judging the beautiful allowed herself to be guided simply by Eros, even when her behavior spelled grief for her husband, her child, and her parents.

Hunt, in the *editio prima*, without the benefit of Lobel's additions, conjectured "surveying" (*perskopousa*) for the dubious word in line 6, where only *persk-* can be clearly distinguished; took *andra* (man) in line 7 to mean Paris, supplied as the necessary verb *krinnen* (judged), and reconstructed *-ston* in line 8 into *ariston* (best). Here is his translation of the sentence, in which I have taken the liberty of italicizing the most doubtful words on the papyrus: "for Helen *observing* well the *beauty* of men *judged the best* to be *that one who destroyed the whole glory* of Troy, nor bethought herself at all of child or parents dear, but through love *Cypris led her astray.*"[3]

Lobel and Denys Page in their 1955 edition of Sappho and Alcaeus, accepted J. U. Powell's conjecture of *perskethoisa* ("surpassing," line 6, with kappa taken to be a scribal error for chi) and with the addition of the fragments from P. Oxy. 2166(a)2 have given us a completely different sentence, in which the emphasis falls not on Helen's choice of Paris but on her desertion of her husband.[4] They show their uneasiness over Hunt's conjecture of *ariston* in line 8 (where only *-ston* is readable in the text) by leaving the dubious word uncorrected; in their apparatus, however, they suggest *pan-*

---

3. *P. Oxy.* 10: 40. See also Wilamowitz (1914) 1971, 386–87. For the problems presented by this reading, see Theander 1934, 64–69. Some of those problems have been rendered moot by Lobel's additions to the papyri, though Lobel's text also raises questions that have not, in my view, been adequately addressed.

4. For the conjecture *perskethoisa*, see Powell 1915, 142–43. Lobel and Page (1955) accept Powell's conjecture "hesitantly" (*dubitanter*), indicating in the conventional way, by dots under *-ethois-*, the questionable status of the word. In Page's *Lyrica Graeca selecta* (Oxford: Clarendon Press, 1955), however, and in his *Sappho and Alcaeus* (1955) the dots have fallen away, leaving the unwary reader with the false impression that *perskethoisa* actually exists on the papyrus. In his commentary on line 6 in *Sappho and Alcaeus* Page notes that "the sense seems positively to demand the reading *perskethoisa*," though he then admits, in his commentary on line 7, that the reading makes for an inelegance in Sappho's "parable."

ariston (best of all). This suggestion, however, originally made exempli gratia, has crept up from the apparatus into the text itself in Page's study of Sappho and Alcaeus and has since become the canonical reading.[5] Anne Pippin Burnett's translation captures the tone and sense of the passage as reconstructed by Lobel and Page: "Herself the perfect gauge of what we know as fair, fair Helen left the best of men and sailed away to Troy, not thinking of her child, forgetting both her cherished parents, gladly led upon a crooked course [by Kypris? By Eros? . . .]."[6]

Disappointing as the loss of the text is at this cardinal point in the ode, its fate offers us a hermeneutic puzzle that replicates in an uncanny way both Helen's career and Sappho's. While the men talk of armadas, the women have quietly slipped away. Equally uncanny, the two editors of the papyrus, Hunt and Lobel, in their divergent readings of the problematic sentence have quite unintentionally articulated the very problem that has always haunted Helen's name, as in fact it has also shadowed Sappho's reputation.

Hunt's reading laid the emphasis on Helen's choice of Paris as the most beautiful object—she "judged him the best who destroyed sacred Troy." Lobel has compelled us to give up that reading and shift our attention from the favored lover to the deserted husband. If we accept Lobel's reading, then *andra* (in line 7) is not simply the unmarked term "man," but the more strongly marked term "husband." In this reading Helen would be guilty of a double crime, since he whom she forsook was both the best of men and the best of husbands, while he whom she preferred was something less than either.[7] Her offense would be even more heinous if we were to accept *panariston* ("best of all," "best in all respects," line

5. Cf. Sappho, *Ode* 16 LP, apparatus to line 6: "fort. [panar]iston supplendum" ("perhaps *panariston* should be supplied") with the text given by Page (1955, 52).

6. 1983, 278, following Voigt's text, which in essentials agrees with Lobel and Page.

7. Ghali-Kahil (1955, 1: 36) makes the implications of this reading explicit by translating lines 7–8 as "Helen, deserting the best of husbands [le meilleur des maris], etc."

8). Thanks apparently to Page's influence, *panariston* has become the canonical reading, leading translators to accentuate Helen's crime by pelting Menelaus with garlands of praise as "the noblest of heroes."[8] In Willis Barnstone's translation the simple *andra* of Sappho's text has become so highly charged that he whom Helen deserted is celebrated not only as Helen's husband and "the best of men"; he has also become Helen's "king."[9]

Lobel's additions to the papyrus, in removing Paris from the text, have also had the unfortunate effect of obscuring an essential point of the ode which was more visible in Hunt's reconstruction; namely, that Sappho, to clinch her argument, has presented us with a famous beauty contest from the mythical tradition in which Helen was not the object, though she was the prize, but the adjudicator. To read the problematic *persk-* in line 6 as *perskethoisa* (surpassing) is to introduce a curious contradiction into the argument, the argument being that in matters of the beautiful there is no absolute but only a subjective judgment determined by desire. Why would Sappho undermine her thesis by describing Helen as "far surpassing humankind in beauty"? Of course Helen was just that—by general consensus the woman of surpassing beauty—but Sappho's objective in this ode is not to uphold the traditional standards of beauty but to turn them upside down, exactly as Helen had done, and pierce through to their subjective core.[10] Helen finds herself in Sappho's ode not because she was the paragon of beauty

8. See Gentili 1988, 89; cf. also Winkler 1990, 176. But cf. Barnard's translation of the ode (1958, no. 41), which disregards Lobel's additions and follows Hunt's reading.

9. Barnstone 1988, 66.

10. Page (1955, 53), while arguing that the sense seems "to demand the reading *perskethoisa*" in line 6, frankly admits its inappropriateness: it "seems then inelegant to begin this parable, the point of which is that Helen found *to kalliston* in her lover, by stating that she herself surpassed all mortals in this very quality." A personal examination of the papyrus has convinced me that *perskethoisa* is almost certainly not Sappho's word. In my view, where Powell's conjecture requires a theta, the visible traces of ink support a lambda or a delta rather than a theta. I am grateful to William Mullen for examining the papyrus with me and to P. J. Parsons for our discussions of the several questions raised by Powell's reading.

but because she was the most famous personage in myth who, in matters of the beautiful, exercised her individual judgment in complete disregard for the social consequences.

If we accept Powell's conjecture *perskethoisa*, we must first assume that Sappho has permitted a certain incongruity to slip into the argument, and then infer as the implicit argument of the sentence that Helen, by general consensus the paragon of beauty, exercised beauty's privilege to overturn the conventional standards of beauty. While Hunt's *perskopousa* (surveying) seems untenable, he had surely a truer sense of the argument, since Powell's conjecture carries the suggestion that Helen was the object and prize of the contest, whereas Hunt's conjecture situates her firmly in place as its judge.

Once we have laid to rest the troublesome *persk-* in line 6, we face an equally vexing problem with regard to another half word, *-ston* in line 8. If Menelaus is indeed the *andra* referred to in line 7, and Sappho had indeed described him as *ariston* (the best), this is enough to make us sit bolt upright in our seats. And if Sappho really wrote *panariston* ("best of all" men or husbands), we cannot help but blink in sheer disbelief. Who in antiquity, besides Sappho, ever thought of Menelaus as the best of husbands? He commanded a significant military force at Troy, but it was not the largest; he was a good warrior, but certainly not the best; and surely none of his comrades would have thought to call him "the best of husbands." True, in the *Odyssey* (at 4.264), Helen finds Menelaus "not lacking in the least in looks or mind." But she is the hostess at her own dinner table, with two young guests to think of, all eyes and ears, and her husband seated across from her. Certainly Sappho was not thinking of this Helen—the penitent wife and gracious hostess, entertaining her husband's friends—when she composed her ode to Anaktoria.

In the traditional triangle, Menelaus usually comes in a poor third after Helen and Paris. When poets think of Helen's regret or her homesickness, they more often remember her daughter, her parents, her home, the friends of her youth, before they remember her husband, if they remember him at all. In the *Iliad*, when Helen acknowledges her shame to Priam (at 3.173–76), she mentions her kin, her daughter, and her friends, but about Menelaus she says not a word. Menelaus may be inferred, to be sure, from Helen's reference to her "chamber" (*thalamos*), which she places first in the catalogue of her delinquencies. But if *thalamos* is to be understood as "bedchamber," the very indirectness of the reference suggests that Helen's mind was more on the shame of the violated marriage bed than on the person of her husband. Alcaeus, musing on Helen's offense, thinks of her leaving her "sumptuous" bed (to borrow Burnett's translation).[11] But this implies, to men's ears at least, that Helen found the bed of Paris even more sumptuous.

In Hesiod's list of Helen's suitors Menelaus hardly strikes the lordly posture that would entitle him to be called the best of men (or husbands). In fact, he did not even present himself among her suitors at the house of Tyndareus; Agamemnon competed in his place.[12] His stature is slightly improved when Hesiod informs us that he won the contest because "he had given the most," but Hesiod immediately undercuts this information by reminding us that Achilles was not a contestant, being too young at the time.[13] Had he competed, Hesiod continues, Menelaus would certainly not have won Helen, nor would any of her other suitors. Such passages sum up fairly accurately what could be said of Menelaus. While *ariston* might be possible in Sappho's ode, to read *panariston* in line 8 is surely to stretch credulity. To be as gallant as possible, one might call Menelaus the perennial second best. As a son of Atreus, he was second to Agamemnon; as a commander of military forces, he was again second after Agamemnon; as a warrior he was second, if not third or fourth, after Achilles, Ajax, or Diomedes; even as Helen's husband (Hesiod takes care to remind us), Menelaus won the prize only because Achilles had not competed.[14]

---

11. Alcaeus, N1 LP; Burnett 1983, 186.
12. Hesiod, frag. 197 MW.
13. Frag. 204.85–92 MW.
14. Cf. Beye 1966, 176, on Menelaus in the *Odyssey*: "Menelaus is again, here as in the *Iliad*, neither overly bright nor overly perceptive." Cf. *Iliad* 17.586–88, where Apollo taunts Hector for shrinking from battle with Menelaus, "who before this was a soft warrior." Menelaus is much the same figure in the whole post-Homeric

Suter's comparison of the Helen-Paris-Menelaus triangle with the Punch and Judy show is very instructive.[15] If Paris serves in the melodrama as the object of abuse, Menelaus is the figure of ridicule. The horned husband will always be a theme for village burlesque. Even in Euripides' *Helen*, which is as much a rehabilitation of Menelaus as it is of Helen, Menelaus is more the buffoon of the comic stage than the tragic hero. If Paris was compromised in respect to the manly virtues by being one of Aphrodite's favorites, Menelaus was compromised too, but in a different way.[16] If he was superior to Paris as a warrior, that was small comfort, since Paris was no warrior but a lover. To wear the horns is not an experience that can be alleviated by "mitigating circumstances." Once cuckolded, in an honor culture, a man is compromised forever.

Granting, however, that Sappho did in fact call Menelaus "the best of husbands" despite his compromised status, we are faced with an interesting twist in the argument of the poem. By introducing Helen and her fateful choice as the exemplum, Sappho has shifted from the generalized beauty contest with which the poem opens to the specific contest with which Helen's name has been forever associated in the poetic tradition, the contest between the good and the beautiful. Whether named or unnamed in the poem, Paris is present by implication; Sappho has made her point clear that Helen, in deserting Menelaus for Paris, preferred beauty above everything else, including virtue.[17]

---

literary tradition. Ghali-Kahil (1955, 1: 37), following Hampe (1951) and Schubart (1938), argues that Sappho was simply following the conventional custom of authors before Euripides in calling Menelaus "the best," but I find it hard to agree. Hampe's suggestion is attractive, however, that when Silenus in Euripides' *Cyclops* (lines 185–86) calls Menelaus *anthrōpion lōiston* (best of fellows), the description is a parody of this passage from Sappho's ode.

15. 1993, 7.

16. See Boedeker 1974, 34–35, for the compromising, feminizing effect of Aphrodite's influence on male heroes. For Helen's similarly compromising influence on Menelaus, cf. the numerous vase paintings (listed in Ghali-Kahil 1955) that represent Menelaus dropping his sword in Helen's presence.

17. Theander (1934, 70) argues that Sappho intended to draw a contrast between Helen's physical beauty and lack of inward beauty. I agree with Page (1955, 56 n. 2)

In any case, in spite of the serious lacunae in the text, we can agree that Sappho in thinking of Anaktoria's beauty has structured her ode in the form of a contest, in which, after several contestants (specifically the cavalry, the infantry, and the fleet) have tried and lost, she awards the crown to Anaktoria. Contests in turn imply spectacles, like the great Panhellenic spectacles at Olympia or Delphi where crowds gathered from far and wide to witness the fierce competition among athletes and musicians to prove themselves "the best." On Lesbos the competitive spirit extended to beauty contests for women.[18] The life of "the good and the beautiful" (*kalos kai agathos*), as the Greek aristocracy named itself, revolved around contests to attain the superlative rank. It was deeply embedded in their inheritance that the goal of human existence was to strive to be or to attain the fairest, the noblest, or the best.[19]

---

that nothing in the poem suggests that Sappho intended such a contrast; as Page remarks, "The context (3–6) requires that Helen shall prove the truth, not the wickedness, of Sappho's theme." In rejecting Theander's interpretation, however, we should not forget that, assuming we have the correct reading, Sappho has pointedly contrasted *aristos* (the best), with its connotations of both physical and moral virtues, with *kallistos* (the most beautiful), primarily used of outward, physical excellence. If Sappho called Menelaus "the best man," in my view she used *aristos* in the conventional sense, to refer to manly virtues: Menelaus was the best warrior not in the absolute sense but in comparison to Paris.

18. On the athletic competitions as the aristocratic venue in which men competed to establish "the best," and therefore "the most beautiful," cf. Ibycus, frag. 282 PMG, where Ibycus highlights the glory of Polykrates by comparing his achievements to the great contest of the *Iliad*. See Nagy 1979; Burnett 1987; Mullen 1982, 46ff. For a woman's beauty contest, held in a sacred precinct on Lesbos, see Alcaeus, frag. G2.27–35 LP. Exiled from the city, Alcaeus finds himself forced to live a rustic's life, longing for the life of the city. In this ode Alcaeus laments his wild state, to be a solitary fugitive hiding in the wolf thickets. His one consolation is that he can hear the cries of the women engaged in the beauty contest in the temenos of the gods, "and the wondrous sound arises all around of women making their sacred *ololugai* [ritual cries]." Cf. also scholiast A on *Iliad* 9.129: "Among the people of Lesbos a beauty contest of women is held in the precinct of Hera, called the *kallisteia*." On this contest, see Page 1955, 168 n. 4; and Nagy 1993 (forthcoming).

19. Loraux 1986 provides an excellent study of this aspect of life in fifth-century Athens; see p. 103 for the significance of *kalon* and *aiskhron* in Pericles' Funeral Oration.

Sappho casts her contest for "the most beautiful" in the form of a priamel, the rhetorical figure so loved of the Greek poets which arranges images or ideas in a ranking system, wherever the possibility of a contest could be found.[20] Pindar, for example, in celebrating Hieron, the tyrant of Syracuse, for his victory in the single-horse race at the Olympian Games, opens his famous *First Olympian* ode with a priamel enumerating a series of noble elements—water, gold, fire blazing in the night. But their splendor gives way to the splendor of Hieron, who is triply crowned in Pindar's sequence of thought—first as a victor; then as victor in the chariot race, the king of races; and finally as victor at Olympia, which was of all fields of contest the most splendid. Hieron, the tyrant of Syracuse, prosperous, generous, victorious with horse and chariot at Olympia, is the final, Panhellenic spectacle to which Pindar draws our eyes.[21]

Pindar uses his priamel to focus our gaze on "the best" (*aristos*), while Sappho's priamel focuses on "the most beautiful" (*kalliston*).[22] But the terms are interchangeable; to attain one was to attain the other. Or rather, ideally, the two terms were synonymous, though in actual fact they were more often in open conflict— witness the *Iliad*, which can be read as the epic confrontation between the good and the beautiful. If Sappho brought the two terms together in such close proximity—assuming we are reading the papyrus correctly—she no doubt expected us to experience the resonance of their interaction. Like the poles of a Heraclitean force field, in Greek thought the good and the beautiful were simultaneously in agreement and at war with each other.[23]

20. On the priamel as a rhetorical figure, see Bundy 1962; Race 1982. For the priamel of this ode, see Page 1955, 55; Burnett 1983, 281; Rissman 1983; Pavlock 1990, 5. Other illustrious examples of the priamel are to be found in the *Homeric Hymn to the Delian Apollo*, in which the priamel is climaxed by the myth of the birth of Apollo; and in the *Hymn to the Delphian Apollo*, in which the priamel leads to the founding of Apollo's temple and shrine at Delphi.
21. On the horse signifying "pedigree" at the Olympian Games, that is, the pedigree of the contestants, see Nagy 1990b, 335ff.
22. On *kalliston* in this ode, see Liebermann 1980.
23. On the problematic relations between the good and the beautiful, we might compare another passage in Sappho (frag. 50 LP): "He who is beautiful [*kalos*] is beautiful to look upon. But he who is good [*agathos*] will also be beautiful [*kalos*]."

Any search in ancient Greece for "the most beautiful" would lead sooner or later to Helen, the very icon of beauty. Musing on beauty and on the inevitable contests that beauty inflicts on us, Sappho takes us back to Homer, and we find ourselves in the third book of the *Iliad*, where Helen is at the heart of the conflict between the good and the beautiful. Ambivalent as always, Helen is the pivot on which Sappho's priamel swings from the military displays of the first stanza to Anaktoria in the fifth, being the classical paradigm of the woman who, in matters of the beautiful, was both the prize and the judge; *sēma* and *sēmantōr*, the sign and the maker of the sign. Would anyone have called Menelaus the best of men, if he had not been the husband of Helen?

When Helen is introduced into the poem, she could be mistaken for a moment as the crowning term of the priamel: the search for the beautiful takes us past the cavalry, the infantry, the fleet, until our eyes light on Helen.[24] This sequence is rendered explicit if we read *perskethoisa* in line 6: the search for the most beautiful that begins in the first stanza leads us in the second stanza to the woman "who far surpassed all humankind in beauty." But no, we have been deceived by our expectations. Helen's function in the ode is as the adjudicator of the contest. Her appearance in the judge's box in this ode reminds us that the contest staged in *Iliad* 3, to which this ode implicitly refers, is in fact two contests mirroring each other. In the one contest, "for the fairest," we gaze with the troops up at the tower, where Priam, acting in loco parentis, presents Helen as the prize. In the second contest, "for the best," we sit with Priam and Helen on the tower itself, to judge the armies arrayed on the field below and mark Helen's two contestants, Menelaus and Paris. Like all mirrors, the two contests both agree and disagree with each other.

Whether named or not, Paris is, implicitly at least, the crowning

24. On the confusion here as to whether Helen is to be read in lines 6–7 as "the fairest" or as the judge of "the fairest," see Koniaris 1967, 263–64; duBois 1984, 96. In my view the confusion between Helen as the prize of the beauty contest and as the judge was central to the portrait of Helen throughout antiquity; Helen was ambiguity itself.

term of Sappho's priamel, since to mention Helen is to remind us of the scene in *Iliad* 3 when she, observing the two contestants fighting for her name and honor, turned her back on the military show and retired to her room, to join Paris in bed. However Helen managed her private shame, no one, whether on the battlefield or among those listening to the bards singing the tale, could be left in doubt as to which of Helen's two lovers was the victor of the duel in book 3. Paris may not have been the best, but surely he was the most beautiful, if we take Aphrodite's intervention on the battlefield seriously and read the bedroom scene at the end of book 3 as his victory celebration.[25]

Paris too yields his pride of place, of course, since the priamel is the rhetorical path leading us to the true object of the ode, Sappho's friend Anaktoria.[26] Here the priamel gives way to the ratio; As Paris was to Helen, Anaktoria is to Sappho. Sappho, supported by Helen's example, is moved to declare Anaktoria the winner in her beauty contest, for whose "lovely step and radiant face" she would not trade "all the chariots of Lydia, with the men and their equipment."[27]

Burnett argues that Sappho presents Paris in this ode "without a

25. See Rissman 1983, 30–54, for an analysis of this ode's relationship to the Homeric *Iliad*. See also Winkler 1990, 174, on Helen as Sappho's paradigm of the "many-mindedness" of a woman moving between the public and the private space; also Pavlock 1990, 5–6. On Paris as "the best," cf. also Isocrates (*Encomium on Helen* 45), who argues that Paris was chosen by the three goddesses to judge their competition because he was conspicuously supreme in birth and looks.

26. Koniaris (1967, 216) suggests that Sappho may have avoided naming Paris in the ode so that "in the aesthetic field of the poem" Anaktoria's name would not suffer any competition. This is a valid suggestion in my view, since the comparison that the poem raises between Paris and Anaktoria is certainly best left only implicit.

27. Page (1955, 57), noting Sappho's implicit contrast between the sparkle of Anaktoria's face and the flash of military armor, admits that the contrast "may seem a little fanciful; but this stanza was either a little fanciful or a little dull." But to find this stanza either fanciful or dull is to miss the Homeric resonance of the ode, particularly the element of shame, which links Sappho and Helen. Sappho's point of view is to "bypass male literary authority," as DeJean (1987, 790) has shown. Helen in this ode is the exemplar of Sappho's own narrative persona, as DeJean sees it—"the desiring subject," that "controls the gaze."

single blemish."[28] This would be true if we accept the reading that removes Paris from the text altogether, but to think of Helen is to think of Paris, and to think of Paris and Helen is to think of blame and blemish. If Paris was the most beautiful of the Trojans, he was a beautiful coward. It is not quite accurate to argue, as Bruno Gentili does, that Sappho reinterprets the Homeric myth "without any concession to the traditional schematism . . . of Helen the adulteress who causes grievous misfortunes and the final ruin of Troy."[29] Sappho certainly supplies enough data in the ode to indict Helen for causing misfortunes for others, particularly if we accept Lobel's reading that she deserted "the best of all husbands," not to mention a child and "dear parents." Sappho's point is that Eros is a force so powerful that it writes its own laws, as Helen did, who chose Paris, though his beauty was her dishonor.

Greece in Sappho's time was still a culture based on honor and shame, as it was in Homer's time, and Sappho was, like Helen, a devotee of the goddess whose favors were won at the expense of shame. She had good reason to think of Helen, whose beauty was synonymous with shame. If Helen could cast her shame aside in favor of the effeminate Paris, Sappho was equally flagrant, if not more so, to reject men altogether and to prefer a woman's (or more probably, a girl's) beauty to the greatest spectacles of male power.

After Claude Calame's discussion of pederasty in ancient Greece, in its socially approved function in initiatory cults, it might seem anachronistic to talk of shame in connection with Sappho's "Anaktoria" ode.[30] But the personal lyric of archaic Greece frequently opposed itself to the public and civic morality, which was based on the code of honor and shame. Archilochus, while a warrior himself in his public persona, in his personal lyric could

28. 1983, 286.
29. 1988, 89.
30. 1977. Even when homosexuality was tolerated in ancient Greece, it was hedged about with many taboos that were dictated by shame. On this point see Dover 1978 and 1984.

blithely confess not only that he had lost his shield in an ignominious retreat from the battlefield but, even worse, that he was
altogether lacking in the sense of shame that a warrior should
experience when faced with such a catastrophe to his honor: "But
what is that shield to me? Let it go. I shall find another, just as
good."[31] This is not the sentiment of a citizen but of a mercenary.

Anacreon was another lyric poet famed for flouting the social
codes. Asked why he composed hymns to boys instead of the more
traditional and serious hymns to the gods, he answered with boy-
ish irreverence, "Because these are our gods."[32] To be helplessly
entangled in the nets of desire, though it was one of Anacreon's
major themes, as it was a constant theme of archaic lyric, was not a
manly attitude, particularly when, as in Anacreon's case, his white
hairs should have betokened a more responsible citizen.[33] In one
ode Anacreon even exposes himself to a double ridicule when he
confesses that the idol of his affection has spurned him on two
counts—first for his white hair, and then because she was from
Lesbos, and her preference was not for a man but for another
woman.[34]

Personal lyric was confessional, and confessions derive their
power from the degree to which what is confessed deviates from
the acceptable social norms. The lyric poets knew shame as well as
anyone. How could they not, living as they did in a culture steeped
in shame? But like their gods, Eros and Aphrodite, they laughed at
shame, as boys laugh at the scruples of their elders.

We should distinguish Sappho's personal voice from her public

31. Frag. 5 IEG.
32. Anacreon, frag. 7 Campbell.
33. But cf. Stigers 1981, 45–49, for a discussion of some of the strategies by which
the male poets could recoup some of the male authority that they would lose when
they surrendered to their erotic infatuations.
34. Frag. 358 PMG. See West 1970 for useful remarks in this context, on Sappho
presenting herself vis-à-vis her beloved much as a male poet like Theognis presented himself vis-à-vis his beloved; also Lefkowitz 1981, 62. But cf. Stigers 1981
on Sappho's need to articulate an attitude toward the erotic that differs from male
attitudes and truly reflects the feminine experience.

function. The epithalamia were her public poetry, but they have suffered even more from the ravages of time than her personal lyrics. The opposite fate befell Pindar. His personal poems have virtually disappeared, while what was preserved were his victory odes for young athletes, in which he celebrated the heroic ethos with extraordinary brilliance. If Sappho had a public function in Mytilene, to be a second Helen, *chorēgos* of the girls' dances, preparing adolescent girls for marriage and adulthood, Anacreon too had his public function at the court of Polykrates, if we accept Lucian's testimony that he had composed choruses for both girls and boys.[35] The aged dandy tottering after winsome youths was not his only persona.[36]

But little of Sappho's public function can be found in her surviving verses. If Ionian and Aeolic fathers sent their daughters to Sappho to study music and the graceful arts, surely they expected them to return with something more in hand than a scroll of Sappho's personal songs yearning for a society of women indifferent to men altogether. However gracefully Sappho might sing such themes, the political ethos of archaic Greece was not built on such a foundation.[37] Calame is careful to distinguish the socially sanctioned homoeroticism that hovers around choral lyric—homoeroticism subjected, as he puts it, to an educative function—

35. Anacreon, frag. 500 PMG. On Sappho's social function, see Hallett 1979 and Stigers's response (1979).
36. It is interesting to compare the ancient literary portraits of Anacreon and Sappho. Both were built up largely from the shame elements, whether these were derived from their own poems or were simply ascribed to them by later gossips. In Sappho's case, it was said that she was a prostitute, that she was short and ugly, that she flung herself into the sea in unrequited love, and so on. On the elements of caricature in Sappho's portrait, see Lefkowitz 1981, 62.
37. On this point, see West 1970, 326–27: if Sappho had a public function on Lesbos to prepare girls for marriage, this function "does not suit the bulk of her own poetry. . . . But it suits the Epithalamia." On the public and the private in Sappho's lyric, see Winkler 1981; also Stigers 1981. I question whether male and female homosexuality in ancient Greece should be considered exactly symmetrical. On this point, see the interesting remarks by Hallett (1979, 449–50) on the marked difference in the treatment of homosexuality in Sappho and in the male poets in the scholarship from Hellenistic to modern times.

and the homosexuality that Sappho advertises as her permanent and constant disposition.[38]

If Sappho's public function in Mytilene was to play the mothering Helen, Helen *kourotrophos*, whom Calame sees celebrated in Alcman's *Partheneion*, this is not the Helen who appears in Sappho's "Anaktoria" ode but the Helen of the epic tradition, "Helen hated of all Greece," as H.D. has her name herself in *Helen in Egypt*.[39] By invoking this more dreaded figure, Sappho elides the simple contest with which *Ode* 16 begins into the baffling, complicated, four-way contest of the *Iliad*, between beauty and ugliness, honor and shame.

If Sappho's attitude toward Paris in this ode, or toward Helen and Paris, is morally neutral, as Burnett and Gentili have argued, shame is nevertheless the context that gives the ode its force, since Sappho has selected as the paradigm to prove her argument the woman whose beauty was her shame.[40] But Eros, Sappho argues, knows no shame. Nemesis is not in his vocabulary, Eros being, like his surrogate Paris, the *puer aeternus*.[41] Sappho argues for her right to be another Helen, the subject who, in controlling the gaze, in Joan DeJean's words, can afford to bid shame a fond adieu.[42] If Helen's gaze lighted upon the beautiful but unmanly Paris, Sappho's gaze found Anaktoria—not a man at all, noble or ignoble, but a girl, to be the object of her desire.

38. 1977, 1: 430.
39. 1.1.24.
40. Worth noting in connection with Sappho's ode is Suter's study (1993), which points out that Paris of the *Iliad*, as an object of abuse, shares many of the characteristics associated later with the shameless Dionysus. Her study contributes significantly to our understanding of Helen's position both in Homer and in the post-Homeric tradition. Cf. also Boedeker 1974, 34–35, on the shame and the effeminacy that the epic tradition associates with Paris and other heroes who enjoyed Aphrodite's favors.
41. For a good discussion of the *puer aeternus* archetype, see Segal 1991.
42. 1987, 790; cf. also duBois 1984, 103, on Sappho's Helen as "an autonomous subject." On the reputation of Helen's gaze in antiquity, cf. Euripides *Trojan Women* 892 (Hekabe speaking): "She seizes the eyes of men."

PART II

THE REVISED HELEN

CHAPTER 3

The Helen of the *Odyssey*

If the *Odyssey* is, to some extent at least, a commentary on the *Iliad*, we could argue that it gives the first major revision of the Helen myth of the *Iliad*. The Trojan War is over; Paris is dead; Menelaus and Helen are husband and wife again, all passion spent, living in domestic rectitude until they are surprised by a visit from a young man who is the very image of their old friend Odysseus. "Our dearest friend," Menelaus calls Odysseus in one of the ploys of the *Odyssey* poet to give Odysseus a status equivalent to that of Achilles, who is the hero of the *Iliad* poet.[1] The Trojan War may be over, but the contest is still on for "the best," and if the contest remains open, Helen herself has still a part to play, since one of her principal functions is to mark "the best." While the Helen of the *Odyssey* is the same person that we see in the *Iliad*, the *Odyssey* poet shifts the light so as to present her in ways that are appropriate and significant for the *Odyssey*.

First, a strong romantic interest is created between Helen and Odysseus. What could be a more romantic introduction to the *Iliad* for young Telemachus, just entering his maturity, than the story that Helen has to tell of his father's secret mission and of the secret tryst between his father and Helen herself deep in the heart of the enemy city (4.240–64)? We cannot help musing here on the very

1. *Odyssey* 4.171–80.

different, yet strangely similar, story told by Hesiod (frag. 198.2–6 MW), that though Odysseus was among Helen's suitors, he did not press his suit by sending gifts "for the slender-ankled maiden, since he knew in his heart that Menelaus would win, since in possessions Menelaus was foremost among the Achaeans." Is Helen's story in the *Odyssey* intended to improve the image of Odysseus as it was presented in the kind of stories that Hesiod tells?

The courtship aspects of Helen's story, though they remain subliminal in the story itself, are reinforced by the other stories in the *Odyssey*, where Odysseus in disguise gains access to the private rooms of a goddess or queen. From Troy to Ithaca, Odysseus lays a trail of such trysts with resourceful, beautiful, and charismatic women—it is one of the repeated, formulaic themes of the poem. By including Helen among these wondrous women, the *Odyssey* reminds us that though the Trojan War is over, beauty still reigns supreme, and Helen still retains her awesome power to determine men's significance. Even the resourceful Odysseus needs Helen to enhance, if not determine, his significance.

Second, with the Trojan War concluded, Helen is safely at home in Sparta again. This Helen of the *Odyssey* W. B. Stanford calls "repentant, industrious, hospitable, domesticated, and still beautiful."[2] Helen is no longer wild; her status has been resolved. She is not wife and mistress, but simply a wife; not Greek and Trojan, but simply Greek. Eros has been caged, and Helen's vagrancy is over once and for all.[3] What passed between Menelaus and Helen when they were face-to-face again after the fall of Troy is not said. Other sources tell of Helen taking refuge in the temple of Aphrodite after the fall of Troy, where Menelaus advanced to kill her, raised sword in hand, but once under the influence of her charisma

2. At *Odyssey* 4.121 in his commentary on the poem.
3. Pausanias (3.15.11) tells of coming on a wooden statue of Aphrodite, with her feet bound in chains, in a shrine at Sparta (in her local cult form, as Morpho). Of the interpretations given of this unusual idol, Pausanias accepts the story that the chains were placed around Aphrodite's feet by Tyndareus to signify the return of his daughter Helen to her proper domestic status.

he dropped his sword (figs. 2 and 3).[4] But Homer leaves the interval between the fall of Troy and the domestic scene in Sparta a blank. How Helen was domesticated is left unsaid. It does not seem to matter. Bygones are bygones. Husband and wife, with youthful excesses behind them, can enjoy a comfortable middle age knowing that though they may grow wiser, they will never grow older.

Third, the *Odyssey* suggests more explicitly Helen's divine nature, though it remains still no more than a suggestion. The *Iliad* removes the most conspicuous aspects of Helen's divinity, leaving her only with an ambiance of divinity, which can be detected in the formulaic language used of her.[5] An uneasy awareness prevails in the *Iliad* that Helen is the mistress of daimonic powers; these powers are made visible and active in the *Odyssey*.

The greatest of Helen's powers we learn from the prophecy that Menelaus won from Proteus in Egypt, that Menelaus would enjoy immortal bliss in Elysium as his reward for being Helen's husband. The *Iliad* never gives the slightest hint that any hero could escape the common human destiny, and it would certainly be a very different *Iliad* if any of the warriors on the field at Troy thought that although death was a very strong probability for himself, Menelaus would escape death entirely for his part in the Trojan affair. Whether Helen will join Menelaus in Elysium or rise to the heavens to join her brothers, the Dioskouroi, the *Odyssey* leaves uncertain; but in any case, marriage to Helen is enough to make Menelaus the son-in-law of Zeus, and this relationship in turn is sufficient to guarantee Menelaus immortal bliss. If Helen in the *Iliad* is a victim in the social system of woman exchange, in the *Odyssey* she has risen above the social system, to become one of the "dread goddesses" whose influence plays a significant part in

4. Ibycus, frag. 296 PMG (= schol. Euripides *Andromache* 631). The silence of the Homeric epic is all the more striking since the meeting of Menelaus and Helen after the fall of Troy was a popular theme in vase painting of the classical period; see Ghali-Kahil 1955, 1: 71–113. See figure 2 in this volume for Menelaus reaching for his sword, and figure 3 for Menelaus dropping his sword.

5. On these formulas, see Clader 1976.

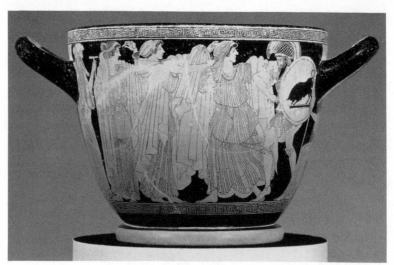

Figure 2. Attic red-figure skyphos signed by Macron as painter and Hieron as potter, about 490–480 B.C.E *Top:* Paris abducting Helen; *bottom:* Helen's return to Menelaus. Museum of Fine Arts, Boston, Acc. #13.186. (Francis Bartlett Fund. Courtesy, Museum of Fine Arts, Boston).

Figure 3. Attic red-figure neck amphora by the Berlin Painter. Menelaus dropping his sword in Helen's presence. Kunsthistorisches Museum, Vienna, Inv. Nr. IV 741. (Courtesy, Kunsthistorisches Museum, Vienna.)

determining the plot of the poem.[6] Perhaps we can attribute this shift, in part at least, to the greater latitude that the *Odyssey* allows for fantasy and romance.

Paradoxically, then, in the *Odyssey* Helen has been both more humanized and deified. We can detect the compromise between the two poles in the medical knowledge that, according to the poem, Helen acquired in Egypt. When Telemachus visits Sparta, and unhappy memories of the past threaten to dampen what should be a festive occasion, Helen has the wisdom to drop into the wine a medicine that alleviates grief and anger and brings blessed amnesia

6. For the significance of the "dread goddess" theme in the *Odyssey*, see Wohl 1993, 23–27; and pp. 34–35, on Helen's power and "numinosity" in the poem.

(*pharmakon nēpenthes*, 4.222–26).[7] The Helen who is treated in the
Iliad as if she were the cause of the Trojan War has now become the
healer, whose analgesic medication, in Homer's description, will
let a man bear the death of father or mother without grief, and even
let him witness his dear brother or son cut down by the sword
before his eyes. This medicine, the *Odyssey* informs us, Helen acquired from Polydamna (She Who Conquers Far and Wide), when
Menelaus and Helen were blown off course on their return from
Troy and forced ashore in Egypt.

Egypt! The mysterious Egypt haunts the Helen myth in our
earliest texts and continues to haunt the myth even into the twentieth century. Egypt was as famed in Homer's time, it seems, for
its ancient and occult learning as it is in our own time, when the
theme of Helen in Egypt has inspired an opera—*Die ägyptische
Helena*, by Hofmannsthal and Strauss—and a long lyric poem—
Helen in Egypt—by the American imagist poet H.D. In Homer,
Egypt is the medical capital of the world: "There the fertile soil
grows medicines [*pharmaka*] in the greatest number, many good,
when mixed, and many grievous. In Egypt every person is a physician, for they are sprung from the stock of Paian, the Healer"
(4.227–32).

Is Homer's story of Helen's Egyptian medicines an allusion to a
cult of Helen in Egypt dating as far back as the early Iron Age, or
even into the Bronze Age? But if Homer knew of a cult of Helen
like the cult that Herodotus reports of Helen worshiped at Memphis as "The Foreign Aphrodite," he has kept it subliminal and

7. On Helen's "good drug," see Bergren 1981; Wohl 1993, 34. Neumann (1963,
300) takes *pharmakon nēpenthes* to be opium, which he associates with the realm of
the Great Mother: "The magical efficacy of the poppy is a secret of the woman."
Helen's administering the drug to the young Telemachus, together with the aspects of Telemachus' journey to Pylos and Sparta that suggest a journey to the
underworld (for which, see Anderson 1958), reinforces the idea that Telemachus
enters into an initiation ceremony at Sparta. Further support for this symbolism is
the story that Menelaus tells of his wrestling with Proteus—the primal spirit of the
deep—to gain the vision of his own access to the Elysian Fields. This knowledge
makes Menelaus himself something of a Proteus when Telemachus comes to Sparta on his vision quest.

humanized it, since Helen the goddess, whether Spartan or Egyptian, would seriously interfere with the plot of Helen at Troy. The *Odyssey* has deftly translated Helen's magic into a medical skill.[8] If Helen has the powers of a dread goddess, she is also no Circe mixing dangerous drugs in the forest primeval. She has become a learned physician. The wildness of pure godhood has been domesticated.

Whatever the reason, in having Menelaus and Helen cast ashore in Egypt and detained there for seven years after the fall of Troy, Homer adds to the aura of mystery surrounding Helen. In Egypt, Menelaus slips the bonds of mortality altogether by mastering the magic of the Leviathan and thus becomes a kind of leviathan himself who can outwrestle Chaos. While he is engaged in this project, Helen studies for her degree in medicine. It is not surprising that the sophistication for which Egypt was famous would gravitate to the Spartan Helen, who in Greek myth was the miracle worker par excellence. The medicines of Polydamna (a title, no doubt, of the Great Goddess) are a reification of Helen's own mind-altering powers.[9] What tradition attributed to her daimonic gaze the *Odyssey* has humanized and historicized by attributing it to Helen's Egyptian learning. Telemachus, too young to have acquired Helen's power to transform the shameful into the beautiful, needs assistance from the medicines of Egypt.

With pain distanced, as it always is in Helen's presence, Helen prescribes another antidote: she suggests that she and Menelaus entertain their guests, Telemachus and his new friend Peisistratos,

8. Cf. Slatkin's study (1991) of the process at work in the epic, by which Thetis is reduced from her status as a major divinity in religious cult to a minor goddess in the *Iliad*.

9. In the *Iliad* Helen's charisma has the power to render her blameless in the eyes of Hector, Priam, and the old men watching the Trojan War from the city gates. As noted already, other stories told of Menelaus (and other men too) advancing on Helen with murderous intentions after the fall of Troy but dropping his sword under her gaze. For the popularity of this "emasculation" theme in classical art, see Ghali-Kahil 1955, 1: 86–93; for the effect of Helen's medicine on the narrative of the *Odyssey*, see Bergren 1981, esp. 207–8; cf. also Zeitlin 1981, 204: "These *pharmaka* belong to the poetics of enchantment."

with stories.[10] As in the *Iliad*, Helen is again a weaver of tales, but "story" in the *Odyssey* takes on a new significance. In the *Iliad* Helen's tapestry marks her impotence, her exclusion as a woman from the contests where men struggle to define meaning. But stories in the *Odyssey* have a generative power; they are the word itself shaping events, the events being in this case the return of Odysseus to his home.[11] The stories told to Telemachus by Nestor at Pylos, and by Helen and Menelaus in Sparta, are as much pre-scriptive as they are commemorative. Through them the name of Odysseus will be revived, he himself will be resurrected from the dead, and his son will come into his heroic inheritance.[12]

Helen, now *logos* maker, the shaper of the story, will instruct Telemachus, to shape the virtually fatherless boy into the son who will be prepared to stand at his father's side when his father returns to claim his throne. Her function in the *Odyssey* suggests her func-tion in cult as *kourotrophos*, "nurse of the young shoot."[13] But, besides instructing or initiating Telemachus, in recalling the Odys-seus who could steal into Troy and wreak damage from within the city walls, Helen will also recreate the Odysseus of the past, who is

10. Murnaghan (1987, 162 n.23) notes that Helen's drug "works as an artificial substitute for the passage of time by creating instantaneous reconciliation to loss." The analgesic effect of stories, of poetry in the broadest sense, was a conventional topic in Greek literature from the earliest period.

11. See Van Groningen 1953; Austin 1966; Bergren 1981.

12. For Helen's educative function in the *Odyssey*, and the sympathetic magic of the stories that Telemachus hears on his journey to Pylos and Sparta, see Austin 1975, 182. On Helen as story (*logos*), and the place of Helen's drug in her *logos*, see Bergren 1981, 1983; Zeitlin 1981, 203–7.

13. See Clader 1976, 70, 74ff., on *koros* (*kouros*) as "young shoot," and Helen's function in cult as *kourotrophos*, "nurse of the young." In Theocritus *Idyll* 18.48ff. (the epithalamium for the marriage of Helen and Menelaus) the girls, singing in Helen's honor at her bedroom door on the morning after the wedding, describe how they will garland a plane tree with a lotus wreath, anoint the tree with oil poured from a silver vessel, and inscribe on its bark "Reverence me. For I am the plant (or shoot) of Helen." As *kourotrophos*, Helen is both the living presence immanent in the tree and its nurse. For further reading on Helen's connection with the young, both male and female, see Calame 1977, 81; Lindsay 1974, chap. 9, "The Nature of Helen."

assumed dead but will soon steal into his own palace and lay waste
to the usurpers and pretenders to his throne.

In Helen's story of the Trojan War, Odysseus, dressed in a
beggar's rags, with self-inflicted welts on his back to complete the
disguise, slips into Troy on a spying mission (4.244–64). No
doubt, if discovered, Odysseus could pass himself off as an abused
runaway from the Greek camp, a Thersites turned deserter. The
story is, of course, a shadow play of the events to come when
Odysseus steals into his own palace, with the same motive (espionage), and the same strategy of insinuation and entrapment.

The strategy was successful at Troy, Helen continues, or rather,
her story opens up several readings. We might say that the strategy
was almost successful or that it was a failure or that Odysseus
managed to snatch victory from failure. Such are the ambiguities
that arise when Helen tells the story, particularly when she is the
principal character in the story. Odysseus, stealing into Troy, escaped the scrutiny of the Trojans—his disguise was so far
successful—but not, of course, Helen, whose gaze no man could
hope to escape, not even Odysseus. Recognizing Odysseus beneath his disguise, Helen leads him to her private rooms, where she
bathes and feeds him, and they then converse as old friends, or
should we say lovers? We cannot help seeing the shadow of another
woman reading the story over Helen's shoulder—Penelope, who
in book 19 will also entertain the wily actor and elicit his secrets
from him.

Helen, charming Odysseus as easily as she charms other men,
swears an oath to do him no harm "until he reached the ships and
stockades of the Achaeans" (4.254–55). We are reminded now of
Circe swearing a similar oath, and of the other goddesses, nymphs,
and queens whose protection Odysseus enjoyed on his homeward
journey. Seduced by a woman apparently wilier and more perspi-
cacious than he, Odysseus then freely divulges the entire plan of
the Greeks (their *noos*, their "mind or intention," line 256). His
mission into Troy was not to divulge but to gather information,
but men's purposes are easily swayed when Helen is in the room.

Odysseus then creeps back to the Greek ships—so Helen concludes her story—but leaving a slaughter of unsuspecting Trojans in his wake. The Trojan women cried aloud for their men, treacherously killed in the night, but "my heart rejoiced," Helen concludes,

> Since it was turned now and bidding me turn homeward,
> And I repented of my infatuation, which Aphrodite
> Had given me, when she brought me there from my dear
> Fatherland, leaving my child, my own roof, my husband—
> A man not lacking in the least, either in mind or body.[14]

The plan, which falters under Helen's gaze, is fortunately put on track again, by Helen herself, collaborating now with Odysseus. This is not the impotent captive of the *Iliad*, but the captive turned double agent, conspiring with the archconspirator of the Greeks— Odysseus himself. Only Helen, with her allegiances on both sides, could move as fluidly between the categories of friend and enemy. The Helen of the *Odyssey* has the fateful gaze attributed to her in the tradition, which can lead Odysseus to spill his secrets like a husband exchanging confidences with his wife, but what has changed between the *Iliad* and the *Odyssey*, we are led to believe, is Helen's allegiance. To accept her reconstruction of the past, if her gaze had the potency to disarm Odysseus, it was nevertheless wholly benevolent in its intentions.

Helen's tale of espionage and conspiracy would hardly suit the *Iliad*, where engagements take place on the open field, in the fierce light of day. The Helen of the *Odyssey* takes us into the inner room, where we share the secrets of a woman marginalized but compensating for her exclusion by undermining the city walls from within, sowing duplicity in all directions. Helen was not to be taken for granted. If men made her a sign, she would prove to be the sign maker, awarding them significance according to her categories and values. Even telling a story about herself, Helen is equivocal. When will her magnet, shifting from Paris to Odysseus to Menelaus, shift to some other pole?

14. 4.260–64.

Helen's memory of her secret rendezvous with the master of guile is a story better saved for an intimate occasion, such as her own dinner party, with only the son of Odysseus as her guest, and help from the medicines of Egypt to soften the effect. It can be told now, *entre nous* as it were, because the war is over, and Helen's charisma is no longer threatening. But, more important, a story in which Odysseus spies on Troy and Helen spies on Odysseus belongs in the *Odyssey*. We have left the military arena of the *Iliad*, where issues are to be definitively settled by sword and spear. Under Helen's guidance Telemachus enters a hermeneutic zone, where signs are obscured in shadow (at the center of the poem his father visits the underworld, which is the theater of shadow and image), where multiplicity of meanings is in order, where stealth is a virtue, and duplicity the proof of a superior mind.[15]

But lest we be completely seduced by Helen's story, Menelaus follows it with another, quite different, story from the Trojan War, which, while also celebrating Helen for her daimonic powers, celebrates Odysseus even more for his power to withstand and outwit her magic. Again the subtext is the meeting of two great minds—Helen and Odysseus. As Helen's was a story of intrigue within Troy, her husband tells of intrigue within the Greek camp, symbolized by the warriors crouched in the belly of the Wooden Horse, who may be contrasted with Odysseus hidden in Helen's private rooms in Helen's story. But to intrigue Menelaus adds counterintrigue, in the person of Helen—who else? Only one person in Troy could conceivably have seen through the trick of the Wooden Horse; namely, Helen, whose gaze was proverbial. Menelaus describes a suspicious Helen circling the Wooden Horse, probing its belly with her hands and, as if intuiting its inner mean-

15. For the intelligence required in the *Odyssey*, which the stories told of Helen and Odysseus in book 4 exemplify, see the study by Detienne and Vernant (1978) on the place of *mētis* in Greek thought. *Mētis*, the intelligence in which Odysseus excels, Detienne and Vernant characterize as a complex of mental attitudes that combines "flair, wisdom, forethought, subtlety of mind, deception, resourcefulness, vigilance, opportunism," applied to shifting, transient, and ambiguous situations that "do not lend themselves to precise measurement" (3). See also Raphals 1992.

ing, calling out to each Greek warrior by name, simulating—such was her power of mimesis—every man's wife in turn.[16] But Helen's treachery was foiled, thanks to Athena's providence in leading Helen away from the Horse, and to the grim determination of Odysseus, who was able to restrain the warriors in the Horse from crying out in answer to Helen's call.

In Helen's story of Odysseus she was a better trickster than he. But now Menelaus revises the portrait with a story that exonerates Odysseus of the slightest inference of shame that he might have incurred in Helen's story. In the story that Helen's husband tells, Odysseus proves to be more clever than Helen on two counts— first for his contribution to the design of the Wooden Horse and then for his ability to prevent Helen's magic from undoing the purposes for which it was built. In Helen's portrait she was a secret collaborator within Troy working on behalf of the Greeks, but Menelaus virtually cancels out that Helen with a story that tells of her open collaboration with the Trojans, her yearning for her former home and husband apparently forgotten. In Helen's story Odysseus divulges the military secrets, while in her husband's story he prevents their disclosure. In one story Odysseus is the seduced; in the other he successfully resists Helen's seduction. In one story Helen's gaze has the power to recognize Odysseus beneath his disguise; in the other story the roles are reversed, and Odysseus, now better disguised, sees through Helen's magic.[17] Menelaus attributes Helen's perfidious behavior around the Wooden Horse to a daimon's influence, a tactful way, perhaps, to shift the blame from Helen. But that is no explanation. Helen's daimon is the problem: it has no reliable axis, no fixed reference point.[18] Aphrodite may be domesticated in city temples, but that is only an illusion: her real temples are in the wild.

16. Zeitlin (1981, 204) calls Helen in the *Odyssey* "mistress of mimesis."
17. On the import of the two Trojan stories, and their relations to the overall theme of the *Odyssey*, see Zeitlin 1981, 203–6; Olson 1989; Wohl 1993, 34–35.
18. Cf. Murnaghan 1987, 121, on Helen as "a figure who epitomizes both female seductiveness and female treachery."

Helen, probing the secret of the Wooden Horse, is accompanied by a Trojan, "godlike Deiphobos" (4.276). Homer adds no further detail about him, but in the post-Homeric tradition Helen became the wife of Deiphobos after the death of Paris. He was her third husband, after Menelaus and Paris; her fourth, if we include Theseus, who raped Helen when she was a girl and kept her in his custody until she was freed by the Dioskouroi. Where are Helen's loyalties now?

"Doubleness," Ann Bergren argues, is Helen's defining characteristic of herself, and adds that the Homeric poems are unique in that "they not only reveal but do not attempt to regulate the doubleness of Helen."[19] Later authors would work to resolve the doubleness, but Homer insists on it. In the *Iliad* Helen's status depends on the viewer. To the Greeks she is a Greek wife, who has been wived according to the proper protocols (with the oaths sworn by all her suitors to protect the contract) but who has now been abducted (or seduced). She must be returned to the marital status assigned to her. But the Trojans, perhaps taking their cue from Priam and Hector, treat Helen as the legitimate wife of Paris.

But "wife," though it may have its place in society, is not a term in Aphrodite's vocabulary. Her province is sex and sexual desire. Hesiod makes the point explicit when he puns on smile and genitals in glossing her epithet "smile-loving."[20] Aphrodite's companions, to continue with Hesiod, are Eros and Himeros, desire and longing; her vocabulary is "girlish whispers, smiles, deceits, sweet pleasure, and the honeyed persuasions of love."[21]

Helen, as Aphrodite's surrogate, and therefore not bound by society's inhibitions, is a woman without a country, though, conversely, she is at home anywhere. Helen's social function, woman-

---

19. 1983, 80. Bergren notes some of the conspicuous double elements in the Helen myth—two abductions (Theseus and Paris); two brothers, with their alternating states of life and death; Helen's dual paternity (Zeus and Tyndareus).

20. *Theogony* 200. I am one of those who accept that a pun is intended here, and am grateful to Frank Romer for sharing with me an unpublished paper on this passage.

21. *Theogony* 200–206.

as-sign, with all its contradictions, alienates her from her own being. But then she is doubly alienated, since the cost for her agreement to play her social function is to be alienated from society—the proverbial contradiction of the prostitute. She must forgo her own shame to play the woman of no shame, yet she would not succeed in her public function if she did not truly understand shame. Paris, with hardly even an embryonic sense of shame, is pretty but uninteresting. The focus of attention is always more on Helen than on Paris.

In the *Odyssey* Helen's social status has been firmly resolved, and her powers to damage Hellenic honor have been drastically curtailed, yet doubleness continues to haunt her character. She is still the story and the storyteller, the spectacle and the spectator. The *Odyssey* shapes Helen's ambiguity to its own purposes. Both Helen's and Menelaus' stories are of the intriguing mind, mind outwitting mind. Helen is the victor in her story, but Menelaus tells of a Helen whose intentions were far from benevolent, once again attempting to seduce Odysseus and his fellow Greeks into betraying their own cause. Never losing sight of its theme, to shape the contest for "the best" in favor of Odysseus, and to celebrate the crafty mind over physical prowess, the *Odyssey* leaves us in no doubt that among men only Odysseus could match Helen in duplicity and charm.[22]

22. Much has been written in recent years regarding the recognition scenes between Odysseus and Penelope in the later books of the *Odyssey*. See Doherty 1994 (forthcoming); Murnaghan 1987; Van Nortwick 1979. It has been pointed out that though Penelope is praised in the poem for her cleverness, her cleverness is still defined in terms of her relationship to her role as the faithful wife. If we compare, however, the story of Helen attempting to seduce the Greek warriors in the Wooden Horse with Penelope's trick of the bed, Penelope proves more cunning than Helen. Helen may be said to have seduced Odysseus in a manner of speaking (in her story of their encounter in Troy), but of all the women and goddesses who fall under Odysseus' spell only Penelope could be said to have truly seduced him into bed. Also worth noting in this context are the comments of Olson (1989, 393), who argues that the sexual tension revealed in the stories that Menelaus and Helen tell foreshadows the warnings given to both Telemachus and Odysseus that Penelope is not to be trusted: "The male bonds of trust between master and servant, father and son, are ultimately accepted as more important—or at least more

To crown Helen's mystery, Menelaus goes on to tell Telemachus that Menelaus himself, as Helen's husband, and therefore
the son-in-law of Zeus, has been granted to dwell in Elysium "at
the boundaries of earth, where the living is most easy; where there
is neither cloud nor heavy snow nor rain, but Ocean sends forth the
breath of Zephyr to refresh mortal beings" (4.561–68). Humiliated
in life, Menelaus is yet to be raised above all other men and rewarded, not for his valor, which is undistinguished, but simply for
accepting his part in Helen's story, as the cuckolded husband.
Where Helen will go the *Odyssey* leaves vague, though we are left
to infer that she too will retire with Menelaus to the Elysian
Fields.[23] Completing their parts in the great spectacle of shame,
they will be compensated by spending eternity in the balmy climate reserved for those few who most closely approximate the
archetypes as signifiers of Being itself, which transcends even
shame.

Who is the real Helen? "In the *Iliad*, at the beginning of her
literary tradition, the figure of Helen is marked by radical undecidability," Mihoko Suzuki aptly remarks.[24] Even in the *Odyssey*,
when Helen is respectable again, she is still marked by undecidability. Is Helen a goddess? Aphrodite's threats in the *Iliad* remind us that Helen is no god if to be a god is to have force; that is,
power and volition. Is she then a human? If so, she belongs to that
class of heroes which has its being in the ambiguous space between

---

secure—than those between husband and wife." For this purpose, to demonstrate
the unreliability of women, Helen was the *Odyssey*'s perfect paradigm. Morgan
(1991) shows, in a few pointed pages, how deeply shame affects the portrait of
Penelope (in contrast to Helen's shamelessness). We might even interpret Penelope
as the revision of Helen, so that the Trojan War can reach the fitting conclusion,
with Helen's shamelessness almost canceled out by Penelope's higher sense of
shame.

23. But here too ambiguity haunts the Helen myth. The tradition variously portrayed Helen after death as living with Achilles on Leuke or joining the Dioskouroi
as a celestial constellation. Even in death Helen's allegiances were never finally
resolved.

24. 1989, 18.

mortality and immortality.[25] Helen is a child in the patriarchy. But she is also a woman who cannot be constrained by the social codes that govern other men and women. Helen is at the center of events, yet marginalized. In the *Odyssey*, she is the perfect wife, when that is expected of her, and in the *Iliad* she is the perfect mistress.

Many separate factors lead almost inevitably to the theory that Helen was once a goddess but has been heroized, trimmed down from goddess to virtual goddess, to fit into the scope of the Homeric epic. We might cite her daimonic power in the Homeric poems, peculiar to itself; her "doubleness"; and her "radical undecidability." We note also the mysterious eclipse of the Dioskouroi by the two sons of Atreus; Helen's parentage, as daughter of Zeus, with her mother never named in Homer; and the confusion in the myths between Leda and Nemesis. Helen's cult of the tree (as immanent presence at Sparta, as tree fetish on Rhodes) and the hints in epic diction of Helen's original Indo-European role as sun-princess, sister of the Twin Riders, are suggestive too. L. R. Farnell, however, objects to the "faded goddess" theory, which was in its heyday in his time, as being "sterile" and "unnatural."[26] Sterile, because the functions ascribed to Helen in the various cults do little to illuminate the character of Helen in the Homeric texts. Where is Helen Dendritis, fetish or goddess of the tree, to be discovered in the *Iliad*? Unnatural, since our earliest certain evidence for Helen is Homer himself, and for him (and his epic tradition) she is not a goddess but a woman like a goddess. Why, Farnell argues with some reason, should we reverse the order of our available evidence and take the myths circulating in the post-Homeric period as representing the pre-Homeric Helen, from which the Helen of epic was derived? Farnell contends instead that Helen was heroized in the same way that the heroes were heroized, as humans commemorated for deeds of heroic stature and elevated to the level of the

25. Nagy in his studies of local versus Panhellenic traditions (1979, 1990b) has shown that the issue of god or hero is a highly complex question. We have to ask, "God or hero where?"
26. 1921, 324ff.

protective, ancestral daimones of local cults. Why should we assume that the heroes were heroized from humans to demigods and daimones, but that Helen was heroized in reverse, from goddess to virtual goddess to human?

Clader revives the goddess theory with new and persuasive arguments. The evidence is mostly circumstantial. Helen Dendritis or the Indo-European sun-princess is certainly not to be discovered in the Helen of epic in any obvious way. Yet Clader's study of the epic diction relating to Helen invokes an undefinable mystery, as alluring as it is terrifying. The silence of the Homeric poems with regard to Helen's mother, their insistence on Helen as "the daughter of Zeus," the glancing allusion of the *Iliad* to Helen's powerful but absent brothers, the Dioskouroi, and the implication of apotheosis with which the *Odyssey* brings the Helen story to a close— such hints betoken a larger Helen myth from which the poetic tradition drew what suited its own purposes. Some of the stories told of Helen in the post-Homeric tradition, like that of her power to render armed men impotent, could certainly be attributed to the influence of epic. But it would be difficult to ascribe a feature of the Helen cults such as the tree fetish on Rhodes simply to clever, hermeneutic readings of the epic. We could imagine a story growing from the epic tradition which told of Helen condemned to death by hanging, but the fetish of a woman hung from a tree suggests an ancient cult of the earliest animistic period, assimilated to the story of Helen of Troy. Gregory Nagy's studies of hero cults and traditions in ancient Greece have made it virtually impossible to distinguish the post-Homeric from the pre-Homeric elements in a traditional myth.[27] Besides, even taking Homer as our earliest Greek document, Nagy has revealed how thoroughly the Homeric tradition is imbued with Indo-European influences extending back long before the Bronze Age.

The Helen that Clader reconstructs, taking the cult and epic traditions together, is truly a daimon. It is certainly tempting to

27. 1979, 1990a.

read in Homer's Helen the epic, Panhellenic translation of the various Helens of local cults—Helen of the tree, princess of the sun, nurse of the young. Clader's hypothesis, based on C. Watkins's derivation of Greek Helene from the Indo-European root *wel-, "twist," that Helen's name is cognate with Anglo-Saxon "willow," is almost irresistible.[28] It would be a pleasure to believe that Homer's Argive Helen is second cousin to the willows gracing English lawns. But if Homer's Helen is really the same person as the Helen in cult, her function as *kourotrophos* has been translated into her terrifying responsibility to seduce brave young men onto the path of individuation, which leads, in the end, to the grave. She is both Aphrodite and Persephone. Yet however Helen was fabricated, whatever historical facts were assimilated into the myth in the course of time, the figure of Helen was born in the age when the archetypes were taken to be not figures of speech but true living presences in the world, and humans derived their reality to the degree that they impersonated the archetypes, as copies of the original.[29]

In contrast to religious cult, where the boundaries were probably more fluid between idol and immanent presence, the epic maintained a clear distinction between god and hero. Zeus could not save his own Sarpedon from death, and Thetis accepted Achilles' death as any mother would, with resignation to a fate that could not be otherwise. Even so, Helen and the hero Herakles represent an unusual degree of indeterminacy between the orders of human and divine, which the myths themselves could not quite resolve. Both Helen and Herakles were curiously double. Herakles was even given a double form after death—as a deathless Being with the other deathless Beings on Mount Olympus, and as an empty idol, which Odysseus saw in the underworld with the other ghosts of the dead. Helen's doubleness lay in being both responsible and not responsible for the thousands who died at Troy in

28. 1976, 80. Worth reading in connection with the cults of Helen as goddess of tree and plant is Frazer 1935, vol. 2, chap. 9, on the pagan worship of trees.
29. Cf. Lacan 1978, 45: "The gods belong to the field of the real."

pursuit of beauty, for which she would stand as both the signifier and the signified.

Whatever her origin, the Helen of our Homeric texts is not a fictional character such as might be composed in the age of rationalism, to which touches of divinity have been added as a cosmetic. For a fictional Helen, we would have to go to Euripides' *Helen*, where the fiction is apparent in every scene (see Chapter 6 in this volume). But that is a very different person from the Helen created in the mythopoeic age. The mythopoeic Helen, with her uncanny powers, her disregard for social mores coupled with her grace in every social situation, her self-determinism even in captivity, was born in the age when gods still walked on the earth, and the daimon could be seen in every tree. Attuned as they were to the physical world, to the here and now, the archaic Greeks nevertheless understood that Nature herself spoke through masks, and therefore to adopt a mask was to approach the highest reaches of Being.[30] Helen is all mask and therefore comes closest to the gods, whose presence, radiating through her, makes her the more real.

The wonder is how the epic tradition shaped the various Helens of cult into the Helen of the Homeric poems, who would illuminate the great themes of the *Iliad* by standing in that light where humans and their archetypes meet, a woman incarnating the goddess, *kourotrophos* of all plant and animal life, while experiencing the shame of such an incarnation. Wherever she appears in Homer, Helen is both goddess and human, an exquisite portrait of what it meant in the Homeric age to be cast as a daimon mediating between Being and Significance, a young woman with a god's image to project, wearing the carefree face of Nemesis on the public stage, while keeping her own cares to herself.

---

30. On the intricate systems of belief that govern the relations between god, mask, and human impersonation, see Levi-Strauss 1975.

CHAPTER 4

Stesichorus and His *Palinode*

It was bound to happen. Helen's humanizing process, once begun, would continue until someone found the way to divest her of all her divinity, to render her more human and therefore more believable. Stesichorus was the first poet on record to construct this new, more human Helen, though his intention was probably the opposite, to transubstantiate the woman—Helen of Troy—into the immaculate goddess of Spartan cult.

While Sappho and Alcaeus were bringing luster to Lesbos on the shores of Anatolia through their personal lyric, in Sicily Stesichorus was gaining great fame for choral lyric. Stesichorus—He Who Stations the Chorus—was a kind of nom de plume, signifying his role as both composer and choreographer in the development of the choral form. He was credited with inventing the triadic structure of the choral ode—strophe, antistrophe, and epode. The terms, meaning "turn," "counterturn," and "song sung in place," reveal the choral ode's original character as dance, a public performance, by a company of dancers, whether women or men, boys or girls.[1]

Several ancient references testify to the high esteem that Stesichorus enjoyed in antiquity, but one piece of evidence is of particu-

---

1. For Greek choral lyric as poetry to be sung and danced, see Nagy 1990b; Mullen 1982, 14ff., also his "Appendix" on pp. 225–30, for the ancient testimony on the choral ode as "triadic dance."

lar interest—the spectacular and famous François Vase. Depicted on the vase is the wedding of Peleus and Thetis, and among the guests are the nine Muses, whose names are inscribed on the vase, so that their identity is unmistakable. All nine Muses are thus named, except that beside the figure who should be Terpsichore (She Who Takes Pleasure in the Dance), the painter, Kleitias, has inscribed the name ΣΤΕΣΙΧΟΡΕ (Stesichore, the feminine form of Stesichorus—She Who Stations the Chorus). In this pun, highly unusual in the history of ancient vase painting, the potter and the painter have conspired first to fuse the Muse of dance with the celebrated choreographer, and then to use the rotund surface of the vase as a primitive moving screen on which to choreograph figures and scenes from the poet's various odes.[2] The François Vase is an impressive object, clearly not intended for practical use but for public, ceremonial display, and its painting is a magnificent tribute to Stesichorus, offered jointly by the patron who commissioned the vase, the painter, and the potter.

Also included among the wedding guests on the François Vase is Dionysus, who is depicted bearing as his gift what Andrew Stewart argues must be the golden urn in which the bones of Achilles were later to be buried. Here the potter and the painter conspire to celebrate themselves and their place in the tradition. The vase waxes self-reflective, like the *Iliad* viewing itself through Helen's tapestry, referring to itself as the traditional wedding and funeral gift via the mythical vase portrayed on the vase itself. By intertwining the names of the Muse and the choreographer, the François Vase elides the art of pottery into the art of the choral ode, and via its allusion to the poet whom the pseudo-Longinus would later group with "the most Homeric" of ancient authors, the painter and the potter advertise their art as being as traditional as epic, and as modern as Stesichorus.[3]

---

2. Stewart (1983) argues that the scenes represented on the François Vase are all references to poems by Stesichorus.

3. [Longinus] *On the Sublime* 13.3. In the context the author uses *homērōtatos* (most Homeric) to convey two senses: that the authors cited, among whom he

In personal lyric, like Sappho's odes, which she would have sung while accompanying herself on the lyre, the setting is intimate, and contemporary events or the poet's personal confessions become the explicit subject matter. While traditional material perfuses all archaic lyric, whether personal or choral, the central theme of personal lyric is the here and now. But choral lyric was intended for a larger public and a wider perspective. It presumed the *khoros*—a public space marked off as the dancing ground. In Sparta the agora was called the Khoros—thus the public space where people gathered for business, politics, and religion was marked as the dancing floor of the city.[4] Choral lyric presumed also a large audience, which was no doubt also expected to be enthusiastic and participatory. The choral art was, artistically speaking, the property not of the private symposium but of the polis; taken as a whole, it reflected in microcosm the society and its hierarchies.[5] Its themes were the mythical traditions of the local families, with their claims of descent from the ancient heroes, or more broadly the polis, the city itself. The emerging city consciousness was at once proudly local and Panhellenic.[6] Even in Pindar's victory odes, which celebrate recent victors in the Panhellenic games, the themes were more likely to be those of the epic and Panhellenic tradition, celebrations of the gods and heroes of

includes Plato himself, had Homeric sublimity; and that they most deliberately studied and imitated Homer. By coincidence, the passage in Plato which prompts this author to link Stesichorus and Plato (*Republic* 586) is the very passage where Plato refers to Stesichorus and the eidolon of Helen.

4. On *khoros*, see Nagy 1990b passim; Mullen 1982. On the Spartan agora as *khoros*, see Pausanias 3.11.9; Nagy, p. 345.

5. For diverse approaches to this public and civic function of choral lyric, see Podlecki 1971; Calame 1977; Mullen 1982; Burnett 1987; Nagy 1990b, 345 and passim.

6. For the complicated relations between the local cults, with their own traditions, and the Panhellenism of epic and choral lyric, see Nagy 1990b. See also Burnett (1988), who discusses the importance of choral poetry in the western colonies of Greece, where the colonists were required to abandon the cults and cult objects of their mother cities and needed new myths and rites that would legitimize the colony, while also proclaiming its Panhellenic traditions.

myth, and their adventures on that luminous horizon where once gods and heroes had met and conversed with each other. Like the François Vase, Pindar's victory odes were commissioned to celebrate a moment in the here and now, but also like the vase, they were composed to stand as monuments conferring glory (*kleos*) for all time as Homer did. Glory being preeminently their theme, their focus still remains on the tradition, even when they digress to supply the local color that would please the victors and their families.

Stesichorus was noted for the grandeur of his themes and style. Quintilian, who praises him for "sustaining on the lyre the weight of epic," remarks that Stesichorus would have been another Homer, "had he but practiced moderation."[7] The historian Ammianus Marcellinus tells a story that Socrates, in prison awaiting his death, overheard a man singing an ode by Stesichorus.[8] Socrates begged the man to teach it to him while he still had time. But what would be the use? the musician asked, since Socrates was to die the following day. "So that I might depart life knowing something more," Socrates replied. Any song might have engaged Socrates' attention in those last days of his life, but this anecdote, even if mostly apocryphal, when taken in conjunction with the high approval that Socrates expresses for Stesichorus in the *Phaedrus*, gives us a gauge to measure where Stesichorus ranked in Socrates' estimation. Socrates would not have misspent his last hours committing to memory a song that was an affront to the dignity of the gods or heroes.

Of Stesichorus' prolific opus, nothing now remains but a handful of grammarians' glosses and a few scattered lines discovered on

7. Quintilian *Institutes* 10.1.62. For Stesichorus in relation to Homer, see Nagy 1990b, 419–23. For other studies of Stesichorus, see Wilamowitz 1913, 233–42; West 1971b; Stewart 1983.

8. 38.4. But cf. the similar story of Solon, begging his nephew to teach him an ode of Sappho's which the boy had just sung (Stobaeus *Florilegium* 29.88). When asked, "What for?" Solon replied, "So that I may learn it and die." Was Socrates following a tradition begun by Solon, or were both stories fictional, belonging to the genre of "final requests"?

papyrus scraps rescued from the rubbish heaps of Egypt. While the scraps give some indication of his themes, they are insufficient to give us any basis for judging the solemnity and melodiousness of his verse, for which he was extraordinarily honored both in his life and after death. For our fuller understanding of the choral ode as the cultural art of the archaic polis, we must rely on the later masters, particularly Bacchylides and Pindar. For Stesichorus, one of the earliest shapers of the choral form, we have only anecdotes and a few scant words from his own compositions.

Thanks to Plato, however, three continuous verses have been preserved that have ensured Stesichorus' enduring fame even after all his odes have crumbled back to dust. These are generally taken to be the prelude of what Plato refers to as "the so-called *Palinode*," an ode that Stesichorus composed as an apology to Helen for slanders that he is said to have spoken about her in an earlier ode.[9]

Stesichorus' first Helen ode has vanished, if indeed it ever existed, so that we cannot say how he may have treated Helen differently from other poets of his time or before him. But a scholiast to Euripides gives us a bit of information that suggests the approach that Stesichorus may have taken toward the Helen theme: "Stesichorus says that Tyndareus, when sacrificing to all the gods, forgot only the Kyprian, the gentle giver. She, angered, made the daughters of Tyndareus bigamists, trigamists, and deserters of husbands."[10]

For his "slander" (*katēgoria*), as Socrates calls it, Stesichorus was

<hr/>

9. The *Palinode* is given as Stesichorus, frag. 192 PMG. Bergk also attributed frag. 241 PMG to the *Palinode* ("I will go to seek another prelude"). For the ancient sources on the *Palinode*, see Page's notes to frags. 192–93 PMG; also frags. 192–93 in Davies 1991; Dale 1967, xvii–xxiv. For further discussion, see Woodbury 1967; Segal 1971; Cingano 1982; Kannicht 1969; Zeitlin 1981, 201–11; Nagy 1990b, 419ff.; Bassi 1993.

10. Frag. 223 PMG (= schol. Euripides *Orestes* 249). In the same fragment, which continues as Hesiod, frag. 176 MW, the scholiast adds some verses from Hesiod that tell a similar story: Aphrodite in her anger at Tyndareus placed his daughters under an "evil curse" (*kakē phēmē*), with the result that "Timandre left her husband Ekhemos for Phyleus; Klytaimestra abandoned Agamemnon and, taking the worse as her husband, slept with Aigisthos. In the same way Helen disgraced the bed of blond Menelaus."

struck blind. But Stesichorus came to understand the truth—so the story goes—and composed a new poem, "the so-called *Palinode*," as Socrates refers to it; literally, his "song re-sung," or his "song reversed." Helen was apparently mollified, since, if we are to believe Socrates, Stesichorus had his eyesight immediately restored.

Plato's story of the *Palinode* occurs in the *Phaedrus* (243a) when Socrates has just completed his speech in praise of the nonlover (or, more accurately, the one masking his erotic intentions by feigning to be the disinterested "friend"), in his attempt to outshine Lysias, of whose speech-making powers Phaedrus was greatly enamored.[11] Now, suddenly repentant, as if coming to his senses, Socrates confesses that he has committed a grave error in speaking in a derogatory way about Eros, in his view one of the greatest of the daimones mediating between the gods in their bliss and our less than blissful world.

"I must purify myself, my friend," Socrates says by way of preface to the quote. "There is an ancient purification," he continues, "for those who err in telling sacred stories [*mythologia*], which Homer did not know, but Stesichorus did. For, being deprived of his eyesight for accusing Helen, Stesichorus, unlike Homer, did not remain in ignorance. Being musical [*mousikos*, "gifted by the Muses"], he recognized the cause. Whereupon he composed the so-called *Palinode*." Here Socrates quotes what has been taken to be the prelude of the poem:

> The story [*logos*] is not true.
> You did not board the well-benched ships,
> You did not reach the towers of Troy.

Invoking Stesichorus as his exemplar of the mythologist who was both virtuous and enlightened, Socrates then purges himself by composing a palinode to Eros, as his expiation for slandering a great benefactor of humankind. As Stesichorus was to Homer, a

11. On the erotic relations between Lysias and Phaedrus, as lover and beloved, and as author and reader, see Svenbro 1988, 219–25.

more truly inspired poet, revising not only his own text but the text of his most inspired predecessor, Socrates would be to Lysias, a more inspired rhetorician, correcting his own errors and those of his rival, to demonstrate how a god or daimon should properly be praised.

The *Palinode* has vanished, along with all the other odes of Stesichorus, except for the three verses quoted by Socrates, or four if we include the verse that T. Bergk conjectured might belong to the *Palinode*.[12] We do not know how Stesichorus treated Helen in the *Palinode*, except that from Plato's allusion in the *Republic* (586c), where he contrasts true pleasures with the mere phantoms of true pleasures, we learn that Stesichorus had explained away Helen at Troy by saying that she whom the Greeks and Trojans took for Helen was in fact only her eidolon (ghost or phantom).

Though the *Palinode* was often cited in antiquity, no one after Plato ever quoted a single verse from the poem until on a papyrus scrap uncovered only in our own era, a commentator on the lyric poets cites the Peripatetic scholar Chamaeleon for his authority that Stesichorus composed not one but two palinodes, and even quotes the first lines of both.[13] This story is hardly credible, but even if it were true that Stesichorus had composed two palinodes, the papyrus sheds no further light on either the structure or the content of the poem or poems. The *Palinode* was more talked of than read, if indeed it was read at all after the time of Plato.

More memorable than the *Palinode* itself were the circumstances of its composition. What was there to say about Helen once it was said that she was not at Troy? But a Helen insulted by a poet and

12. Bergk conjectured that both frag. 241 ("I will seek another prelude") and frag. 257 ("speaking foolish things") might belong to the *Palinode*. See Page's note to frag. 241 PMG. This produces in some translations a fourth, introductory verse to the passage quoted by Plato: "I spoke foolishness; I will go and seek another prelude."

13. Stesichorus, frag. 193 PMG (= P. Oxy. 2506, frag. 26, col. i). Bassi (1993) is the most recent scholar to join several others in accepting both assertions of this papyrus, that Stesichorus composed two palinodes and that he located Helen in Egypt during the Trojan War. I remain skeptical on both counts.

taking her revenge for his blasphemy—that was a story to be remembered. It had the properties of an archetypal myth: a man unwittingly offending a great goddess and suffering nemesis at her hands; a mythologist blinded for political insensitivity but restored to sight when he had corrected his myth; Helen proofreading, indeed dictating, her own biography; and finally the celebrated Helen of Troy replaced by a phantom. A topos of such rich implications—"a haunting theme," as my friend James Merrill called it in private conversation—was bound to develop variants in the course of time, the confusions inherent in the natural course of gossip being exacerbated in this case by the enigmatic nature of the subject. The reputation of the *Palinode* has far outlived the poem itself, and Stesichorus, though now hardly more than a name, has achieved his immortality for being the first poet to see that Helen of Troy was a pure fiction.

If the *Palinode* was intended to resolve the mystery of Homer's Helen, it succeeded only in provoking new mysteries. The differences among the various later commentators, while shedding little light, alas, on the actual structure or contents of the *Palinode*, reveal much about the problems that any revision of the Helen myth entailed. The first problem presented by the *Palinode* was the eidolon itself. Given that it was the key to the whole revision, where and when could it be plausibly inserted into the plot? In the later tradition, some claimed that the eidolon was introduced into the story in Egypt.[14] According to one version of the events, Stesicho-

---

14. For the assertion that Stesichorus had dispatched Helen to Egypt for the duration of the Trojan War, see Stesichorus, frag. 193.12–16 PMG (= P. Oxy. 2506, frag. 26, col. i): "Stesichorus himself says that the eidolon went to Troy, but Helen remained with Proteus (i.e., in Egypt)." Dale (1967, xx) understands that a Helen confiscated in Egypt is no solution to the problem; yet, on p. xxi, she is inclined to accept the authority of this late source, though it seriously compromises the rehabilitative intent of the *Palinode*. See also Ghali-Kahil 1955, 1: 286–90; Kannicht 1969, 1: 26–33; Bowra 1970; Bassi 1993. While I cannot feel comfortable with Bowra's arguments in support of this papyrus, he gives one of the clearest expositions of a highly complicated topic. The fragment, in my view, is symptomatic of the confusion that surrounded the *Palinode* in late antiquity. For the process by which the confusions arose, see Dio Chrysostom *Orations* 11 (*On the Trojan Story*),

rus had Paris abducting Helen from Sparta and reaching Egypt, where he was detained by Proteus (for more on whom, see Chapter 5 in this volume). But there Proteus confiscated Helen and sent Paris on his mindless way with Helen's idol. How the offended Helen would have been satisfied with this apology and accepted it as an adequate recantation is not explained.

Another problem presents itself. Once we have decided where the eidolon was introduced, we must fix on an agent and a motive. Who could be plausibly invoked as the author, and what could be the possible motive for a revision of such magnitude? The Egyptian story posits Proteus (long familiar from Homer's *Odyssey*) as the author who separated Helen from her image and dispatched Paris to Troy hallucinating her empty form. Detaining Helen in Egypt we can understand, since it removes Helen to the margin of the scandalous Homeric text and nicely positions her for her later elevation into the goddess of the local cult in Egypt. But what motives would have inspired an Egyptian to sow hallucination in all directions, for Greeks and Trojans alike? Granted, Proteus, as remembered from the *Odyssey*, had credentials that could be used in support of such a revision. A shapeshifter himself, he could be plausibly credited as the author of this new plot to separate Helen's Platonic Eidos from her all too human eidolon, but cui bono?

A delightful spin was put on this Egyptian story by a scholiast commenting on Aristeides' *Orations*.[15] According to this authority, Proteus, after separating Helen and Paris, thoughtfully provided the frustrated Paris with a painting of Helen—an art object to pacify a lover's unfulfilled libido. But a theory that Helen of Troy was no more than a painting—this sounds very late indeed, surely later than Stesichorus. Prosperous suburban villas come to mind, with large wall surfaces, where painters could treat the Trojan War in a painterly fashion, with the final Alexandrian touch being to

---

37ff. See also Chapter 5 in this volume.
15. Schol. Aristeides *Orations* 3.150; see Page's note at Stesichorus, frag. 192 PMG.

make Helen the painting at the center of the painting, much as the self-referential François Vase places Achilles' funeral urn at the center of its composition. Whoever was the author of this fanciful hypothesis, it is the first instance in European letters of pornography.

Even after the *Palinode*'s forthright repudiation of the Homeric myth, ambiguities continue to cluster even around the *Palinode*, as if any version of the Helen story quickly foliates under the pressure of an ambiguity that escapes resolution. If the explicit intention of the *Palinode* was to restore Helen to her dignity as the goddess of Spartan cult, its covert intention was to rehabilitate the tarnished reputation of the Homeric Helen and reinstate the fallen woman as the immaculate Greek wife that she should have been.[16] Need we add that if Stesichorus had intended only to restore Helen to divine status, her marital infidelity should have presented no more than a minor problem? Infidelity among gods and heroes was not unknown; even for a goddess, there were precedents. The matter at stake was less Helen's divinity than her human modesty, or lack of it. Only one question, in the end, held any force: Was Helen ever in another man's bed who was not her husband? Sparta, Egypt, Troy—who cared about the place? The question was not *where* but *whether*.

From the verses that Socrates quotes from the *Palinode* we may infer that Stesichorus proposed a definitive solution: "You did not board the well-benched ships; you did not reach the towers of Troy." The talk of Egypt and a compassionate pharaoh intervening in the plot was probably later elaboration, whether at the insistence of certain Greeks residing in Egypt or because a flaw was discov-

16. Bassi (1993, 52–53) questions the conventional view that Stesichorus intended to clear Helen's name and "reclaim her divine status," since she cannot see anything in the story as told by Socrates that indicates "a moral or religious conversion on the part of the poet." While I agree with Bassi that the *Palinode* was not successful in replacing the Homeric text, I cannot see any other motive for Stesichorus to compose the *Palinode* than to clear both Helen's name and his own, and in my view the passage in the *Phaedrus* that is our primary source for the *Palinode* is couched in language of ethical and religious significance.

ered in the original revision. If Helen had never reached Troy, it was equally improper for her to be left to sit out the war in Sparta. The "where" was significant not in itself but for the question it implied: Was Helen being "Helen" somewhere else while Troy fell? Confusion also arose as to the agent of Stesichorus' blindness. In the version of the *Palinode* story as told by Pausanias, Helen herself was the angry deity who struck Stesichorus blind.[17] In his story, a certain Leonymos of Kroton, on a pilgrimage to the island of Leuke in the Black Sea to solicit the healing powers of the heroized Ajax, found Helen also on the island, who was then living with Achilles. She gave Leonymos her personal instructions to visit Stesichorus in Sicily on his return home and inform him that she was the offended party who was the cause of his blindness. But why a Helen who was sensitive to her honor would have been living out of wedlock with Achilles, even if only as ghosts, is not explained. To remove Helen from her illicit Trojan bed only to have her reappear in the Black Sea after the Trojan War with yet another lover—this is an interesting rehabilitation. It points out that Helen's transgression was not so much that she abandoned Menelaus as that she preferred a Trojan lover to her Greek husband. Achilles as her lover was a more acceptable revision, even if propriety demanded that he could not become her lover until after his death.[18]

Horace attributes the punishment of Stesichorus to Helen's brothers, the Dioscuri (Dioskouroi in Greek).[19] He may have his sources confused, or his version may reflect the prominence of the cult of the Dioscuri at Rome.[20] But he was expressing, perhaps

17. 3.19.11.
18. This posthumous affair between Helen and Achilles is foreshadowed at Hesiod, frag. 204.87–92 MW, where we are told that Achilles had been too young to be one of Helen's suitors, but had he competed with the other suitors, he would certainly have won. Some revisionist understood the necessary symmetry: Achilles, excluded from among Helen's suitors at the beginning of the story, would have to be included as her lover at the end of the story. H.D.'s *Helen in Egypt* makes much of the arcane affinities that destined Helen and Achilles to become lovers after death.
19. *Epodes* 17.42.
20. For the prominence of the cult of the Dioscuri under Augustus and his heirs, see Poulsen 1991.

without realizing it, the thoughts that easily arise around Helen's name. Why would Helen need to hasten to her own defense? Did she not have two mighty brothers to defend her honor? Variants also arose as to how the truth was vouchsafed to Stesichorus. In Pausanias, Helen sent Leonymos of Kroton as her personal emissary to inform Stesichorus that she was responsible for his punishment. Other sources said that Helen revealed the truth to Stesichorus in a dream. Yet others attributed the revelation to the Dioskouroi, whom once again we discover hovering close at hand, persistently there and not there at the same time.[21]

Even in the recantation of the old story, which should have laid all doubts to rest, some uncertainty lingers regarding the Dioskouroi and their part in their sister's rehabilitation. They were needed in the story once the *Iliad* had called attention to the shame of their absence at Troy, yet they could not be included in such a way as to present a serious conflict with the authorized story (Homer's), in which they had not participated. Giving them a peripheral role in the *Palinode* story, whether as Helen's celestial avengers blinding Stesichorus for his blasphemy or as the supernatural spirits revealing the truth to the errant poet, was a sagacious move. If Stesichorus had not included the Dioskouroi in the *Palinode*, sooner or later someone would have noticed the omission and added them to the story, to ensure that Helen's brothers had not sat on the sideline completely idle while her reputation was at stake. It was imperative—so at least it must have seemed to some of Helen's revisionists—that the Dioskouroi, as Helen's brothers and her traditional saviors, be appointed the keepers of the story.

In late antiquity the story had become so muddled that the commentator in the papyrus fragment referred to above has Ste-

---

21. For the Dioskouroi as the traditional saviors of Helen, see Euripides *Helen* 1494–1511; and Chapter 6 in this volume. Pliny (*Natural History* 2.101) gives an interesting example of the way in which the tradition linked Helen with the Dioskouroi, while distinguishing her from them at the same time. In talking of St. Elmo's fire, which was traditionally associated with the Dioskouroi, Pliny distinguishes two forms of the phenomenon. The single flame, named Helena, is menacing (*dira ac minax*); the double flame, called the Dioscuri, is "salutary" (*salutares*).

sichorus composing two palinodes.[22] That must mean, if the word
palinode still retains any of its original meaning, that Stesichorus
twice committed blasphemy, whether both times against Helen or
against two separate figures of the traditional mythology, and
twice recanted his heresy. And, the fragment adds, Stesichorus
used one recantation to critique Homer, and the other to critique
Hesiod. Bewildering as this copious duplication seems, the case is
made more convincing because the commentator quotes the opening words of the two palinodes. One began "Hither, O Goddess,
lover of dance"; the other: "O Golden-winged Maiden." Much ink
has been spent in speculations about these two palinodes, but the
questions are moot. Only one palinode was celebrated in antiquity,
as Leonard Woodbury notes, the ode that Socrates identified as
"the so-called *Palinode*" by Stesichorus.[23]

---

22. Stesichorus, frag. 193 PMG. See above, note 13.
23. 1967; see also Dale 1967, xvii–xxiv; Podlecki 1971; Kannicht 1969, vol. 1;
Bowra 1970; Bassi 1993. Apart from this fragmentary commentary, dating from
the first or second century B.C.E., no one in antiquity added so much as a single
verse to the three quoted by Socrates in the *Phaedrus*—a reason to suspect that the
Palinode was a topic of gossip long after the poem itself had disappeared. If Stesichorus had simply criticized Hesiod's treatment of a traditional myth, that would
hardly deserve the name "Palinode." The *Palinode* to which Socrates alludes in the
Phaedrus was so called not because it was a critique of the Homeric tradition,
though it was that, but because in it Stesichorus recanted his own former position.
Are we to believe that Stesichorus repeated his offense twice; that he blasphemed
two major figures in the tradition; that he was twice punished; that he was twice
purged of his error; and that, in purging himself, he criticized the two major poets
of the epic tradition? The symmetries are too neat. They point in another direction:
the poet who proposed a definitive resolution of Helen's duplicity was himself
divided into two by later gossips and was said to have twice misspoken himself in
his treatment of epic themes and was twice obliged to make a public volte-face.
Page (1963, 36) is prepared to accept the testimony of frag. 193 on both counts,
that Stesichorus composed two palinodes and that he told of Proteus detaining
Helen in Egypt during the Trojan War: "We have no particular reason to distrust
this new evidence." In my view we have considerable reason to distrust a source as
late as this papyrus when the topic is the polymorphous Helen story. Bowra (1970)
gives an articulate defense of the two-palinode theory, but the theory must remain
highly speculative, given the lateness of its source and the meager information
supplied by this late papyrus. The assertion of another papyrus fragment (Hesiod,
frag. 358 MW), that Hesiod had introduced the eidolon into the story, is also
symptomatic of confusions that arose in connection with the phantom-Helen
theme.

The dramatic, indeed mythic, aspects of the *Palinode* story made the verse that Bergk tentatively attributed to the *Palinode* a commonplace (frag. 241 PMG: "As Stesichorus says, 'I will go seek another prelude'"). And "palinode" itself became a rhetorical figure, whether to signify recantation of a position taken or as the classic example of men fighting over shadows. Socrates cites the story with his customary irony, yet we cannot miss his serious intent when he lauds Stesichorus for understanding, as Homer did not, the need for purification for those who err in telling the sacred stories, and the mode of purification required of such storytellers, that they should do as Stesichorus did—correct the error and sing the song anew. Any correction that reduced the scandals imputed to gods and heroes in the canonical traditions would be sure to engage Socrates' approval. And Helen, whether read as daimon or human, was a scandal.

The central theme of the *Palinode*, as in the Homeric story, was still Helen's shame. The revision that Stesichorus proposed would erase both her shame and her impotence (or the shame and impotence of her brothers, if we prefer that version of the *Palinode*). Thus revised, Helen would no longer be the passive spectator watching men quarrel over her meaning, but the goddess who "controls the gaze" (to borrow from DeJean). In the anecdote of the *Palinode*, Helen's gaze has assumed the power to visit punishment on a poet with the same violence attributed to the gods and goddesses in traditional myths when their honor was in question. Isocrates talks of Stesichorus "blaspheming" Helen, a religious term that signifies much more than simply maligning a human person.[24] The *Palinode* belongs to that subset within the corpus of Greek myth in which the unwary traveler, often a devotee of the goddess herself, stumbles into the precinct of the goddess at an inopportune moment, or offends her dignity in some other way, whether intentionally or unintentionally, and is promptly punished. The power to blind or to restore sight, while appropriate for

---

24. Isocrates *Encomium on Helen* 64. LSJ defines the Greek verb *blasphēmeō* as "to speak profanely of sacred things."

any goddess (compare Athena and Artemis), has particular significance in reference to Helen, since that was her ancient power, to
open men's eyes or to blind them at her pleasure.

But we moderns are not easily fooled by tales of goddesses
visiting punishment on men who expose their nakedness. Helen's
anger we read as a code for other, to us more cogent, motives that
would lead to such a drastic revision of the most canonical of all the
traditional texts. Had Helen, who had endured blasphemies for
centuries in the epic tradition, suddenly grown tender at insults to
her dignity? With the Helen of the *Iliad* known throughout the
Greek world, what reputation had she to lose?

In oral cultures, myths abound in variants, prompted by numerous kinds of pressures. Myths are public property, to be passed
from one storyteller to the next, though a Darwinian struggle no
doubt obtains, in which variants compete for that degree of au-
thenticity which grants them canonical status.[25] But the *Palinode*,
though it may arise from a local cult, presents itself not as a variant
but as a repudiation of the epic tradition. What would the Trojan
War be without Helen? Poets were given a wide latitude to shape
the traditional myths as they chose, but no one else in antiquity
dared as radical a revision of a traditional myth as Stesichorus
proposed. Even Sappho, thinking of Helen, thinks not of the
Helen deified at Sparta but of Homer's Helen.

As one of the earliest instances in Greek poetry, and certainly the
most celebrated, of an outright revision of a canonical text, the
Palinode opens a window onto the pressures affecting the traditional corpus of myth in the archaic period. Some no doubt were
frankly political, radiating from Sparta and perhaps from other
cities where Helen's cult was maintained. But the *Palinode* was also
the expression of the new spirit of rationalism that was moving
through archaic Greece of the seventh and sixth centuries.

Perhaps Stesichorus did not himself invent the story of Helen's
eidolon. A late scholiast, whose information R. Merkelbach and

25. On this contest for local myths to achieve global status, see Nagy 1990b.

M. L. West include among Hesiod's *fragmenta dubia* as fragment 358, attributes the introduction of the eidolon to Hesiod.[26] But this information is highly suspect. How would the story of Helen's eidolon (which is a rehabilitation story) comport with fragment 176 MW, in which Hesiod itemizes the profligacies of the daughters of Tyndareus—Timandre deserted Ekhemos for Phyleus; Klytaimestra deserted Agamemnon for Aigisthos, "who was the lesser husband"; and "likewise Helen disgraced the bed of blond Menelaus"? The reputation of these infamous daughters, the fragment explains, was the curse (*kakē phēmē*) laid on Tyndareus by Aphrodite, because he had overlooked her in his sacrifices to the gods.[27] Are we to believe that Hesiod too blasphemed Helen but came to his senses, recanted, and published a revised version of the Trojan War?

What Socrates calls "the so-called *Palinode*" would not have been so memorable in antiquity if Hesiod, who was as canonical as Homer, had already anticipated Stesichorus by telling of a phantom Helen at Troy. Some modern scholars have read fragment 358 MW as a simple scribal error, Hesiod being confused with Stesichorus.[28] But the problem is deeper, in my view, than scribal error. The *Paraphrasis* to Lycophron, to which we owe this notice, has not only confused the two poets; it has also conflated two separate eidola, the one substituted for Iphigeneia at Aulis, and the other substituted for Helen at Troy.

By good fortune, another fragment from Hesiod, which Merkelbach and West attribute to his *Catalogue of Women*, helps us to pinpoint the source of the error with reasonable certainty. In this

26. Hesiod, frag. 358 MW: "Hesiod first told of the eidolon of Helen." For arguments in favor of this attribution, see Ghali-Kahil 1955, 1: 286–87.

27. We note the semantic collusion between *phēmē* (saying, utterance) and the daughters' reputation. The evil *phēmē* in this Helen story is both the utterance voiced by the god and, on the human plane, the gossip that surrounded the daughters of Tyndareus.

28. West (1985, 134) considers the fragment "suspect." Cf. Dale 1967, xxiii: "Marckscheffel, the editor of Hesiod, was, in default of further evidence, quite justified in treating 'Hesiod' as a mere blunder for 'Stesichorus.'"

passage (frag. 23a MW) Hesiod brings us, through a catalogue of noble women (wives, mothers, and sisters of the heroes), to the verge of the Trojan War. The fragment begins uncertainly, but as Merkelbach and West have reconstructed it, it talks of the marriage of Leda and Tyndareus and names their daughters—Timandre, Klytaimestra, and Phylonoe. Here the text falters, leaving us to surmise that "the violet-tressed"—namely, Artemis—did something to Phylonoe. Merkelbach and West conjecture that line 12 reads that Artemis made Phylonoe "ageless and deathless for all time." If this is the correct reading, we cannot help but ponder the curious symmetry that has Artemis favoring first the sister of Klytaimestra (Phylonoe) with immortality, and a few verses later granting the same favor to Klytaimestra's daughter, Iphimede.

Be that as it may, the name that we might expect to find in a list of the daughters of Leda and Tyndareus is suspiciously absent; ancient texts have an inclination to wobble, and some even to dissolve clean away, when Helen's name appears or should appear. But a scholiast commenting on Pindar's *Nemean Ode* 10.150a (= Hesiod, frag. 24 MW) clears up the problem by supplying a piece of information that could explain Helen's absence from this list: "Hesiod, however, puts it that Helen was the daughter of neither Leda nor Nemesis but of a daughter of Okeanos and Zeus." But this is the kind of information that only engulfs us in a surfeit of new problems. How did Okeanos and his daughter enter the Helen story? Certainly elsewhere in Hesiod's *Catalogue* Helen is treated as one of the daughters of Tyndareus—Helen's suitors are repeatedly said to ply the house of Tyndareus with messengers and gifts, though the contest itself seems to be have been organized by Helen's brothers, Castor and Pollux (see frags. 196–99, 204 MW).[29]

29. In frag. 196.4–8, Helen is to be inferred as the "*korē* who had the form of golden Aphrodite," who also has some connection with "the house of Tyndareus." In frag. 197 Castor and Pollux arrange the contest among Helen's suitors; in frag. 198 the Dioskouroi are again named as the masters of the contest of Helen's suitors; in frag. 199 suitors ply the home of Tyndareus with messengers and gifts, "for great was the fame [*kleos*] of the woman"; in frag. 204.61 Helen is certainly resident in the house of Tyndareus. See West 1985, 123, 133–34.

However Hesiod may have later brought Helen into the family of Tyndareus, we return to the papyrus, where, after the lacuna where we might expect Helen's name, we resume the narrative at line 13.[30] Once the story of Phylonoe has been briefly told (lines 11–12), Hesiod reverts to Klytaimestra and proceeds to give us her history: she married Agamemnon and bore "fair-ankled Iphimede and Electra, who rivaled the goddesses in form." He then picks up the history of Iphimede—Iphigeneia as we know her (lines 17ff):

> Iphimede they slaughtered, the well-greaved Achaeans,   17
> On the altar of Artemis of the sounding golden spindle,
> On that day when in ships they sailed for Troy
> To exact reparations for the fair-ankled Argeione—   20
> an eidolon.   21

"The fair-ankled Argeione" can be none other than Helen, elsewhere named "Helen of Argos" or "the Argive woman." But we are surprised to see her appear so casually in line 20, syntactically subordinated to Iphimede, so soon after the daughters of Tyndareus have been named, among whom she was not included.[31] Within the space of fourteen verses we have moved in Hesiod's *Catalogue* from Leda to Tyndareus, and thence to the three women who played fateful parts in the Trojan War—Klytaimestra, Iphimede (Iphigeneia), and Helen. Helen has at least been introduced, but no sooner is she sighted than Hesiod turns our attention away from her—she is but a parenthesis—to correct the erroneous impression that has been on our minds since line 17, that the Achaeans had sacrificed Iphimede at Aulis. In fact, we now learn, they sacrificed not Iphimede but only her eidolon (line 21).

30. West (1985, 43) assumes that "Helen's birth must have been mentioned" in the context of frag. 23a; on p. 96 he assumes that it would have appeared later in the narrative, specifically in the lacuna at lines 38ff., where Zeus would have been introduced into the story to account for the births of Helen and her brother Polydeukes, whose name appears at line 39.
31. See Hesiod, frags. 200ff. MW, for "Helen of Argos" as a regular formula for "Helen." She seems to be named again as "fair-ankled Argeione" in frag. 136.10 MW.

Iphimede they slaughtered . . .   17

. . . .

. . . reparations for the fair-ankled Argeione—   20
an eidolon. But herself the violet-tressed   21
goddess easily saved and distilled sweet ambrosia over her
head that her flesh might stay firm,
And she made her deathless and ageless all her days.
Now human tribes on earth call her Artemis of the   25
Road, and Keeper of the Gate for the Glorious Goddess
of the Violet Tresses.

Pausanias explains the last piece of information as a reference to the
cult of Iphigeneia as Hekate: "I know that Hesiod proposed that
Iphigeneia did not die but by the intention of Artemis became
Hekate."[32]

Eidōlon, the first word of line 21, is a clever use of both necessary
and apparent enjambment. In necessary enjambment the syntax
carries the sentence across the break at the end of one line and into
the first part of the subsequent line; the spill-over word or phrase is
necessary to complete the thought. In apparent enjambment, syntax and meter coincide; the thought is complete when a line is
done. But the paratactic drift of the epic style allows the poet to
add a qualification, an afterthought to a thought already completed.

A cursory reading of lines 20–21, particularly for readers versed
in the epic style, could easily mistake eidōlon as the qualification
added to Argeione in line 20—fair-ankled Helen—particularly since
the name is in the genitive case, which, construed as a possessive,
could leave the reader with a first impression that the Achaeans had
sailed to Troy to exact reparations for "Helen's eidolon." But no,
the enjambment directs us to overlook Helen and return to Iphimede, who is named four hexameters earlier. But even so, when
we have the eidolon attached to its proper subject, it still continues
to play on our nerves as both an apparent and a necessary enjambment. Technically, eidōlon is not necessary to complete the sentence

32. 1.43.1 (= Hesiod, frag. 23b MW).

in which Hesiod describes the sacrifice of Iphimede at Aulis (lines 17–20). It is inserted at the beginning of line 21 as if it were an ornamentation added to a thought already completed. In fact the addition of the word *eidōlon* completely undermines the whole sentence. The sacrifice of Iphimede at Aulis was, it now transpires, a false assumption. With the introduction of *eidōlon* in line 21, we are obliged to trace our steps back to the beginning of the sentence and correct our error.

What may be safely inferred from this fragment is that Hesiod was the first poet to introduce the eidolon into the Iphigeneia story. Thanks to the hazards of time, a papyrus find in Egypt has given us the very passage in the *Catalogue of Women* where Hesiod first stated the story of the sacrifice of Iphigeneia but then, seven lines later, retracted it by introducing her eidolon. But, given the apparent but false enjambment of *Argeione* and *eidōlon* in lines 20–21, a reader, especially one familiar with the parataxis of epic, could be forgiven for misremembering the passage and confusing the two eidola, or perhaps even thinking that Hesiod had introduced two eidola into the story, the eidolon of Iphimede at Aulis and the eidolon of Helen at Troy.

The eidolon aside, the whole passage from Hesiod's *Catalogue* is a thicket of duplications. If Merkelbach and West have reconstructed the passage accurately, the violet-tressed goddess twice removes a woman and makes her an immortal (Phylonoe, Iphimede). Artemis herself is duplicated, via Iphimede, who becomes a second Artemis—"Artemis of the Road." Iphimede is duplicated, as herself (*autēn*) and as her eidolon. Add that Phylonoe, sister of Klytaimestra seems suspiciously similar to Klytaimestra's daughter Iphimede, and at the same time a kind of shadow form of Helen, and it takes a certain concentration to remember that there was only one eidolon in this passage, and it was not Helen's. After Stesichorus, when the two revisions of the traditional story had become familiar topics, it would be easy for a scholiast to confuse the two revisions and imagine that both had been proposed first by Hesiod.

Given that Helen's eidolon is almost impossible to reconcile with Hesiod's version of the Trojan War, we can assume that Hesiod was the earliest literary authority to use an eidolon to rescue Iphigeneia at Aulis, and Stesichorus, in the absence of any stronger evidence than the dubious Hesiod fragment 358 MW, was the first to use the same strategy to rescue Helen from Troy. West dates Hesiod's *Catalogue* to 600 B.C.E., or perhaps even as late as the mid–sixth century. Noting that the eidolon of Aeneas in the *Iliad* and the eidolon of Herakles which Odysseus sees in the underworld (in the *Odyssey*) have been suspected as late interpolations, West suggests that the two Homeric instances, together with Iphimede's eidolon in Hesiod fragment 23a MW, and Helen's eidolon in Stesichorus, are all examples of the new trend in myth interpretation in the sixth century. Assuming Hesiod and Stesichorus to be roughly contemporary, West suggests that either poet could have borrowed the idea of the eidolon from the other.[33]

But in oral traditions interpolations are moot, since they imply an already fixed, canonical text, rather than one in the process of continuous refinement and revision.[34] Hesiod's account of Iphimede worshiped as "Artemis of the Road," while presented in Hesiod's narrative as though it were a revision of a traditional myth, suggests an ancient local cult. The four eidola to which West refers play various functions; all four may represent local traditions making their way in the archaic period into the canonical tradition. But to substitute an eidolon temporarily for a warrior on the field, as Aphrodite substitutes the eidolon of Aeneas in the *Iliad*, is very different from substituting an eidolon for Helen at Troy, which would entirely nullify the traditional plot. If the eidolon of Aeneas is a poetic device allowing for a hero's temporary disappearance from the field, to replace Helen at Troy with her eidolon is to put her into permanent eclipse.

33. 1985, 130–35. But cf. Skutsch (1987, 189), who suggests that the eidolon substituted for Helen may be an extremely old motif. He bases his suggestion on the association of the Indo-European Twins, the Asvins, with a woman (the princess of the sun) who was replaced by her eidolon.
34. See Nagy 1979 on the problematic relations of the text and the tradition.

Helen's eidolon may represent a genuine local tradition circulating in Sparta, or in regions with Spartan affiliations.[35] Yet West is surely correct to see the eidolon emerging in the archaic age as a rationalistic device that might be employed "to save the appearances" of a traditional myth by subtracting its offensive elements. Whatever the origins of Helen's eidolon, the term carried a new significance in the sixth century, as we can infer from the notoriety that accrued to Stesichorus for his *Palinode*. In Homer, eidola are simply ghosts of the dead, except for the single instance when Aphrodite temporarily substitutes an eidolon for Aeneas on the battlefield and thus saves him from imminent death (*Iliad* 8.549–53). But at the moment when Stesichorus was proposing that Helen herself was only an eidolon, Xenophanes was arguing that even the gods are no more than idols, self-projections of humans, who venerate them as gods.[36] Projection and representation were emerging as key concepts in philosophical discourse. Debates arose, among both poets and philosophers, as to the correct reading of traditional myths. Xenophanes had only ridicule for the cloudy and beclouded images of the divine in Homer and Hesiod. A piece of gossip from antiquity told of the brother of Stesichorus associating with the philosopher Thales and studying geometry.[37] Perhaps both brothers, the mathematician and the poet, were influenced by the new scientific thinking of their age.

Whatever the local traditions that lie behind the *Palinode*, it surfaces significantly in the age when the lyric poets were viewing the epic tradition more skeptically or with local allegiances. The story that Helen of Troy was not a woman but a false image mistaken for the woman has even today a modern ring, which no doubt it had when Stesichorus first proposed it as the genuine Helen myth. Though an eidolon of Helen could be seen as an extension of

35. On Stesichorus and Sparta, see Bowra 1961, 76; West 1969, 147–49; Podlecki 1971.
36. Xenophanes, frags. 169–72 KR.
37. Proclus *In primum Euclidis librum commentarius* 65.11 Friedl.; see "Stesichorus," *RE* 2.3 (1929), 2458–59.

Homeric practice, in fact it has more in common with the false images of the gods that Xenophanes attributes to human perception and vanity, since the function of Helen's eidolon is to declare the whole issue of the Trojan War a perceptual error.[38] If Homer permitted Aphrodite to introduce a phantom onto the battlefield to confuse the warriors, Homer himself was not confused by false images. Hallucination affects only his characters. But if Helen of Troy had been a hallucination from beginning to end, Homer was as much affected by the hallucination as his benighted warriors were.

The *Palinode* thus calls Homer's authority into question, and for this Stesichorus received special commendation from Socrates, as a poet who understood *mythologia*, the art of the sacred story. To underline the point made in the *Phaedrus*, another tradition explained Homer's blindness as his punishment for defaming Helen in his story of Helen at Troy.[39] The blinding of Stesichorus is almost less noteworthy than the restoration of his sight, since every poet who had followed the Homeric tradition in singing the fall of Troy had been blind. Stesichorus too had followed Homer blindly at first, but, thanks to Helen's personal intervention, he became the first poet to see Helen in her full lucidity.[40] In the verses quoted by Socrates, Stesichorus rejects the traditional story (the *logos*) as not genuine (*etumos*). His Helen, he claimed, was the genuine Helen.

Homer's Trojan War was no longer thought rational, at least in some quarters. Would two great armies have warred for ten long years for a woman's beauty? Would a Greek man worthy of the name permit his wife to be seduced by an Asiatic libertine? In such an event, would Hellas sacrifice its noblest youths to retrieve a

---

38. Nagy 1990b, 419: the Stesichorean Helen myth "contrasts its own adherence to one particular localized version with the syncretism of the Homeric *Helen* tradition of the *Iliad* and the *Odyssey*." See also Zeitlin 1981, 202–3, and Bassi 1993 on the political motives implicit in the *Palinode*.
39. Nagy 1990b, 421; the story is told in the *Life of Homer* 6.51–57 Allen.
40. On the blindness as metaphor or poetic device to signify Stesichorus' inner blindness, see Woodbury 1967.

woman of Helen's easy virtue? Would they then, though suffering as much damage as they inflicted, with no more ado accept Helen's return to her wifely bed in Sparta? If the Trojan War defied common sense, so did Helen, as Homer portrayed her. A new reading of the traditional myth was needed; some wanted it to be more rational; others wanted perhaps a more sympathetic portrait of Helen; and yet others, applying higher ethical standards, wanted their Homer expurgated.[41]

Helen and Menelaus were the cult heroes of Sparta. The Dorians who occupied the region after the Mycenean era seem to have adopted Menelaus and Helen and made them as much their own as the original Myceneans had. These Dorians, expanding westward to Sicily and Magna Graecia, took their cults with them, including the cults of Helen and the Dioskouroi. Stesichorus was responding, it seems, with Doric anxieties to a myth that, in their eyes, had long been overworked.[42] Had Spartans grown weary of jests about light-footed Spartan wives and their engagingly inattentive husbands?

In attributing the blinding of Stesichorus to Castor and Pollux, Horace shows a sound instinct. If Helen's shame was the problem, her brothers were as much implicated in the debacle as she was, as Homer had pointed out.[43] In Horace's version of the *Palinode* the

41. Woodbury (1967, 166) notes "the changing climate of opinion," requiring that the old story "had to be altered by any writer who wished to present Helen sympathetically." Others have commented that while Homer passes no judgment on Helen, the poets of the archaic age (e.g., Alcaeus, Ibycus) were painting her portrait in more pejorative terms.

42. Nagy (1990b, 420) notes that the revised Helen myth of the *Palinode* represents a local tradition, common to Kroton in Magna Graecia and Himera in Sicily (the traditional provenience of Stesichorus). He observes that "the recantation of Stesichorus, featuring the restoration of his vision, not only denies the Homeric tradition but also reaffirms another tradition that happens to acknowledge explicitly the thought patterns associated with the cult of Helen as a local goddess." See also Bowra 1934.

43. On this point, cf. Dio Chrysostom *Orations* 11.71. Dio's Egyptian informant, who gives an alleged Egyptian reading of the *Iliad*, condemns the absence of the Dioskouroi from Troy as one of Homer's blunders, which Homer only made worse when he had Helen point to the flaw. The Dioskouroi, he notes, were "the

Dioskouroi were acting as they conspicuously did not in the *Iliad*, rescuing not only Helen but themselves. With the story thus revised, the Dioskouroi could be excused for their absence from Troy, since they were in fact not needed. When they *were* needed, however, to punish an errant poet for his blasphemy, they were on the spot at once.

The *Palinode* found a solution to the question of Helen's honor as radical as it was rational. Helen would be divided into two forms, the real and the imaginary; the real, that is the honorable, Helen would be left in Sparta, or at least safely outside the field of action; while the imaginary Helen would be dispatched to Troy, to serve as the false and dishonorable sign for which the Greeks and Trojans brought down their civilizations.[44] The Helen we remember, weaving the Trojan War on her loom, gazed at by the murmuring elders, inspecting the troops with Priam from the city walls, pleading with Hector to pay her a visit, concluding the dirge over Hector's body, weaving her spells on Odysseus in Troy and Telemachus in Sparta—the several Helens of the epic were at one stroke removed from the text and replaced with their phantom.

Helen's ambiguities were thus cleanly dissolved. Helen of Troy, with her deadly and daimonic ways, was declared imaginary, while Helen herself remained immaculate, overtly the goddess of Spartan cult but implicitly the now-tethered wife of Menelaus. Helen's transcendence in the Homeric epic, which gave her a god's permission to overlook her own shame, to abandon her husband and take

---

most insulted" (*hubrismenous*) by Helen's capture, and it would strain credulity to suppose that they had not been in the forefront of those who sailed to Troy to avenge such an insult. Dio's Egyptian had his own explanation for their absence in the Homeric story: Paris was one of Helen's suitors and, pressing his suit very persuasively, was declared the winner. Helen became his legitimate wife. The nonsense of Aphrodite and the Judgment of Paris, and a shameless Helen engaged in erotic dalliance—all such improprieties were thus removed. Given this revision, the Dioskouroi had no insult to complain of. Menelaus, however, smarting from his imagined loss, stirred up the other Greeks, until they came to believe that his loss was their loss and sailed to war, convinced that all Hellas had been insulted by Helen's mismarriage to Paris.

44. On this point see Zeitlin 1981, 202–3; Bassi 1993.

a lover, to watch Troy burn to the ground around her feet, and then return to her husband as if returning from a visit to her cousins, would no longer disturb the narrative. Helen, circumscribed, would be no longer daimon but simply a woman.

Bergren notes, quite correctly, that "Stesichorus did not invent the doubleness of Helen and her *logos*. For doubleness is the distinguishing mark of her entire tradition."[45] But, such is Helen's paradox, the intention of the *Palinode* was not to create a double Helen with a twofold *logos*, but to do the opposite—eliminate the oscillation of Helen's twofold *logos* by reducing it to one. Stesichorus thus created, or thought he had created, not two *logoi* but one genuine *logos* and one apparent *logos*—the false *logos* objectified as the eidolon. Homer was thus reduced to a composer of fictions, while Stesichorus could claim for himself the authentic poet's mantle.

While the *Palinode* overtly recuperates Helen's reputation as a goddess who visits a ruthless punishment on Stesichorus for his blasphemy, in fact the Helen revealed to Stesichorus was no goddess at all but a simple human.[46] Nor would this revised Helen be any longer both wife and mistress, or both Greek and Trojan. She would be all Greek, and a wife plain and simple, with her deadly gaze and her wayward libido displaced onto her idol. Helen, divested of all false projections, would be a whole woman at last. Her enigmatic appearances in Homer were just that—*appearances*. Helen, completing her trajectory from human to divine, was now truly domesticated. The woman was now demarcated from her value as sign, and all her duplicity was ascribed to her sign.

So Stesichorus vindicated Helen's honor. But honor is a family affair, and Helen's honor, thanks to the influence of the epic tradition, became by Panhellenic extension a Greek affair. Greeks, so

45. 1983, 91.
46. Kannicht (1969, 1: 60) argues the opposite, that Stesichorus has simply rendered the Helen of epic into a pure goddess (who would be the goddess of the local cults at Sparta, Rhodes, and elsewhere). But the *Palinode* reveals a twofold intention: its overt intention, to restore Helen to her status as a goddess, is negated by the contrary intention, which was to strip Helen of her power and remove her from the stage.

widely dispersed throughout the Mediterranean in the archaic age, were finding their identity not only in their common cults and traditions but in their relations as Greeks to the great imperial powers pressing on their borders—Lydia, Persia, Egypt, Phoenicia, Carthage.

The Persians, the Phoenicians, and the Egyptians had their own versions of the Helen myth, if we accept the testimony of Herodotus, and Herodotus makes the Trojan War, together with earlier instances of woman-stealing between Greece and its eastern neighbors, the frontispiece to his *Histories*.[47] Though he will not commit himself personally, he reports that the Persians date the hostilities between the Greeks and the Persians to the Greek expedition against Troy. With the Helen story at the forefront of his mind, as one of the earliest and most significant episodes in the long history of the hostile actions between Greece and Asia, Herodotus, so affably garrulous, is always open to a variant story, another *logos*, and we are the beneficiaries.[48]

Seen through Persian eyes (as quoted by Herodotus), the Trojans were certainly to blame in the Trojan affair, but, that admitted, the blame then falls curiously on the Greeks, whom the Persians indict for bearing the major responsibility for the long and devastating conflict between Greece and Persia. From the Persian side the Greeks, in mounting a massive retaliation for the theft of Helen, cut a foolish figure: "They consider the seizing of young women the act of lawless men; but to put great energy into revenge, once women have been seized, is the act of witless men, there being, in fact, no opportunity for sensible and self-respecting women [*sōphrones*] to be seized."[49] The Trojans had, in the alleged

---

47. 1.1–4, for the Persian and Phoenician versions; 2.112, for the version told to Herodotus by the priests at the temple of Proteus in Memphis. The veracity of Herodotus' accounts is still a vexed question. For the modern scholarship on his "Persian" accounts of the Trojan War, see Vandiver 1991, 114ff.
48. For the dependence of Herodotus' *Histories* on the Homeric epic, see Nagy 1990b, 227ff. For Herodotus' estimation of the importance of the Trojan War in relation to the Persian Wars of his own time, see Vandiver 1991, and Chapter 5 in this volume.
49. Herodotus 1.4.

Persian view of the incident, at least the grandeur of ambition; monumental crimes command a certain admiration. But a thousand ships and a ten-year war were, by Persian standards, a preposterous overreaction to an event admittedly unlawful but of no great significance in international affairs.

The incident at Troy, trivial as it might seem from the Asian side, was not trivial to the Greeks, or to certain Greeks, since it was the story of their own shame and dishonor. We can imagine Greek sailors, Dorians at least, facing down the chuckles in countless harbor taverns when Helen's name was mentioned. Stesichorus obviated the joke, or thought he had. With Helen removed from Troy, Greek womanhood was vindicated. But, better yet, with Helen at last genuinely rescued, before she even fell into bed with Paris, the men's honor was saved. If Greek men had been fools to destroy themselves at Troy for a phantom, that was more excusable than to destroy themselves for a woman of easy virtue, as Homer's Helen so conspicuously was. Greek manhood was at risk, or perhaps it was more Spartan manhood, but in any case Stesichorus saved the day. Helen had not betrayed her husband. She had never slept in a foreigner's bed. With all suggestion of impropriety removed, Helen was made whole, simplified where she had once been complex. Helen's reward for her cooperation was that her name was cleared and she herself was no longer confused by divided loyalties. In revealing her authentic self to Stesichorus, Helen saved not only herself and Stesichorus but Sparta, and indeed all Hellas, from disgrace.

CHAPTER 5

Herodotus and Helen in Egypt

A hundred years or so after the death of Stesichorus, with rationalism in full stride, Herodotus found yet another Helen story, similar in some respects to the *Palinode* version yet with a significant difference that points to another variant, or at any rate to another inventive revisionist.

Herodotus takes us on his peripatetic search for the many strands, dispersed across the Mediterranean from Sicily to the Black Sea, connecting the Trojan War with the great conflict of his own time between Greece and Persia.[1] Following this thread, we arrive in Egypt, where Herodotus is our guide in a tour of the sights of Memphis. Just south of the temple of Hephaistos he has discovered the hallowed precinct of the Egyptian pharaoh, one long dead but now immortalized through the cult maintained at his shrine. This pharaoh's name Herodotus translates into Greek as "Proteus"—our first hint that we are on the trail of the true Helen story.[2] The pharaoh's temple precinct, beautifully constructed and

---

1. See Immerwahr 1966, 234 n. 133, on the Trojan War as "parallel and analogue," in the mind of Herodotus, to the Persian Wars. Vandiver (1991, 121) sees the Trojan War as emblematic for Herodotus of an *ergon* (deed or fact), which has given rise to several differing *logoi*. See Vandiver, pp. 114ff., for the scholarship on Herodotus' use of Persian sources for the Helen story.

2. 2.112–20. For discussion of this passage, see How and Wells 1957 ad loc.; Dale 1967, xvii–xxiv; Lloyd 1988, 3: 46–48; Fornara 1971, 20; Örtel 1970; Vandiver 1991, 114ff.

adorned, was in the neighborhood of the city known as the Camp
of the Tyrians, so called because it had been settled by Phoenicians
from Tyre. "Camp" (*stratopedon*) was the Egyptian name for foreign settlements, perhaps because the first settlements of each ethnic group had the look of a military camp or a squatters' colony.

Walking into the sanctuary, Herodotus sights a shrine dedicated
to "The Foreign Aphrodite." The dedication, if there was a written
dedication, would not have been in Greek, and it is doubtful
whether Herodotus could have read the dedication in a non-Greek
language. But whatever the linguistic problems, Herodotus has no
difficulty translating this idol's unusual title into the Greek *xeinē*,
"stranger or guest."

The shrine catches Herodotus' attention because in all his travels
he has never heard of Aphrodite worshiped as "The Stranger" or
"The Guest" at any other of her many shrines. With Helen never
far from his mind (see 1.1–4), Herodotus, with suspicious speed,
surmises that the foreign Aphrodite honored in the pharaoh's sacred precinct can be none other than the Greek Helen, daughter of
Tyndareus.

Having just walked into the precinct of a pharaoh who turns out
to be the Proteus familiar to us from the *Odyssey*, and having just
finished deciphering a dedication in a foreign language to a foreign
goddess who turns out to be our own Helen of Sparta, we are
suddenly launched into a conversation between Herodotus and the
priests at the temple. The subject is Helen of course, since she, we
now begin to understand, was the reason for our visit to the pharaoh's shrine. This is the story, if we can believe Herodotus, that
the priests had to tell of the Spartan Helen.

Paris had indeed captured Helen and eloped with her—so much,
alas, for the *Palinode* and its forlorn hopes to redeem Helen's hon-
or. But her honor, admittedly compromised, was not past repair.
A storm arose that cast Paris ashore on the salt flats at the Canobic
mouth of the Nile. On the shore stood a temple to Hephaistos (still
standing in Herodotus' day), where runaway slaves were granted
asylum if they were willing to be branded with the stigmata mark-

ing their servitude to the god. There the slaves of Paris, who were more honorable than he, fled and, given asylum, poured forth a tale of great sacrilege perpetrated by their master.

Present at their confession was the guard stationed at that mouth of the Nile, a certain Thonis. If Thonis had in fact been the guard, and not a mere factotum, his Egyptian title would have been very impressive: "Overseer of the Gate of the Foreign Lands of the Great Green."[3] This honorable gentleman (the gentlemen are honorable in this tale, at least on the Egyptian side) sent messengers posthaste upriver to Memphis to inquire of the pharaoh's pleasure: "A stranger has arrived on our shores, a Trojan by birth, who has committed great sacrilege against Hellas. He has deceived the wife of his own host and is now here with the woman and much treasure besides [the stolen treasure always figuring prominently in the story], having been swept by the winds onto your shores. Are we to give him liberty to sail without hindrance? Or should we confiscate his goods?" To which the pharaoh replied: "This man, whoever he is, who has acted against his own host with such impiety, seize him and bring him before me so that I may see for myself what he will say."

Paris was arrested and brought before the pharaoh. Under interrogation he spun a wandering tale, which was easily exposed by his own slaves, who, now slaves to the pharaoh, told a different tale. The pharaoh was greatly angered, and, had it not been for the pharaoh's ethical scruples against harming any person cast on his shores, Paris would have come to a quick and sorry end. Instead, the pharaoh confiscated Helen and the treasures and gave Paris three days to be gone from the country. Helen he promised to keep in safe custody until her rightful husband should come to reclaim her.

What did the priests think of the Greek version of the Trojan War? Herodotus asked—by which he meant Homer's Panhellenic story. Did they think it was "foolish talk"? Herodotus wondered.[4]

3. Lloyd 1988, 3: 49.
4. For "foolish talk" Herodotus uses *mataios logos*. By coincidence, the *Etymologicum Magnum*, in glossing *matēn* as "foolishness," cites Stesichorus for its use

Indeed, they did. So prompted, the priests then gave Herotodus—the reason for our visit to the pharaoh's tomb fully disclosed at last—their story of the Trojan War. The priests based their story on original Egyptian sources, for the events that took place in Egypt; but, for the events at Troy, they claimed no less a source than Menelaus himself, a claim certainly Homer had never dared to make.

Their story went as follows. With Helen confiscated in Egypt, Paris sailed home empty-handed. But the Greeks, ignorant of the new complication in the plot, mustered their fleet and embarked for Troy. At Troy they sent messengers to the city, Menelaus among them (our alleged source for this—the Trojan part—of our story), to demand Helen's release and punitive damages. The Trojans replied in all truth that Helen was not in Troy but was being held in custody in Egypt. The Greeks, thinking themselves mocked, laid siege to the city until they had razed it to the ground, but even then Helen was not to be found. The Trojans, with nothing more to lose, continued to insist on their original story until finally the Greeks, having no alternative, accepted the Trojan version of the events. Menelaus was dispatched to Egypt, and there he found Helen intact, exactly as the Trojans said he would.

But a story in Herodotus is not complete without its final spin. In this Egyptian story, if the pharaoh was a gentleman, the same could not be said, alas, of Menelaus. With his ships becalmed in Egypt, Menelaus repaid the pharaoh's generosity poorly by sacrificing two of the local youths to gain a fair sailing. For this sacrilege he was hounded from the country. The priests knew that he had reached Libya, but beyond that they could not say.

But our Egyptian informants are no longer necessary. With Helen recuperated from Egypt, we can thank our Egyptian friends for their gracious assistance in the plot and return to our own

---

(= Stesichorus, frag. 257 PMG: "speaking foolishness"). If Bergk's attribution of this fragment to the *Palinode* can be accepted, *mataios logos* in Herodotus may be the historian's oblique acknowledgment of Stesichorus.

domestic version in *Odyssey* 4, where Helen is comfortably domiciled in Sparta again, with the threats from both Troy and Egypt safely behind her.

The story that Menelaus and Helen had been detained in Egypt was known from Homer of course, and this seems sufficient reason for Herodotus to nod in agreement when he hears an Egyptian story of Helen detained in Egypt for the duration of the Trojan War. No matter that in Homer the detention occurs after the fall of Troy, whereas in the Egyptian story it occupies the full ten years of the Trojan War—detention was already part of the traditional story. The coincidences were more persuasive than the differences, and Herotodus was convinced that he had at last found in Egypt the true Helen story.

Did Herodotus travel to Memphis already a believer in the revised Helen story? In leaping to the far from obvious conclusion that the Egyptians (or Egypto-Phoenicians) had set up an idol of the Greek Helen in the pharaoh's sacred grounds, where they worshiped her as "The Foreign Aphrodite," he gives his hand away. Translators generally render this title as "The Foreign Aphrodite," but it would be more in alignment with Herodotus' intention to think of this goddess as "Aphrodite Our Guest," since "guest" would be more appropriate than "stranger" if the function of the cult title was to signify the Greek Helen. If this idol were the Spartan Helen, or could be construed as such, the Egyptian story would not need to, indeed should not, talk of Helen's foreignness. Instead, it should tell how the most beautiful woman in Hellas, if not in the world, came to be the distinguished guest of the pharaoh for the ten years of the Trojan War. Surely Herodotus has arrived in Memphis with this story already in hand, which requires a pharaoh's tomb, an honorable pharaoh, a strange local cult, where perhaps the Phoenician Astarte had been fused with Helen of Sparta, and priests who could spin these cross-cultural threads— Phoenician, Egyptian, and Greek—into a palinode that would "save the appearances," as philosophers might put it, of the Trojan War, while also salvaging Hellenic honor. Whether following the trail of his predecessor Hekataios or in someone else's footsteps, Herodotus knew what he expected to find when he walked into the sanctuary. The topography was already familiar, whoever had mapped it for him. Here in Memphis, exactly where he expected it, was the sanctuary of the immortalized pharaoh (Proteus!). And here, inside the sanctuary, was the very shrine to "Aphrodite Our Guest" (our Helen, of course!). And here were the obliging priests and scribes with their version of the "Rehabilitation of Helen."

Be that as it may, the Egyptian connection in *Odyssey* 4, and the Phoenician connection in the *Iliad* (when Sidon opened its harbor to the fugitive couple, Paris and Helen, in their flight from Sparta to Troy)—such threads, fragile as they were—were sufficient to persuade Herodotus that Homer too knew the story of the real Helen but had excluded it from his plot for artistic reasons. Here Herodotus defines himself vis-à-vis Homer much as Stesichorus had done. As Stesichorus asserted the superiority of his Helen story as myth, Herodotus asserts the superiority of his kind of storytelling over Homer's as history. Homer is relegated to being no more than a poet who would sacrifice historical truth to romantic fancy—poetry's stock is now in decline, while history's is on the rise. Herodotus, turning to the sages of Egypt, found the way to preserve the history of the Trojan War while eliminating the romance. It was simple: all that was necessary was to remove Helen from the action, and romance would no longer disturb the equilibrium.

The Egyptian story, which opens so favorably with Helen's rescue, concludes on a note of shame, when Menelaus rudely repays the pharaoh's hospitality by slaughtering two of the local youth. This peccadillo will be shortly revised by Euripides, to correct its politics, but Herodotus, unlike Euripides, is studiously pro-Egyptian. In his story, Helen's honor, though certainly tarnished, is redeemed thanks to the kindly supervision of the pharaoh, who takes it upon himself to act as a court of international law to put a stop to Paris and his vagrant libido. But Menelaus is stripped of even the little honor Homer had allowed him, and then further disgraced by his outrageous return for the pharaoh's hospitality.

Oblivious to this glaring imperfection, Herodotus found "Helen in Egypt" a credible reading of the Trojan War. If Helen had been in Troy, he argued (weighing the Egyptian *logos* against the Greek), the Trojans would certainly have surrendered her to the Greeks, with or without Paris' consent, for Priam and his people were not so mad as to put themselves, their children, and their city in jeopardy so that Paris might live with Helen. As their casualties mounted, had Helen been the consort of Priam himself, he would have returned her to the Greeks. Besides, Paris was not the heir to the throne, but Hector, and Hector would not have tolerated his younger brother's behavior when the cost to himself and the throne was so high.

Who were these priests, who seem to have agreed with Herodotus when he surmised that the Aphrodite whom they had welcomed as a guest into the pharaoh's shrine was Helen of Sparta, and then gave Herodotus a story of the Trojan War with Helen removed from the plot and placed in the custody of their own pharaoh? "We would dearly like to know," A. M. Dale says, the language in which these priests and Herodotus conversed, and what questions from Herodotus elicited their story.[5] Did Herodotus know enough Egyptian to discuss the Helen story? Did the priests know Greek? Were any interpreters present? And how Egyptian were they after centuries of foreign settlements in the city?

The priests asserted the accuracy of their story, as being founded on genuine firsthand knowledge (*epistēmē*). But their epistemology, while satisfying Herodotus, would not satisfy our modern standards, since the eyewitnesses in this case were Menelaus and Helen, dead and gone centuries before the priests were born.[6] Can

5. 1967, xviii. That Herodotus could converse in any language but Greek is, by scholarly consensus, dubious. For further discussion of this episode in Herodotus, see Hartog 1988, 238–39; Lloyd 1988, 3: 43–52.

6. But cf. Dio Chrysostom *Orations* 11.40. Dio has also found an Egyptian priest who claims to know the true Helen story. His informant also attributes his information to Menelaus himself, but, alas, his story is quite different from the story told to Herodotus by his Egyptian authorities.

we really believe that an idol of Helen stood in the very precinct of the pharaoh? That the priests had in their temple lore their own, authentic Helen cult dating back to the Bronze Age? That Menelaus was kind enough to leave with the hospitable pharaoh the record of his misadventure at Troy?

But these questions are moot. More important is the question why the Egyptians would have needed a revised Helen story that only partially exonerated Helen while it appropriated to Egypt the major share of the honor for her rescue. Of this "Helen in Egypt" story we cannot but ask, Cui bono? It was not the Egyptians but the Greeks, or certain Greeks at least, who needed a new Helen story. The underlying motives in this story seem suspiciously Greek, even if they have been varnished over by other motives to highlight Egyptian integrity. The obvious motive is to remove Helen from the canonical text (the *Iliad*). Equally obvious is the related motive to repair Helen's fallen reputation and rehabilitate her into the goddess that she was meant to be, though in this case she would be a Greco-Egyptian goddess. The Egyptian motives for such a revision are more difficult to fathom. Why would Egyptians have worshiped as their visiting Aphrodite a Greek woman whose sole achievement was her abstinence, reinforced by their own pharaoh, from the company of Aphrodite for exactly the ten-year period of the Trojan War?

Whether Herodotus really discussed Helen with the priests in Memphis, he has borrowed them as authorities, to lend credence to his Helen story. The Egyptians were scrupulous historians, at least in Herodotus' eyes. His word for "historians" is *logioi*, which Nagy translates as "masters of speech," but I would call them "masters of the story."[7] The Egyptians Herodotus calls "the supreme masters of the story" (*logiotatoi*).[8] To revise Helen from her fallen estate into the peerless goddess required a most cunning storyteller.

W. W. How and J. Wells, in their commentary on Herodotus, conjecture that "The Foreign Aphrodite" was Astarte, whom the

---

7. 1990b, 221.
8. 2.77.1. On *logos* in Herodotus, see also Hartog 1988, 295–97.

Phoenician settlers had brought with them, called "foreign" to distinguish her from the Egyptian Aphrodite, Hathor.[9] In the ecumenical spirit of the ancient Near East, the Phoenician Aphrodite had been given her place of honor within the very precinct of the Egyptian king. But if the priests at the pharaoh's shrine were willing to accept Herodotus' identification of the Phoenician Astarte with the Greek Helen, how secure was the authority of their *logos* in other respects?

How and Wells further surmise that Herodotus may have identified the Proteus of Greek myth with the Egyptian title "Proutï." They suggest also that Proteus, a sea god in Greek myth, may have been identified with Dagon, the fish god whom the Tyrians may have brought with them to their settlement.[10] The Egyptian *logos* becomes less secure with every question. Whatever our speculations, they do nothing to explain how the Egyptians had their own version of Helen of Greece, if indeed they had one, and Herodotus had not, like a ventriloquist, put a story into their mouths. The Egyptian bias of the story is indisputable, yet that is precisely what attracts our suspicion. The Egyptians seem to have obliged whoever among the Greeks was sensitive to the problem of Helen's compromised honor, by writing their own pharaoh into the story, as the necessary deus ex machina to do for Helen what her family and people had dismally failed to do.[11] The pharaoh's behavior in

9. 1957, at 2.112.2; Kannicht 1969, 1: 43.

10. Lloyd (1988, 3: 46) disagrees, arguing that Proteus cannot be connected with any Egyptian word and must be purely Greek. On the other hand, he notes that Egyptian iconography depicts the king as the Nile gods are depicted. To equate the Greek Leviathan, with his powers of metamorphosis, with the Egyptian pharaoh would not be difficult in a time when gods were fluid by definition.

11. See Dale 1967, xviii. Von Fritz (1967, 166) claims that in "every sentence" this story of Helen in Egypt has the marks of "a genuine Egyptian story [*Geschichte*]." Fehling ([1971], 1989, 59–65), while accepting the Egyptian coloring "on the level of description," argues that even that aspect of the story we owe to Herodotus' own invention. In my view the Egyptian bias is certainly strong, yet the underlying Hellenic motives may be even stronger. Perhaps we should assume both Hellenic and Egyptian influences here—the cult of Helen being first introduced into Egypt by Greeks settling at Naukratis, but then embellished in time by Egyptians to give greater prominence to the Egyptian contribution.

this story is impeccable, yet we are skeptical, if only because his honor is the necessary element to complete the revision that Stesichorus had left only partially complete in his *Palinode*. Herodotus, or whoever supplied him with this revised Helen story, understood that if Helen was to be removed from Troy, she must also be removed from Sparta. Then, once removed, she would need a guardian of flawless virtue, or her honor would again fall into question. In short, Helen's absolute quarantine was essential to the plot, and for this purpose a quarantine officer of unimpeachable integrity was needed.

Herodotus, in questioning the priests as to their view of the Greek story, seems to assume a single, authorized Greek story—Homer's version, with Helen at Troy—yet his question itself implies another, less canonical story. Why else would Herodotus question the Egyptians if he did not already know of another story, in which Helen had not sailed to Troy? It has been argued that Herodotus took the story without acknowledgment from his predecessor Hekataios.[12] We would be sorry if Herodotus had not in fact visited the temple in Memphis or quizzed the priests for their Helen story but had plagiarized the story wholesale from his illustrious predecessor and rival. But others have argued that the fragments ascribed to Hekataios which allude to the same story were late forgeries attributed to the historian, whose name had canonical authority in the field of early historiography.

Whether Herodotus was aware of the *Palinode* or not, the Egyptian story differs from the *Palinode* in one respect: there is no eidolon in the Egyptian story, not even, alas, so much as the painting of Helen ascribed to Proteus by the scholiast on Aristeides. Herodotus, had he known of the eidolon story, as I suspect he did, may

12. See Diels 1887, 441–44, a view shared by Lloyd 1988, 3: 43–52. For further discussion of the questions raised by Herodotus' account of Helen in Egypt (2.112–20), see Benardete 1969, 47–51. For the extreme skeptical position regarding Herodotus and his alleged use of his sources, see Fehling (1971) 1989; Vandiver 1991. Fornara (1971, 20) also takes the story to be Herodotus' invention. Interesting in this connection is Hartog 1988, though Hartog's study concentrates on Herodotus' representation of the Scythians.

have excluded it for his own reasons, but had it been part of the priestly lore in Memphis, surely the priests would have mentioned it. The eidolon was, after all, the conspicuous and memorable element in the *Palinode*'s revision of the Helen myth. In fact, the eidolon is absent from the Egyptian story because "Helen in Egypt" is a correction of the original revision, intended to eliminate the embarrassment that Stesichorus had introduced with his talk of a ghostly Helen at Troy. Though created for admirable reasons, the eidolon was, when all is said and done, a primitive device, and the Helen problem called for a more sophisticated solution.

The function of an eidolon is to induce hallucinations. But hallucination plays no part in the Egyptian story; everything is clear and direct. Theirs was the rational Helen story. In their version the pharaoh was above board in all his dealings. How would it have fitted the story to have the high-minded pharaoh dispatch Paris to Troy hallucinating Helen? The Trojans, in the Egyptian story, told the Greeks the simple truth, which the Greeks refused to believe, reasonably enough, but their problems were not compounded by hallucination. The presence of the eidolon would vitiate the Egyptian story, since the point here was to present another plot in which the eidolon was no longer necessary.

If Stesichorus had removed Helen to Egypt, as the commentator of P. Oxy. 2506 (= Stesichorus, frag. 193 PMG) asserts, how would his ode merit the name "Palinode"? Egypt was not a required element in his revision; in fact, it would have been an additional complication.[13] All that was required to rescue Helen from her disgrace was to remove her from Troy, and for that purpose her ghost served well enough. To introduce Egypt into the plot would have left Helen's name still beclouded. Helen rendered into a ghost at Troy and Helen deposited in Egypt are two separate revisions, competing with each other.

Dio Chrysostom's *Trojan Oration* sheds light on the process by

---

13. For further discussion of this testimony, see Dale 1967, xxiii; Bassi 1993; and Chapter 4 in this volume.

which confusions crept into the story of the *Palinode*. Little could
Herodotus have suspected that centuries after his visit to the shrine
in Memphis another Greek—Dio Chrysostom, like Herodotus
reincarnated—would also find an Egyptian priest who would tell
him the true story of the Trojan War.[14] In this case the priest is
described as "a very old man in Onuphis" (11.37), and this priest too
claims that the source of his information is none other than Menelaus
himself. At this point, however, Dio's informant and Herodotus
diverge, and Dio gives us another Helen story quite different from
the one that Herodotus attributes to the priests in Memphis. The
Egyptian priests were remarkably busy, it seems, in reworking the
Helen tapestry, century after century.

But before Dio gives us the true Helen story, we are treated to a
diatribe from the old priest in Onuphis on Greek gullibility. Dio's
informant cites Homer's story of the Trojan War as a prime example
of the Greek partiality for romance over history. The lack of a true
historical sense was, to the old Egyptian, a profound defect in the
Greek character. This theme we can trace in the Egyptian Helen
story that Herodotus tells, but Dio gives it even greater rhetorical
elaboration.

According to Dio's Egyptian priest, the Greeks were so easily
deceived by poetry that they were prepared to swear an oath to the
truth of Homer's romance, of Helen falling in love with Paris while
married to Menelaus, and of Agamemnon destroying the city of
Troy. But as if that were not foolish enough, the Egyptian priest was
amused to discover that the Greeks told of yet another poet—
"Stesichorus I believe"—who was blinded by Helen for following
Homer's account but recovered his sight when he recanted. Such
was their addiction to fantasy, and so great their indifference to
truth, in the eyes of Dio's Egyptian sage, that the Greeks were quite
able to believe both Homer and Stesichorus simultaneously. But
worse still, the Greeks could not even agree as to the terms of the
revision that Stesichorus had introduced in his *Palinode* (11.41):

14. Dio Chrysostom *Orations* 11.37ff.

"They say that Stesichorus in his second ode said that Helen sailed nowhere at all; but others say that she was captured by Paris and came here to live with us in Egypt."

Dio's Egyptian informant may be a fiction. His knowledge of Homer's *Iliad* and *Odyssey*, not to mention the tradition outside the Homeric texts, is suspicious; even more suspicious is his careful critique of the *Iliad*, almost episode by episode. Yet his amusement may well reflect an Egyptian's amusement at the welter of conflicting Helen stories circulating among the Greeks who had settled in Egypt. Some settlers brought the *Iliad* with them, and it was their Bible. But others brought a cult of Helen the goddess with them from Sparta or from other Doric cities. At first no doubt the two Helens coexisted quite amicably in Egypt, since Greek mythology was far from dogmatic. But then Stesichorus, responding to the pressures exerted by the contradictions between the two myths, definitively separated the goddess from the woman, and thus yet another Helen story was generated, in which Helen of Troy was only a phantom.

In time Stesichorus' revision was revised again, now under specifically Greco-Egyptian pressures. Some Greeks in Egypt, loath to see Helen dropped from the traditional Homeric story altogether— Egypt had, after all, a venerable link with the story in the epic tradition—generated a compromise, in which Stesichorus had indeed removed Helen from Troy but had deposited her in Egypt. Even here variations arose, since the Egyptian Greeks could not agree as to whether Helen had been kidnapped to Egypt by Paris or dispatched to Egypt by miraculous and supernatural agencies. Thus the original palinode became two. That Dio could talk of so many contradictory Helen stories and of two contradictory palinodes circulating among the Greeks in Egypt, all staking their claims to absolute authority, is another suggestion that the *Palinode* no longer existed, though it continued to be cited as a major authority.

The Egyptian Greeks apparently had not noticed, or if they had, they did not care, that Stesichorus was credited with two entirely different revisions of the Helen story. In one version told of the

Palinode, Stesichorus had saved Helen's honor absolutely by removing her from the story altogether. But in the other version, in order to hallow Helen's connection with Egypt, Stesichorus had allowed her honor to be temporarily eclipsed in Egypt but finally recovered. The Greeks in Egypt had several Helen stories, all conflicting with each other but all equally believed, the reason for the confusion being, in the eyes of Dio's Egyptian sage, "the Hellenic love of pleasure: if it is sweet to the ear, they take whatever anyone says for the truth, and they call it their poets' privilege to say any lie they wish" (11.42).

But the most amusing point of Dio's story is that, in the sophisticated eyes of Dio's informant, all the Greek versions of the Helen story were false. Only the Egyptian priest himself knew the true story, which he was kind enough to pass on to Dio. In his story, Paris was one of Helen's suitors and won her hand in a fair competition. But Menelaus, feeling himself slighted, persuaded the other Greeks that his loss was their loss, and eventually they sailed to Troy, convinced that all Hellas had a legitimate grievance against Paris (11.43–67). Dio's revision certainly offers certain advantages over the other Helen stories, not least of which is that it salvages the honor of Helen's brothers, the Dioskouroi, better than any of the other stories.[15] But to return to Herodotus: little suspecting that five centuries later another Greek would find another Helen story in Egypt, Herodotus believed that his Egyptian authorities had given him the best recipe for removing Helen from the text, and on that basis he voted for theirs as the true story.[16]

Some late sources claimed that Proteus had manufactured the

---

15. See Chapter 4, note 44.

16. Kannicht (1969, 1:46) argues that dropping the eidolon was Herodotus' contribution to the story, to demystify the version given by Stesichorus and give it a more rational, "pragmatic" (i.e., factual), appearance. But if Herodotus thought his version of the Trojan War was the most rational reading, Dio Chrysostom showed that rationality had a long way yet to go. His reading of the Trojan War makes Herodotus as ignorant and naive as Homer, since, for all his rationality, Herodotus still believed in the patriotic fiction of Helen seized from her husband's bed by a foreign trespasser.

eidolon. The Homeric Proteus being himself polymorphic, it was easy to attribute to the pharaoh whom Herodotus had assimilated to Proteus the power to change Helen's shape as well. But such scholiasts had not read their Herodotus carefully enough or had mixed up the various revisions, as we might expect for a story that needed so many corrections. The Egyptian story required Paris to arrive in Egypt with stolen goods—Helen and the Spartan treasures—but to be sent on his way without them, thanks to the pharaoh's intervention. Replacing Helen with her ghost would not have satisfied this plot. A polymorphous creature of the deep was not needed here but a surrogate father, a second Priam but of nobler mettle, to thwart the aggressive libido of the wayward Paris.

Egypt, we may surmise, was added to the story only after the flaw in Stesichorus' *Palinode* was discovered, that Helen could not have been left to her own devices when she was displaced from the text. If she was not at Troy, she must have been deposited somewhere else, but where? Sparta was out of the question. Though it was her final destination, another venue was needed where Helen could be completely separated from the plot so that when the time was ripe, she could reenter the text as the goddess that the story calls for.

Homer, Stesichorus, Herodotus—we now have three Helens in the literary tradition, two of them perhaps originating in local cults but both proposed as revisions of the Helen of the epic tradition. In Homer the Spartan goddess had become a fallen woman. Stesichorus ostensibly remedied this error and restored her to her divine status by substituting a phantom Helen at Troy. But when the phantom disclosed its flimsy construction, yet another Helen was needed—Helen in Egypt. Helen of Troy, Helen in Egypt, and Helen of Sparta have become three entirely separate Helens, though the intention of the revisionists was to erase the ambiguities and duplicity of the Homeric Helen. But each revision to construct a single Helen, detached from her images and projections, only multiplied her images.

Herodotus offers Helen in Egypt as the most rational story

(though later Dio Chrysostom was to discover another, even more rational Egyptian story), but all three versions can rightly be called rational; each attempts in its own way to rationalize the Helen enigma. Perhaps Homer's Helen, or the several Helens assimilated into his Helen, was once worshiped with the simple piety that has no need to rationalize mystery. But Homer is a long way from such simplicity. In humanizing Helen, the Homeric tradition brought the daimonic into the human context, endowing it with human form and motives. The mysteries of the Mother, if we are authorized to read Helen as one of the icons of the Mother, have been translated into the male quest for beauty and honor, into the study of the function of beauty and its effect on the libido in human behavior. To identify the libido as such, and to weave it into a plot that is the ground of the *Iliad*, was a great feat of the human imagination. But when Olympus crumbled, and the gods were toppled from their thrones, the plot came to seem too naive for the more serious intellects.

Already in Homer, Helen has been recognized as a sign, if not the major sign, within a code that determined and calibrated every aspect of life in the Mycenaean age. As an icon transcending almost all other human icons, the Homeric Helen is inevitably something of a phantom, as Helen herself seems to suggest when she wonders if her former life ever happened.[17] This Helen understands that though she is a woman, she must function as the woman-as-sign, outwardly the icon for men and women to behold and shudder at, inwardly a woman hiding her self behind the mask of shamelessness, to play her part in the dramaturgy composed on Mount Olympus.

But the contradictions that could remain in a delicate equilibrium in Homer's Helen eventually exploded under the newer political and philosophical pressures of the archaic age. Stesichorus, rationalizing Homer, divorced the virtuous Helen from her less virtuous icon and thus separated the signifier from its subject. It

17. *Iliad* 6.180.

was a bold, modernist reinterpretation of an ancient myth that had lost its credibility, at least in some quarters. Stesichorus left the virtuous Helen where she belonged, in Sparta, or in any case well outside the arena, so that the contest would be purely semiotic, without Helen's person to confuse the issue. If Homer understood that the Trojan War was fought for a sign, Stesichorus showed that the sign was a mere ghost of what it was intended to signify. Helen, we are told, was pleased with the semiotic distinction, which restored to her person her virtue and displaced all her ambiguity onto her sign.

But Stesichorus had, unawares, created a new plot: the "case of the missing Helen," which would not take long for some clever critic to discover. With Helen dissociated from her sign, where was Helen while her ghost mesmerized all Hellas and Troy? It would be an absurd revision that left Helen in Sparta while the Greeks fought for her honor at Troy. With Helen still the chatelaine in Sparta, managing the palace affairs and raising little Hermione, we would be credulous indeed to accept that in ten long years not a whisper of the truth reached her husband's ears. It would have been one of the best kept secrets in the history of international diplomacy.

No, the plot could not accommodate two Helens—Helen playing the homemaker in Sparta (and it would be only playacting) while her ghost played the other Helen at Troy. Helen must be removed from the scene altogether. Yet she must be firmly situated somewhere, since the point of the revision was to put a stop to Helen's vagrancy. And, wherever she was placed, Helen could not be left unattended (remember Paris). It would be irregular for any Greek queen, and certainly for this queen, to drift with the currents around the Mediterranean while her husband made a fool of himself at Troy, since drift was precisely her problem.

The solution? Egypt, of course! Land of the hieroglyph and royal portraiture.[18] Whoever the author of this revision, it was a

---

18. See Nagy 1990b, 43, for a similar problem in the *Homeric Hymn to Dionysus* (I) regarding the birthplace of Dionysus. In the *Hymn* all possible birthplaces within Greece are rejected, and the only location found acceptable is outside Greece altogether, on Mount Nyse, "near the streams of the river Aigyptos." Here too, as

clever strategy.[19] The Egyptians, assuming it was they, gave Herodotus a story that removed the primitive elements—both Homer's quarrelsome gods and the phantom Helen of the *Palinode*—thus allowing the events to follow their natural human sequence (as if the sequence of events in Homer were not sufficiently human). Better yet, Helen's honor was now absolutely assured. There would be no hint of Helen's interference in the action, no whisper of impropriety, no drift of the libido, not, at least, once Helen reached Egypt. With Helen quarantined, no word of her confinement could possible leak to the outside world, to embarrass either Helen's husband or the revisionists. Egypt, famed for its marvels, land of the *logos* above all other lands, had much to recommend it as the most promising venue for Helen's restoration.

In this way Helen was still abducted (Herodotus mining the ore of myth for the gold of history), first but only briefly by Paris, but then by the friendliest of foreigners, whose watchful eye gave Helen no second opportunity to lose her honor. She was not left to defend herself, as she had been obliged to defend her honor in the *Palinode* story. In fact, she could not be trusted to do so (remember Paris). She was given into the safekeeping of a surrogate father whose righteousness would guarantee her absence. With Helen securely hidden in Egypt, and her eidolon dropped from the plot, the whole Trojan War became then a human catastrophe.

Herodotus still interpreted the Trojan War as the grand spectacle designed by those whom he designates in the traditional fashion as the gods, to illuminate the cosmic truth, that the gods visit great crimes with terrible penalties.[20] With gods no longer intervening directly in the plot, and phantoms whisked away, the Egyptian

---

Nagy has suggested, Egypt is a compromise, a neutral, Panhellenic solution to the welter of rival claims within Greece.

19. Fornara 1971, 20: "The story is a clever piece of rationalistic criticism at once ironic and amusing. . . . Stesichorus' *eidolon* is whisked out of its insubstantial existence; Helen is sent to Egypt and nothing to Troy. Still Troy was destroyed. The paradoxical flavour and wit of the story is perspicuous."

20. Vandiver 1991 calls Herodotus a "revisionist," where the details of the Helen story were concerned, but a "traditionalist" in regard to the overall meaning behind the old myth.

version of the Trojan War certainly has plausibility on its side. The motives become human motives. Could Paris have stolen the wife of Menelaus? Could the winds have driven him ashore in Egypt? Could the pharaoh, thinking perhaps of an alliance with the king of Mycenae, have acted on behalf of injured Hellas? Certainly. Could the Trojans have destroyed their own city for the sake of one woman, however beautiful? No. Humans are more rational. Perhaps the Greeks and the Trojans fought for an idol of Helen? No, that would only complicate matters. Goodness knows, the point was not to duplicate, much less triplicate, Helen but to reduce the several Helens down to one. By the time Herodotus had his turn with the story it had transpired, whether to him, to a predecessor, or to his alleged Egyptian informants, that a successful revision required both Helen and her phantom to be removed, so that the last echo of scandal might be stilled. So the improbable fantasy of the mythopoeic age was rewritten, with the help of certain anonymous Egyptian priests, into a more plausible history of international diplomacy.

Herodotus gravitates to the Egyptians as the masters of the *logos*. But, being a Greek, ever mindful of his Hellenic heritage, he must have recognized that the portrait of Helen that the Greeks had inherited from Homer begged for serious cosmetic improvement. Peerless as they were in the art of the *logos*, the Egyptians were also masters of the royal portrait. In Egypt was to be found the catharsis that would purge the illogical from the story and cleanse the imperfections from the portrait. Like the Nefertiti bust, which Camille Paglia marks as the foundation of Western art, the Helen who emerges from the studios of Egypt is a marvel of Egyptian cosmetics.[21] The new "Helen in Egypt" is a woman of high status, imperial, with no blot or blemish, but with most of her mystery removed, particularly the mysteries associated with Aphrodite.

21. 1990, 66–71.

CHAPTER 6

Euripides' *Helen*:
The Final Revision

A few years after Herodotus had discovered his Helen in Egypt, Euripides took the next step, as inevitable as it was impossible, to reconstruct the original Helen who had been divided into three in the name of rationalism. What rationalism had separated, rationalism could also reunite.[1]

The flaws in the various revisions were obvious. If Homer had made Helen duplicitous, Stesichorus, thinking to eliminate her duplicity, had instead multiplied Helen almost to infinity by casting her as a ghost, but when Herotodus tried a different tack, to subtract both Helen and her ghost from the story, that only multiplied Helen once again. And, for all her Egyptian cosmetics, the new Helen whom Herodotus had found was still far from perfect. Revision called for revision after revision.[2]

In 412/411 B.C.E., after producing several tragedies in which

1. Kannicht (1969, 1: 47) considers that Stesichorus did not so much rationalize the Homeric Helen as restore her to her status as the Spartan goddess. He argues that Herodotus rationalized and demystified the Stesichorus story by removing the eidolon, thus leaving the Greeks and Trojans to war over something less than an eidolon, "a Nothing" ("eines 'Nichts'"). While I agree with Kannicht, I have also discussed in Chapter 5 why I take Stesichorus' *Palinode* to be also a rationalizing of the traditional myth. On Euripides' *Helen* as a synthesis of Stesichorus and Herodotus, see Ghali-Kahil 1955, 1: 296–301.

2. Cf. how, centuries later, Dio Chrysostom (*Orations* 11.37ff.) found an Egyptian whose mind boggled at all the revisions that the Greeks in Egypt proposed as corrections of the traditional Helen story.

137

Helen plays her traditional role as the perfidious woman, Euripides produced his own palinode to Helen in the play simply called *Helen*. It is an odd play. It provided material for Aristophanes to parody the following year and was later used to comic effect by Menander and Plautus.[3] But if the play was less than successful as a tragedy, we should also judge it by its ambition, which was to carry the revision to its final stage and present Helen completely rationalized, a woman at last, pure and simple.

Stesichorus and Herodotus sowed the necessary seeds. Stesichorus supplied the eidolon, thereby adding to the confusion by making a sharp division where only a fluid distinction had existed before, between goddess and woman, person and image, dichotomizing Homer's Helen into her Spartan self—goddess, wife, mother, sister, as faultless in character as in beauty—and the other Helen, the false and perfidious Helen of Troy. Rationalism abhors indeterminacy, and indeterminacy was Helen's besetting fault. But when it became apparent that Stesichorus had only compounded Helen's indeterminacy, which was the reason for her revision, someone stepped forward with a venue where Helen's indeterminacies could be eradicated once and for all. Egypt was added to the recipe, with its rainbow aura of marvel, mystery, and—for the intellects—logic. In Egypt, metamorphosis and resurrection had been raised to very high levels of sophistication.

It was left to Euripides to develop the bare facts suggested by Stesichorus and Herodotus into a full plot. Exactly what drew Euripides to the phantom Helen we cannot say. In his earlier plays on the Trojan theme, Helen was the stock villain of the Trojan War; she "is never spoken of by actor or sung of by Chorus," Dale notes, "without a passing curse of hatred and illwill, venomous or hopeless according to the mood."[4] In Euripides' *Trojan Women* Helen is universally detested, by men and women, Greeks and Trojans alike. The speech that Euripides allows Helen to make to

3. For Aristophanes' parody of the play, see Kannicht 1969, 1: 79ff.; Zeitlin 1981, 186–203.
4. 1967, viii. All citations of the play are based on Dale's text, though Kannicht's edition is invaluable.

Menelaus in her own defense, in which she lays the blame for the Trojan War first on Andromache (for bearing Paris), then on Priam (for not killing Paris when he was born), then on the contest of the three goddesses, then on Aphrodite, and finally on Menelaus himself (for leaving Helen unprotected when Paris was visiting Sparta), we can hardly take for anything more than the cheapest courtroom pleading.[5]

Is the *Helen* really Euripides' own palinode for his past transgressions? Is the curse with which Teukros spits the name of Helen from his mouth the last vestige of the old Euripides, who late in life had come to his senses and, like Stesichorus, perceived that the Trojan War was fought not for Helen but for her sign? If the *Helen* is a palinode, an apology as Socrates meant his praise of Eros to be an apology, it is a strange form of homage to Helen, having more in common with the New Comedy of the Hellenistic age than with fifth-century Athenian tragedy.

Dated to the winter just following the Athenian disaster at Syracuse, when Athenian spirits and fortunes were at their lowest, some have read the *Helen* as Euripides' lament over the delusions that send men to war.[6] But war is incidental to this play, in contrast to other Euripidean plays, like *The Trojan Women*, in which war is the central fact. In the *Helen*, war is something that happened elsewhere and in another time, a distant thunder that will not seriously disturb the afternoon's entertainment.

The tragic effects of human delusion, however genuinely felt they may be, have insufficient gravity to offset the fairy-tale atmosphere, where the whole Helen myth is cleared up in an afternoon's jeu d'esprit.[7] It is difficult to point to anything in the play that could be read as an allusion, direct or indirect, to the conflict between Athens and Sparta. On the contrary, Athens and Sparta

5. Euripides *Trojan Women* 914–65.
6. For the date of the production, see Dale 1967, xxivff.; Kannicht 1969, 1: 78ff.
7. Burnett (1971, 100) calls the play a jeu d'esprit. Zeitlin (1981, 187) refers to the play's "brilliant energy." For the varied discussions of the play's tone and intention, see Dale 1967, vii-xvi; Lattimore's introduction to his translation (1959, 261–64); Griffith 1953; Burnett 1960, 1971; Segal 1971; Wolff 1973; Solmsen 1934; Zeitlin, pp. 186–217.

are united in a common purpose (symbolized by Hera and the Egyptian princess Theonoë, standing in for Athena), and the common enemy is the Phrygian goddess Aphrodite. The political message, such as it is, is rather the celebration of Greek honor and ingenuity over the brutishness of the barbarian.

The play is set in Egypt—a good beginning, inasmuch as Egypt is where we must go, since Herodotus at least, to find the real Helen. The time is seventeen years after the Greeks sailed for Troy. Helen, displaced from Troy during the full ten years of the Trojan War, still waits in the wings for her one moment on stage, though it has been another seven long years since the fall of Troy. The influence of the *Odyssey* is apparent: the new Helen will be another Penelope; the play will be another "faithful wife" story, of a woman's unflagging fidelity to her knight-errant.

Though enjoying the hospitality of the great pharaoh's court, this Helen has been kept ignorant of world affairs. She knows that the Greeks sailed to Troy to avenge her honor and that great disasters have been visited upon both Trojans and Greeks in her name. She knows too that at some time the confusions will all be swept away: she will be returned to Sparta, Menelaus will learn that his wife never betrayed his bed, and everything will be turned back exactly as it was before the Trojan War. This information she received from no less a source than Hermes himself, the very god of information, on the day when he seized her from the circle of her friends and exiled her from the text. In the tedious years of her exile Helen has heard not a word, either from her family in Sparta or from her husband at Troy. After seventeen years of a silence as absolute as the grave, Helen assumes her husband dead.

While Euripides has borrowed the eidolon and the Egyptian setting from his predecessors, the rest of the plot is his free invention. This plot is a fiction, quite unlike the products of the mythopoeic age, since it owes its turns and counterturns to the rational attempt to purge a primitive myth of its indecencies.[8] Seeing the

---

8. Sansone (1985, 18) notes that the *Helen* is as close to free invention as anything in classical literature, but does not analyze why such inventiveness was required: the play could be seen as the triumph of rationalism over myth.

human drama in a Helen confronted with her own idol, with Menelaus playing a confused third hand at the board, Euripides invented a plot to disguise the lack of one, since the real plot depends for its vitality on Homer from beginning to end: for without Homer's Helen in the plot, even if only as a ghost of herself, who would pay to see the expurgated "Helen in Egypt"?

The play opens. Helen enters and, in Euripidean fashion, speaks the prologue. Euripides' practice of having one of the dramatic personae step forward to explain the plot gains in pathos when Helen is asked to play prologue to herself, particularly in this case, where she will be speaking of herself as a ghost. Did she not have personas enough without taking on another? Well, we are all ears.

In the manner of prologues, Helen first sets the scene. Here, spread at our feet, are "the fair virgin streams" of the Nile (*kalliparthenoi roai*, line 1), our first clue to Helen's imminent transformation into a fair maiden again—though not in Egypt—thanks to the Dioskouroi. Perhaps these are the hundred mouths of the majestic river dividing as it reaches the Mediterranean. Or perhaps we are upriver where the river first branches into its separate tributaries—Memphis, of course. We have read Herodotus. But no, it is Pharos Island, which is a tribute to Homer's story. Space is plastic on the stage, and it does not trouble us that this stage must represent Pharos, to accommodate the Homeric Proteus, and Memphis, to accommodate Herodotus. In any case the exotic setting is sufficient to signify the first plot, which is to fix Helen somewhere off the page.

But Euripides has revised the Egyptian story, as told by Herodotus, to remove the noble pharaoh and replace him with his wicked son, who has no intention of releasing Helen to her lawful husband. Proteus, the good pharaoh, who was Helen's savior and for seventeen years her protector—a character borrowed from Herodotus—is now dead. He is survived by two children—Theoklymenos, who has become the new regent of the land, and his sister Theonoe. Theoklymenos, we will quickly learn, is as corrupt as his father was upright. But Theonoe, fortunately, has inherited her father's character. That, and her gift of second sight, will see

Helen through every peril. From her ancestor Nereus—Euripides making up the plot as he goes—Theonoe had inherited the power to discern "the things of the gods," which, Helen glosses, is to see "things as they are [*ta onta*, the fifth-century term for reality], and things as they will be." Through Theonoe's wonderful insight, we will see Helen at last as she truly is and always will be.

But since the plot that Euripides had inherited had eliminated Helen from the conflict, leaving all conflict to her ghost, Euripides' contribution was to reinvest Helen with conflict, since a Helen story without conflict would be a flimsy sham. This is our second plot. Hence Theoklymenos, who will be called upon to play the part of the defeated foreign prince so that the role played by Paris in the Homeric story might be rubbed out and rewritten.

With the scene now drawn before our eyes, Helen identifies herself. Her "fatherland is not without name" (line 16); it is Sparta; her father, Tyndareus. Here the plot is inlaid with yet another plot—to return Helen to the Father—but Helen elides this plot into a bemused skepticism regarding the story of her other father, Zeus, who took a swan's form to seduce her mother, Leda—"if this *logos* be credible" (line 21). Helen's skepticism regarding the story of her birth is, as Dale noted, unsettling.[9] But equally unsettling is the issue of her double paternity, raised by Helen herself, and in the play that intends to resolve the several Helens into one.

But Helen's Spartan past, checkered as it was, is needed for the fourth, if it is not already the fifth or sixth, plot. In this plot Helen must be restored to her proper place and function in Sparta, where she was once wedded to Menelaus, with the marriage contract ratified by all the youth of Hellas. The domestic Helen must haunt the play if the play is to hold our interest. Troy itself would fade away without Sparta to spotlight its full significance. Without her father, in this case her two fathers, abandoned, not to mention husband and daughter, Helen at Troy would lose much of her appeal. Likewise for Helen in Egypt: she too must have aban-

9. 1967, at lines 16ff.

doned, or rather, since this Helen is but a copy of the Trojan Helen, she must at least seem to have abandoned father, husband, home, and family.

One story leads to another. Helen, dropping the swan-and-egg story, continues with another hoary tale—the famous beauty contest of the three goddesses, when Paris was the judge and Helen's beauty the bribe, if, Helen adds, "to be misfortunate is beautiful" (*kalon*, line 27). Here sounds the first note of the major plot, since, wherever the "Judgment of Paris" is mentioned, we can be sure that the "Judgment of Helen" cannot be far behind. Helen drops the first clue that the old fable will be rewritten, to have Paris and Aphrodite excluded from the story, after which it follows that the Judgment of Helen will be reversed, and Helen will be acquitted of even the smallest hint of complicity in that odious event.[10]

Helen's acquittal being the primary intention of the play, for an intention of such magnitude a fitting author must be found—Hera was a good candidate, for her long-standing quarrel with Aphrodite over Helen was well known. Though Aphrodite won the contest, Helen continues supplying us with the background information necessary to this revision, Hera made Aphrodite's promise to Paris null and void by fashioning from the sky (*ouranos*) a living, breathing idol of Helen, which she placed in Helen's bed in Sparta. Herodotus stands corrected. The barbarian's libido is spent on the empty air, and Aphrodite dissolves from the story as easily as a cloud from the sky. "Barbarian" is a term of major significance throughout the play and is frequently linked with "beds" to drive home the point, which is to remove Helen's body from all foreign beds once and forever, and to purge the story of its unsavory foreign influences.[11]

10. The connections between the "Judgment of Paris" and the "Judgment of Helen" are made most explicitly at lines 1506–8, where the Chorus calls to the Dioskouroi to remove the "ill fame of barbarian beds" that had accrued to their sister "from the contests on Mount Ida." For further discussion of the influence of the Judgment of Paris on the plot of the *Helen*, see Sansone 1985, 21–24; Wolff 1973, 62.

11. The *Thesaurus linguae Graecae* gives twenty-six instances of "barbarian" in the

To remove the offending bed turns out to be a marvel of simplicity. All that was required was a small cloud, than which for a compliant deity like Hera nothing could be simpler. Paris, so Helen continues, believed himself in possession of Helen, but it was only his opinion (*dokēsis*). Here we are pointed to the next plot. *Dokēsis*—from the verb "to seem (to others), to seem (to oneself), to believe"—had become one of the key terms in the fifth-century discourse on Seeming and Being. Helen's use of the term in the prologue forewarns us that she has been placed at the center of the philosophical debates on Being and Seeming, Meaning and Being (*onoma/sōma*, *onoma/pragma*, *ta onta/dokēsis*, etc.), which were current when the play was produced. This new Helen is not the daimon of the naive epic but a modernist, living in an age when phenomenology was on every thinker's and would-be thinker's lips. But, and here is Euripides' greatest contribution to the plot, Helen herself is the eidolon who stands in the middle, the ghost mediating between the thesis and the antithesis, Being and Seeming, Meaning and Being. This was her function, to be sure, in the Homeric story too, but she has been updated and speaks now the language of the sophists, to give her greater credibility in a more intellectual age.

Though Paris had returned to Troy from Helen's bed with only a phantom, so Helen continues her prologue (everything is contained in the prologue), the Greeks went to war, never suspecting the true facts, since it was the will of Zeus to thin the world's population, and at the same time to show forth the strength of Hellas—a Homeric touch, reminding us of the importance of *kleos* in the scheme of things.[12] These would be contradictory purposes,

---

Helen, not all of them necessarily pejorative to be sure; but the play leaves us in no doubt that the "barbarian's bed" is the major issue. Note especially lines 1505ff., where the Chorus urges the Dioskouroi "to send the breath of Zeus and wipe away the ill fame of barbarian beds from your sister." Earlier studies of the play have not, in my view, given sufficient consideration to its pro-Hellenic and xenophobic bias. But cf. here Taplin 1992, 110: "From the fifth century BC onwards the Trojans became equated with the alien East, and the *Iliad* became a nationalist epic."
12. The motive for the Trojan War, as fulfilling the plan of Zeus to depopulate the world, is to be found first in Hesiod, frag. 204. 95ff. MW. See also West 1985, 119–

we might think, but we should not press the logic too closely. For all its appearance of logic, the *Helen* is romance, and in romance we do not expect the same grim rules of necessity that govern the tragic stage. In romance, rules can be freely bent, broken, or ignored. The important point was to keep Helen safely distanced from the scene so that the play could continue between the name and the body without Helen's interference.

A deity was needed to lend credence to the story. Hera was happy to oblige, to play the aggrieved goddess who would accept the responsibility for the plot. This Hera, in substituting the phantom Helen in Sparta rather than in Egypt, effectively erases Paris from Egypt and thus removes the last suggestion of misconduct from Helen's character. But if it was necessary to edit Paris out of Egypt, Egypt still remained essential to the revision, as the mediating term between the domestic Helen in Sparta and the wild Helen of Troy. Ergo, another cloud is introduced, by another obliging deity—Hermes the trickster, who is also a credible choice, since the whole play is a bag of tricks.[13] Borrowing Hera's way with clouds, Hermes gathered Helen up into a cloud bank and wafted her into "the folds of Ether" while she was but a young bride, picking roses for Athena.[14]

The Ether (Aither in Greek) was the highest, brightest, purest region of Sky. In the cosmological debates of archaic and classical

---

21. The same motive for the Trojan War is given by Herodotus in his story of Helen in Egypt.

13. Sansone 1985 reminds us that Hermes was included in the old Judgment of Paris story; all the more reason to find him a role in the revisionist story. Cf. the *Homeric Hymn to Aphrodite* (V) 117–21, where Aphrodite, appearing to Anchises disguised as the most beautiful of virgins, claims that Hermes seized her up from the chorus of Artemis, "when we were playing, many brides and virgins, and a great crowd garlanded us." Hermes carried her, so Aphrodite continues, far over barren lands, "so that I thought I would never step on living earth again," much as Helen now laments that Hermes exiled her from her own fertile soil to a barbarian land.

14. For Hermes' part, see lines 43–48, 241–51. In this play Hera and Hermes have both borrowed Aphrodite's tricks. She is the goddess in the epic who wraps up her favorites in cloud and spirits them from the field; cf. how she rescues Paris by hiding him "in a great mist" and depositing him in "his fragrant chamber" (*Iliad* 3.381–82).

Greek it had come to figure as the term for the highest and rarest of the prime elements. Hermes' intentions are transparent. In folding her into the Ether, he was delivering Helen back into the primal element, from which she would be reborn completely spiritualized.[15] This was yet another plot to be worked into the play.

With the eidolon of Helen now safely ensconced at Troy, made, like Helen, of the finest elements ("not me," Helen says, "but a breathing likeness composed of airy Sky," line 34), Hermes carefully removed Helen herself, wrapped in cloud, to Egypt and placed her in the palace of Proteus, the pharaoh, whom he judged to be the most honorable and self-restrained of all human beings, as he would have to be to figure in this very ethereal plot. The problem of the old plot was precisely the lack of self-restraint, whether on Helen's part or on the part of Aphrodite or on the part of Aphrodite's barbarian princeling. But all three parts are now to be rewritten. The barbarian goddess will be removed, and likewise her promiscuous darling; and Helen will be restored to Sparta uncontaminated, where her self-restraint will be her undying fame. This new Helen will be a second Penelope, but with the advantage not given to Penelope, that she will have the pharaoh's inflexible eye to keep her honor inviolate, at least until the last minute. Penelope was left to her own devices, but we can quickly see that to leave Helen to her own devices would put us right back into the old Helen story, and so defeat our purposes.

Here all the plots converge. Helen's body could not be allowed to reside in Troy, nor could it be left in Sparta. It must be sent to Egypt. But how? Helen was not a woman to disappear easily. She was *disappeared*. Again, a task of great magnitude was, as it turned out, simplicity itself. All that was needed was a second cloud, in which Helen's body could be wrapped, and the trickster entering

15. For the completion of this process, see the choral ode at lines 1479ff., where, with Helen safely out to sea, the Chorus first commands the migratory birds to carry the happy message to Sparta. Then, in the final strophe (lines 1495–1511), the Chorus invokes the Dioskouroi, as Helen's saviors, to "descend through the Ether," clear their sister of "the ill repute of barbarian beds," and proclaim that Helen had never been "to the Phoebic towers of Ilium."

on cue, to deposit the precious body, now transformed into the rarest of substances, into the gentlest of prisons. Thus rarified, Helen disappeared, and no one was the wiser.

But enough of such obfuscation. Helen, still speaking the prologue, returns our attention to the matter at hand, which is, as always, her shame. Alas, her longtime protector, the good Proteus, is dead, and honor is gone with him. His son, Theoklymenos, lacking his father's temperance, "hunts" Helen down to make her his wife. We could have guessed as much. What would the Helen story be without the hunt? While it may have satisfied earlier revisionists to fix Helen directly under the pharaoh's eye, that was not finally acceptable. How would it look to posterity that the Greeks needed an Egyptian to guard Helen's honor and, worse, that the Greeks misspent their force on a phantom at Troy while Helen herself sat idle in Egypt? Hence Theoklymenos—to play the parts of the lusting foreigner, the foiled suitor, and the wicked king who has, in effect if not in fact, usurped the throne of the "good pharaoh," his own father of blessed memory.

Helen, still contextualizing herself, directs our eyes now to the tomb of the revered Proteus, and by clinging to it she reminds us that his presence, if not his body, is still needed in the plot. Helen has taken hold of his tomb to claim asylum from the lust of his son, to avail herself of whatever potency the pharaoh can still exert from the grave (which, fortunately, is considerable, since this is a ghost story). The earlier revisions needed a guardian of eminent rank and honesty so that Helen would not be left unprotected. But Euripides saw that a moment must occur when Helen's honor falls into jeopardy if the new Helen is to be a persuasive copy of the old Helen. The several intentions of the play are dramatically represented on the stage when Helen, concluding her prologue, falls prostrate at the feet of the honorable but ghostly father and calls her gesture an act of honor to her "former husband."

The moment of truth has now arrived. With the good pharaoh dead, and his feckless son wielding the power in his place, Helen's honor is for the moment—and it can be only a moment, given

Helen's character—placed in the greatest peril. But from Hermes Helen has learned that all will be well in the end. She will return with Menelaus to Sparta, and he will be convinced that Helen never, in her words, "spread another man's bed" (line 59). But seventeen years without news is a long wait. Like Penelope, Helen is at the end of her resources and thinks of suicide.[16] Her last hope is to cling to the tomb of the dead pharaoh "so that my bed may be saved for my husband. If I bear a name that is a byword throughout Hellas for infamy [*dusklees*], let not my body at least incur any disgrace" (lines 65–67).

On this note Helen concludes the prologue. Her story of the three goddesses vying in beauty, framed by "beauty" in the opening line of her prologue ("the beautiful virgin streams of the Nile"), and by "disgrace" (*aiskhrē*) in the final line, shows us that the old story is still uppermost in our minds. Beauty and ugliness, honor and shame, are still the motives that drive the plot. Helen's function here is to dissipate the shame, while saving the beauty, of the old Helen.

Everything will happen exactly as it should. If Theoklymenos is the villain in the piece, his sister Theonoe is the fairy godmother, thanks to whose assistance the wicked prince, presuming himself to be the almighty pharaoh, will have his sails trimmed, and he will be left with the phantom.[17] Helen's honor, so long preserved, will not be sacrificed at the last to a barbarian's lust. Helen and Menelaus will be reunited, and Menelaus will understand the truth. Theonoe will officiate at their nuptials; Theoklymenos will be called on to play both the jilted lover and the father surrendering

16. See Loraux 1985, 42–43, 54, for the significance of Helen's talk of suicide, with its connections to "shame" and "husband." In the context of ancient Greek tragedy, suicide was a woman's honorable exit if she had been disgraced or had brought disgrace on others. The revised Helen cannot, of course, commit suicide, since one of the necessities of the plot is to bring her back alive to Sparta. But since, even in this revision, Helen is a woman dishonored, if only by her eidolon, she will be allowed to talk of her suicide, to give it a shadowy reality, so that she can earn her place on the stage as a "tragic heroine."

17. Sansone 1985, 24: Theoklymenos' expected marriage to Helen will turn out to be "fiction."

his daughter to the successful suitor; the Dioskouroi will fly in to add the gods' blessings on the couple; and the honeymoon will be celebrated at sea, with full Egyptian regalia. And after the honeymoon Helen will arrive in Sparta as fresh as the day she left, a goddess again, but entirely Greek. But all that is in the future; at the moment the threat is from the barbarian, who, like Paris, knows nothing of self-restraint or honor.

It is a clever plot, and by the time Helen has concluded her prologue we are on the edge of our seats, particularly since we are about to witness, as the ancient Athenians themselves were hardly aware, the birth of fiction. We might call the *Helen* the first novel in Greek literature, since it is a tissue of plots and subplots, with fictitious gods, a fictitious pharaoh, a fictitious priestess, invented specifically to improve on a myth that had come to seem primitive, indecorous, and even preposterous.

With Helen's prologue completed, and the several plots and subplots at least briefly delineated, a sailor stumbles onto the stage looking for Theonoe. He is, it turns out, Teukros, son of Telamon and brother of the famous Ajax of Salamis. He has been banished from Salamis by Telamon, who was angered that Teukros had the indecency to return home from the Trojan War safe and sound, when Ajax, his more illustrious brother, committed suicide in shame that he had not been awarded the arms of Achilles. Whether Ajax acted honorably or dishonorably in killing himself may have been a debatable point, but, that act aside, it was certainly a disgrace for the lesser brother to return home unscathed. Disgrace, exile, and innocence too, not to mention the aggrieved father—all these apply to Helen no less than to Teukros.[18] Teukros is a sympathetic character. He too needs a new home, and a new story.

Teukros has been buffeted about the Mediterranean trying to make a landing on Cyprus, where Apollo has instructed him to found the new Salamis—the weaker, disgraced brother will thus redeem his own and his family's fame, when Salamis in Cyprus

18. Burnett 1971, 76.

grows as famous as the mother city. He has come to Egypt to seek
Theonoe's assistance, whose powers to rewrite destiny are apparently widely known.

Teukros is astounded to find himself standing outside portals so
awesome that they can only be compared with the gates of Ploutos,
Death himself. This is the pharaoh's palace, but it is also the *heroon*,
the sanctuary of the dead pharaoh, which Herodotus visited in
Memphis, where the good Proteus was immortalized. It makes
little difference whether we take the *skēnē* to represent the palace or
the sanctuary, Pharos or Memphis, but it adds to the irony to have
Teukros believe himself gazing upon the very gates of death when
he is in simple fact standing in the graveyard. We, with our wider
perspective, know that the graveyard in which Teukros finds himself is the hallowed ground where the old Helen will be laid to rest
and the new Helen resurrected to an immortality unsullied by the
weakness of the flesh. Like Homer's heroes, she will be translated
out of biology altogether, since biology was her failing, and made
a radiant and eternal *logos*, a pure story.

Even more astounding, however, is the sight of a woman who is
the very replica of the person whom Teukros had seen Menelaus
dragging from Troy. In his ignorance Teukros has just seen "The
Foreign Aphrodite," whose shrine Herodotus puzzled over in
Memphis, though he has the advantage over Herodotus in that he
is witnessing the cult idol in the flesh and not just hearing of her
reputation from the temple priests. Violated by the sight, Teukros
spits Helen's name through his teeth, as one spits against the evil
eye in the Mediterranean. He is incorrect when he supposes that
this is Helen's phantom. His first instinct was correct, before reason came to its rescue: he is gazing on Helen herself, Helen in all
her luminous reality. Yes, this is the pre-Trojan Helen, almost
identical to the Trojan Helen, but with one significant difference.
She has Helen's charisma, but it has been reduced below the
threshold of danger, since it is a requirement of the plot that the
new Helen be placed where she will be no danger either to herself
or to others. The first scene of the play marks that mission accom-

plished. Helen's charisma has been detoxified; it is now pure grace.[19]

Helen, for her part, is astonished to hear herself cursed for a crime that is not of her doing. Teukros apologizes for his mistake (the palinode theme). His rage (*orgē*), he says, led him to see a false resemblance between the woman at Troy and the woman in Egypt, no insult intended. This is the requisite vilification theme, familiar from Euripides' earlier plays, but now softened, displaced onto the phantom, and reduced to a mere echo, though the echo will no doubt haunt Helen wherever she goes.

Helen grieves to hear of the damage done at Troy in her name. The play, as we might have guessed from its subject matter (the revised Helen myth) and its date of production (late fifth- century Athens), is a study in semiotics, which was the popular topic among the sophists of the day. No plot could be more topical than the enigmatic relations between the person and her name, particularly when the semiotician would be Helen herself, asked to decipher her own script.

The anger of Teukros is a useful reminder to Helen, should she need one, of what the price would have been, had she sailed to Troy with Paris. On the other hand, though she has now been revised out of the story, she must still pay for the transgressions of her eidolon, while being innocent of all actions imputed to it. She might as well have been the phantom Helen if she was to be blamed for its misbehavior. But all will be resolved in the end: the phantom will be jettisoned, Helen will be reinstated, and her transgressions will appear for what they are, a cloud of empty accusations.

But we are at an early point in the drama, long before the separate Helens have been resolved into one. At this point, Helen, though grieving that she must bear the shame for the behavior of the eidolon, takes some satisfaction that if she will be cursed, she will be cursed not for herself but only for her resemblance. She

19. Segal (1971) notes the frequency of *charis* (grace) in the play.

accepts her scapegoat function, to bear the fault attributed to her, to seem to be a woman of easy virtue when she is not. This Helen knows, and it was no small consolation in her shame culture, that, whatever else she may be, she is not that other Helen, who was mistakenly thought to have slept in a barbarian's bed.

Helen accepts Teukros' apology, and a dialogue begins. Helen, allowed for the first time in many years to converse with a fellow countryman, and one who participated in the very actions from which she was excluded, presses Teukros for news. This is not Homer's Helen, weaving the Trojan War into her tapestry, but a woman banished from the theater altogether, forced to rely on others for her *logos*, as they may chance by with this or that piece of information. And, alas, the spin here is that the *logos*, when Helen hears it, is almost invariably incorrect. But all will be well, we need to remind ourselves, before we sink into despair.

Did Teukros really sail to Troy? Yes, "and we brought it low and destroyed it utterly, leaving not even the trace of a wall still standing" (lines 105ff.).

"Ah, wretched Helen," Helen sighs, "through you the Phrygians were destroyed. But go on."

"And many Achaeans too," Teukros adds.

"And you took the Spartan woman?" Helen asks, getting to the point. She is as fascinated as we are, no doubt even more so, because while both we and she are spectators, she is still, as always, also the spectacle.

Yes, Teukros replies; he had seen Menelaus dragging the woman herself by the hair. Helen is forewarned. Menelaus will not be easily persuaded that the woman whom he dragged from the barbarian's city to his own Greek ship was completely insubstantial. Helen dwells on the point. Had Teukros seen Helen herself, or had he heard the story? Teukros is insistent. He saw Menelaus dragging Helen as clearly as he now sees the woman in front of him. Helen dragged by the hair is a spectacle forever impressed upon Teukros' memory—and what would Helen be without the spectacle? Had Teukros perhaps mistaken a likeness of Helen for Helen herself?

Perhaps it was an appearance, a mistaken opinion (*dokēsis*)? But no, Teukros saw Helen with his own eyes, and "the mind [*nous*] sees," he adds cryptically.[20]

Teukros begs Helen to change the subject. She turns to him for news of her family. Leda, she learns, is dead. What was the cause? Was it in shame for her daughter's behavior? So they say, Teukros admits. She hanged herself. And Menelaus? With no sign of him at Sparta, so many years after the fall of Troy, he is presumed dead. And her brothers, the Dioskouroi? Both dead and not dead, Teukros answers; "there are two stories" (*logoi*, line 138). He tells them both.

In one story the Dioskouroi have been elevated to godhood and transformed into stars (as we find in Horace's version). In the other, quite opposite, story, they too committed suicide in shame. It is not a pretty picture: at least one suicide in the family, possibly three, from shame, and a husband presumed drowned at sea—yet another consequence and source of family shame. So much shame must be added to make the new Helen credible, since she could hardly be Helen if the plot were entirely free of shame.[21]

But enough of stories. Teukros explains his own mission, to consult the seer Theonoe regarding his search for Cyprus, where Apollo has instructed him to found the new Salamis. The alarm rings. "Let sailing itself be your sign," Helen cries, as she urges Teukros to flee the land before he is discovered by the wicked Theoklymenos, who threatens to kill any Greeks found on his soil. But why? Ask no more. Helen's lips are sealed.

20. Teukros may be alluding to a famous line by Epicharmus or demonstrating his knowledge of the philosophical issues of his day. Dale (1967, at lines 121–22) finds the point absurd and would delete the line from the text.

21. See Loraux 1985 on the catastrophes that are requisite for the woman on the tragic stage. In fact, however, as the play progresses, we find that the Dioskouroi did not die in shame, and Menelaus was not drowned at sea. The only "real" catastrophe in the play, then, is Leda's suicide. This is the suicide that is almost a requisite for the tragic heroine if she is to achieve tragic stature. But since Helen is being revived from the dead, the tragic suicide is conveniently displaced onto her mother, who never figured prominently in the Helen story and was thus easily expendable.

But ours are not. Teukros is an old Mycenean warrior who has just walked in on a plot in progress. Stupified as he may be, since he has fallen under Helen's spell more than he imagines, he would brook no violence against a Greek woman as beautiful as Helen; even more beautiful, if that were possible, since this is the new, flawless Helen. Besides, he stands sorely in need of an action to redeem his own name. But the sword raised to defend Helen's honor cannot be handed to a minor character; it belongs more properly to Menelaus. Teukros must be hurried off the stage before Menelaus blunders on.

Exit Teukros in great alarm, stopping only to offer his own humble palinode to the virtuous Helen (lines 161–62): "You have Helen's body but not her mind. Yours is very different." That is true. Helen's body was transported to Egypt, but who knows where her mind was displaced?

The hapless Teukros is an anachronism, a relic dragged willy-nilly from Homer's world into the sophisticated circles of fifth-century Athens. His epistemology is hopelessly outdated. He knows nothing about the unreliability of the senses. He has not read his Parmenides or overheard Socrates ruminating on the good and the beautiful with the young athletes in the gymnasium. He is the old-fashioned man in the street, who believes what he sees, a quaint hero of a bygone age who has unwittingly stepped into the philosophers' den.

Helen, remaining alone on stage, sings a haunting aria to the Sirens, "the winged virgin daughters of Earth" (the recurrent virginity theme), to bring their music, and adds a prayer that Persephone, in her grace, will grant them permission to assist her in singing the lament that will bring grace to the dead. This is a lovely ode, and with a tragic beauty, since Helen, even when excused from the story, must still sing the final dirge of the Trojan War, as she sings the final dirge for Hector in the *Iliad*.

The Chorus—Spartan women exiled to Egypt like Helen—enters, hearing her cry, and sings another lovely ode (a *kommos*), with Helen as their soloist, in which they express a woman's sympathy for a woman's fate, to be excluded from her life yet blamed for every event in it. Helen recapitulates for them the latest news: her mother has committed suicide, her husband is assumed dead, and her brothers probably died in shame; in any case, they are gone (though they are Helen's traditional "saviors"). The Chorus, ever mindful of the play's intention, sorrows at the injustice that a rumor, and false at that, that Helen had slept "in barbarian beds" (line 225), could cause such devastation.

Even if, against all probability, Menelaus were to arrive and return Helen to Sparta, Helen continues, her problems would not be over, since everyone would take her for the false Helen, whatever she might say. No matter how flawlessly she is reconstructed, Helen will be forever unpersuasive. People will not accept her being over their story. Faced with this truth, Helen has but one alternative: to yield to the barbarian's lust. But that would be no escape, for, Helen poignantly observes, when the gods took her from her fatherland and set her down on barbarian soil, they made her a slave, though she had been freeborn. "Among barbarians everyone is a slave, but one," she adds (line 296), voicing the sentiments appropriate to an Athenian in the age of democracy.

Helen's point is well taken, and the legitimacy of her complaint almost conceals the subplot, which calls for a wicked pharaoh to enter the picture so that a Greek warrior can play the part that Herodotus had erroneously assigned to the Egyptians. Herodotus' mistake was to remove Menelaus, except as the transgressor at the conclusion of the story. But the new Menelaus will have a more honorable function. He will steal from the pharaoh, though it will not be seen as theft but simple nemesis, to pay the pharaoh back for too much honor granted him by Herodotus. And, even more satisfying, Menelaus will no longer be only the cuckolded husband or the fool who went to war for a phantom. He will be made over into the man he should have been—Helen's husband, lover, and savior.

"Savior," that is, in a manner of speaking. As it turns out, when Menelaus arrives on stage, Helen will save him rather than vice versa, but that is because at least two subplots interfere with each other. In one plot, all that is required for Helen's salvation is simply the appearance of Menelaus—see lines 277–78, where Menelaus is Helen's last hope and only anchor. In this plot Menelaus is needed only incidentally for his warrior function, which was never very impressive; more significant is his function as husband. Helen's story still needs a husband, ineffectual as he may be, to blot out that other story, in which Helen did not need a husband and chose, if that is the word, to take a foreign lover, or be taken by one. On the other hand, Menelaus' warrior function must not be completely eliminated—that was the fault in Herodotus' story. A small conspiracy will be contrived, by Helen herself, with Menelaus playing Helen's brave defender, to rescue her body intact from the barbarian. It had been recovered, but not intact, in Herodotus. What Herodotus had left only half corrected Euripides would bring to a perfect finish.

Exeunt Helen and Chorus, with Helen at her wits' end and planning suicide, but with the Chorus encouraging her to consult Theonoe before taking any precipitous action on the basis of the information just relayed. She was correct to see that in being sent to Egypt she had been sent into slavery. But she was wrong to implicate the gods. They had nothing to do with it. She should have blamed her revisionists, who banished her so that they might correct the text without her interference.

Onto the stage stumbles another battered sailor, also a Greek. This is a red-letter day in Memphis—two Greek visitors arriving on a single day. This latest arrival is Menelaus, but in a much worse case than Teukros. He has been shipwrecked—the ancient novelists' favorite trick for moving their characters around the Mediterranean and having them reappear in unexpected places. Menelaus has lost almost everything. He has managed to recuperate from the sea a few scraps of jetsam, which serve him as a minimal covering, a few friends, and, of course, Helen. If the new Helen is another Penelope, Menelaus is her Odysseus, both the Odysseus arriving naked before Nausikaa and the later Odysseus arriving before Penelope disguised in a beggar's rags.

This Menelaus has been reading his *Odyssey*. Like Odysseus stowing his treasures in the cave of the nymphs when he arrives on Ithacan soil, Menelaus too has stowed his small treasure saved from the deep in a cave at the seashore. In his case the treasure is Helen, or rather, the ghost that was substituted for Helen when she was removed from the plot. Like Teukros, Menelaus has been taken from Homer's quaint setting and inserted into another story, the story of the eidolon, about which he knows nothing, not even after traveling about the Mediterranean for seven years with the very phantom in question. He also knows nothing of his wife's sudden departure from Sparta. To have a cloud substituted for his wife without his being any the wiser—Menelaus is always a little behind in the plot, though the poets play him up as best they can.[22] Perhaps he is more sophisticated than Teukros, but not by much. He does not know yet that he has landed in Egypt, much less that Helen, far from being under lock and key in a seaside cave, has been awaiting his arrival, as a guest of the pharaoh, for seventeen idle years.

Alone on stage, Menelaus identifies himself. Being a new and significant character, he too plays prologue to himself, to explain his dire and humiliating circumstances. Indeed, he is a sorry spectacle. Everything went down in a storm—he keeps drawing our eyes to his almost total nakedness.[23] Euripides has placed Menelaus one small cut above Homer's Odysseus, who had only an olive branch to hide his shame from Nausikaa's stare. The new Menelaus has at least what can pass for clothes, however primitive.

Menelaus laments at length the dignity so rudely snatched from him, weeping to think of the splendid robes that went down in the wreck. Once he walked in the purple, but now he is ashamed to expose himself to local ridicule in the town. Dignity is very much

22. Even as a suitor, Menelaus was somehow deficient. Cf. Hesiod, frag. 197.5 MW, where Agamemnon courts Helen as a surrogate suitor for his brother; and frag. 204.87–92 MW, where Hesiod informs us that Achilles was too young to present himself as one of Helen's suitors; had Achilles competed in the contest, however, Menelaus certainly would not have won Helen.
23. Burnett (1971, 80) discusses Menelaus' nakedness in its connection with the general portrait painted of him in his first stage appearance.

on his mind throughout the play, as it is on the mind of Helen, and it is the major consideration even in Theonoe's mind.[24] Alas, for all his thinking on his dignity, Menelaus will not be allowed much. The splendid robes taken from him will never be restored. To play his part as the new Menelaus to the new Helen, Menelaus will be asked to shed what little dignity Homer had allowed him.

His prologue finished, Menelaus discovers the palace. He knocks on the gates. The old doorkeeper, the stock beldam from comedy, barks at him and even begins to shove him from the door. Greeks are not wanted here, she growls. Later she softens, saying that she herself is partial to Greeks, but her master is not, but that comes at the end of the exchange, when Menelaus' humiliation has been adequately exposed (to be compensated for later, when Menelaus robs the pharaoh's palace), and the barbarian's inhospitality sufficiently underlined.

The exchange between the doorkeeper and Menelaus (lines 437–514) is what we would expect to find in vaudeville. Menelaus cringes now before an old woman (*graus*, in Greek), who rains vaudeville blows on his head as if he were a common vagrant. The world-famous hero, the sacker of Troy and Helen's savior—were people to see him in his proper dress—is in Egypt a nobody. But a greater humiliation lies ahead. He is about to discover that he was a nobody even at Troy. What glory was there in being seen dragging a cloud by the hair? But the worst is yet to come: the only escape from this cruel plot is for Menelaus, having first been exposed as a nobody at Troy, then to play a nobody like Odysseus. In the plan of escape, which Helen will devise, Menelaus will be asked to play a corpse of himself; or rather, something less than a corpse—a rumor of a corpse; and he will need to play the part convincingly. The gods never promised Menelaus an easy road to Elysium.

Why would the pharaoh be so inhospitable to the Hellenes, Menelaus asks, as he ducks the blows from the old concierge, whose crusty language hides a softer heart. A proscription on the

24. A point forcefully made by Sansone 1985, 25.

brave and mighty Hellenes is incomprehensible. Who in the world could resist a Greek, particularly when he is the doughty Menelaus? The beldam, relenting, explains: inside the palace is Helen, daughter of Zeus. Helen? Yes, the very Helen, whose father was Tyndareus. We need not pause again over Helen's double paternity; more complex problems command our attention.

"What sort of *logos* is this?" Menelaus asks (line 473), as well he might, since he has just walked in on a revision of his own story. Where did this Helen come from? Sparta, the old doorkeeper replies. Does she mean to say that Helen has been lifted from her cave on the seashore? No, no, no, this Helen arrived even before the Achaeans sailed to Troy.

Poor Menelaus—

> For like a foolishe noddie
> He thinkes the shadow that he sees, to be a lively boddie.
> Ovid *Metamorphoses* 3.522–23 (trans. Golding)

The riddle of Seeming and Being served up to Teukros was simple compared with the riddle now facing Menelaus. Teukros saw Helen with his eyes, but Menelaus holds Helen secured in a cave. The eyes can secure much, but not the body itself, and Helen's body is the issue, not her image. Can it be that in the pharaoh's palace is another woman with both his wife's name and her confused double paternity?

But perhaps, Menelaus muses, in Egypt "Zeus" is a man's name (the border between man and god being very fluid in Egypt), though to be sure there is only one Zeus on high. In his desperation Menelaus separates Zeus into the uppercase Zeus (God) and the lowercase zeus (a man), struggling to grasp the semiotics of this revisionist plot. Menelaus has become our fifth-century traveler, like Herodotus, discovering amazing cross-cultural correspondences in the course of his foreign travels. Perhaps there is another city called Sparta? A second Lakedaimon, a second Troy? Two men called Tyndareus, each with a daughter named Helen, and each of

them married to a man called Menelaus—we are in the theater of
Ionesco.

Whether Euripides intended the exchange between the old doorkeeper and the conquering hero to be as comic as we find it, a
man's discovery of another woman with his wife's name and peculiar history would have a comic side that would be difficult to
exclude from the story. The comic possibilities would only in-
crease if the wife in question was the famous Helen of Troy, especially if it transpired that she had been excused from the Trojan
War. But still another plot intrudes here, which appears even in the
Odyssey, though it is more delicately handled in Homer. Write the
story of Helen and Menelaus as we will, Menelaus will always
appear the foolish one, and Helen his more clever, if not better,
half. The Phoenicians, if Herodotus is to be believed, thought
Menelaus a fool for chasing after his wife, since they did not believe
that decent wives would play their husbands false, nor would they
be given the opportunity to do so. But if Stesichorus solved that
problem by removing Helen from Troy, sending Menelaus to Troy
in quixotic pursuit of a cloud did nothing to enhance his stature.
But why would Euripides then add to the humiliation by having
Menelaus hallucinate Helen for seven years after the fall of Troy?
The nakedness that Menelaus fears to expose to public ridicule is
no metaphor. Menelaus is stripped of his dignity because the new
plot calls for Helen to be clever, and her husband to play the fool.
In the revised story Helen is to play Being, leaving Menelaus to
play Seeming, and in late fifth-century Athens only simpletons
lived in the world of Seeming.

Helen reenters the stage, returning to her sanctuary at the pharaoh's tomb. She has been put in a happier mood by Theonoe's
reading that Menelaus is still alive, and even now close at hand.
And lo! Here he is, nearly as naked as Odysseus. Here begins what
we would expect to be the great recognition scene of all time—
Menelaus and Helen discovering each other again after seventeen
years, and all that history between them, particularly since Helen
has tantalized us earlier with talk of "secret tokens" by which

Menelaus will recognize her as his true wife. Can her secret token better Penelope's? The reunion of Odysseus and Penelope pales beside this reunion, since Penelope was never called upon to play a ghost of herself, as Helen is.

The couple begin with the consternations usual in such scenes, with Menelaus flabbergasted to see the ghost of his wife, and Helen fearing for her honor at the hands of a desperado. Each discovers that the other is Greek (a great relief). But Helen looks remarkably like the wife of Menelaus—she would be recognizable anywhere, the more so since she has not aged a day since she left Sparta. But that cannot be, since the real Helen is locked well out of sight in her seaside cave. And to Helen, Menelaus, though indeed no better dressed than a desperado, looks remarkably like her long-awaited husband. Can it be?

"Oh timely have you come to your wife's arms," Helen begins (lines 566ff.).

"Wife? What wife? Hands off, I say!"

"*Your* wife, whom Tyndareus gave you."

"O Hekate, send me a kind apparition!"

"I am no Hekate. This is no phantom of the night you see before you."

"I say. Am I, a single man, the husband of two wives?"

"*Two* wives? What foreign beds have you mastered?"

"The woman in the cave, whom I have brought from Troy."

"You have no other wife than me."

So it goes. Helen pleads with Menelaus to trust the evidence of his own eyes, but Menelaus is not to be fooled, like Teukros, by coincidence and resemblance. His ontology is based on stronger arguments than the evidence of the eyes. He has read his philosophers and knows the difference between the name and the fact, because he possesses, if not Helen's good name, at least her body, dragged by his own hand from Troy and most positively stowed in a seaside cave.

But no, Helen explains, that was not her body but an eidolon. An eidolon? And who, Menelaus asks, floundering, "can make bodies come alive?" The Ether, Helen explains, from which he is in possession of "a god-worked bed" (line 584).

What god would make such beds? Hera, of course, goddess of the marriage bed. Helen explains: Hera exchanged Helen's phantom for her body at Sparta so that Paris would believe himself enjoying Helen's body while her body itself was safely deposited out of harm's way. At the risk of being thought ungracious, we might question the motives for such bed making, which leaves Menelaus with a cloud for his bedmate in order to punish Paris. But this is not a theological tract; it is a matinee performance made, like Helen's ghost, of the air itself. Matinee idols are to be taken for what they are, the sweets that help us while away the afternoon; and plots are invented solely for our delight. If we thought that Euripides was to present us with a logical solution, we were mistaken; though, seen from another angle, his *Helen* is a masterpiece of logic.

"And how were you here and in Troy at the same time?" Menelaus continues (line 587).

"The name may be in many places, but not the body," Helen answers (line 588), as the teacher might repeat the lesson for one of her slower pupils. The name and the body, things in themselves and their appearances, Meaning and Being—Menelaus is a long way out of his depth. He may have mistakenly fought at Troy for a phantom—the woman-as-name—since he did not see her but only assumed she was in Troy. But to ask him to believe that for the past seven years he has enjoyed not Helen's body but her name is to impose on him an ontology too steep for his comprehension. Like Teukros, Menelaus has been pulled, without his knowing it, from the Homeric text where he was, if not dignified, at least on familiar ground, and made to impersonate an altogether different character, the novice in the school of philosophy.

It will take time for Menelaus to understand that what he so insistently holds in the cave is no more than a name. Being but a character in the play, and not one of the quickest, Menelaus could not see that the point was to remove Helen's body, as much from him as from Paris, since it was the original source of contention. That mission is almost accomplished. The eidolon, having served to cloud the issue, will be dropped from the text, as no longer necessary; as, in fact, a distinct embarrassment. The precious body, so long quarantined in Egypt against all contamination, can now be retrieved and reinserted in the text, without danger either to itself or to the text. If Menelaus was confused, so are we. It is a nimble and witty plot.

Finding himself beached in Egypt, with a ghost claiming to be his wife and, even more incredible, arguing that his very real Helen is in fact no more than a cloud—there is witchery in the air. Menelaus has had his fill of Egyptian epistemology, and he turns to make for the shore. Helen too is distraught, but for different reasons. Her only anchor is about to be weighed, and Helen herself will be left ashore, to face dishonor or suicide. "Surely you will not leave us for an empty bed," Helen pleads (line 590), but Menelaus wants no more talk from phantoms calling his bed a phantom. He will place his trust in personal experience (which, he will soon find, is less correct, in this case at least, than the evidence of the eyes).

The historic recognition would have been aborted then and there, with Menelaus fleeing the real Helen as if she were one of Hekate's ghosts, had not another Greek—this time a slave—burst onto the scene and saved the day. Breathless from searching the countryside for his master, and fearing the usual consequences for bearing bad news, the slave blurts out to Menelaus that the Helen whom he was guarding in the seaside cave simply evaporated into the Ether, pausing only long enough to explain herself and her mission. She was, she explained, not Helen at all but a cloud, fashioned by the clever Hera to substitute for Helen's body at Troy. But, being now superfluous to the plot, the cloud bid the stupefied sailors a fond farewell, the slave continues, and returned to its father sky (*ouranos*).

The slave, dazed by the reverse epiphany that he has just witnessed at the shore, is dazed again to see Helen herself standing beside her husband. His relief is enormous, though tempered by some annoyance that she would play such a trick (lines 616–21):

> O, hail, daughter of Leda!
> So you were here!
> And I was just reporting that you had ascended to the stars,
> Though I was unaware that your body had wings. But I will
> Not allow you to mock us again; you gave trouble enough
> At Troy to your husband and his allies.

Even when guards are stationed, Helen's vagrancy will have its way it seems. But this is a reference to the old Helen. We know, though the slave does not, that the new Helen has no invisible wings, no magical powers to transubstantiate herself or transport herself hither and yon. The new Helen has no powers at all. They were given to the good pharaoh for safekeeping. The slave's reference to the stars is a prophetic reference (out of the mouths of slaves!) to the apotheosis in store, when the expurgated Helen will join her brothers as a celestial constellation. This happy event will be Helen's prize for accepting the full and absolute revision of her biography.[25] Not a story is to be omitted from this plot of Helen's self-substantiation.

Thanks to the eidolon's illumination, the recognition reaches its grand finale. Helen's wild assertions are proven true, if proof is the word. The cloud has passed, and the husband and wife see each other as they really are and have been ever since the beginning of the story. The diapason peals, and the joyous couple raise their anthem of thanksgiving.

But epistemological doubts still worry Menelaus. How did Helen arrive in Egypt? That is a painful subject, Helen replies, but Menelaus presses for details; after what he has suffered, he is prepared for the worst. Her transfer to Egypt was—Helen puts this fact in emphatic first position, to relieve Menelaus at once of any

---

25. Bowra (1934) cites Horace *Epodes* 17.40–44 as evidence that Stesichorus had included this element in his *Palinode*.

lingering doubts—not (God forbid!) so that she might lie in "a barbarian's bed" (lines 666–78). A kind deity brought her to Egypt, if we can call Hermes kind (lines 670–71).

But Hera was the mastermind of the whole plot, Helen explains, taking Menelaus back to the Judgment of Paris, and leading him step by step through the incredible plot in which he has played his ignorant and not very noble part these many years. Menelaus is baffled. The Judgment of Paris is new to him, and certainly it contains enough to keep his thoughts busy for some time. We are baffled too, but for a different reason. We are bemused to see the Judgment of Paris so easily rewritten, to have Hera declared the winner, and Aphrodite the loser.

And thus, Helen concludes her story of the famous beauty contest, she herself was removed to Egypt, though ever so softly. Menelaus tries to comprehend that what he has for seven years taken for a woman is an idol made of air. But Helen enumerates the other, equally dire consequences of the plot—Leda's suicide, and perhaps the suicide of the Dioskouroi too. Their daughter Hermione remains still unmarried and childless, lamenting her mother's "marriage that is no marriage" (line 690). Shame prevents Hermione's marriage, and her marriageless state is yet another reason for shame. Their house has been ruined, and Achaeans have died in the tens of thousands, all for a phantom, a mere name. But at least Helen can take credit, if the credit is due to her and not to the now-dead pharaoh, that she herself did not do what was ascribed to her name: she did not abandon Menelaus "for a disgraceful marriage" (line 697).

Aiskhros—"disgrace" is the penultimate word in Helen's tale, and the term with which the paean of thanksgiving offered up by Menelaus and Helen closes. Shame was the determining factor that led to the amazing story of Menelaus swept off to Troy in pursuit of a phantom, and Helen swept to Egypt—the whole intricate and, on the face of it, absurd plot written to recuperate Helen's shame. In the uncanny way of ghosts and phantoms, Helen's eidolon was the secret token that made it all possible. Menelaus recognizes that he has been sleeping with but a name, compounded of conceits and lies. When the Greek beholds his own wife at last, she is Greek to the core, without a trace of vagrancy in her character.

But wait. Helen's presence in Egypt might suggest a last hint of vagrancy floating in the air—even in the fifth century wives probably did not travel much about the Mediterranean unattended—hence Menelaus' anxiety to know how Helen reached Egypt and, more important, why. Egypt thankfully turns out to be only an apparent vagrancy. Helen was absent from Sparta, true; but she was not a vagrant. Again Egypt is the convenient venue for mediating the contradictions.[26] The solicitous husband and the faithful wife—Greek is united with Greek again, a perfect match, and the ugly rumor that had some impudent foreigner come between them vanishes whence it came, into the air.

The slave, happy to discover that his hallucination on the beach bodes no ill, especially for him, begs to be included in the rejoicing. The story is repeated again for his benefit, as it will be repeated no doubt again and again wherever Helen goes. The cloud, which he witnessed dissolving into the Ether, told the gods' own truth; it was, in fact, "a cloud statue," Menelaus explains to the uncomprehending slave, a fictive Helen formed by the gods to obscure their own ethereal purposes. And yes, this woman here before him is the true Helen. "Trust my words," Menelaus concludes (line 710).

The slave has some obvious remarks to make regarding the incomprehensibility of the god, and how the rain falls on the just and the unjust, and so forth. But lo! Everything has turned out in the best possible way, all of its own accord, automatically (*automata*, line 719). The slave's loyalty and his joy at his masters' good fortune are admirable proof of his own nobility—he hopes that he will be numbered among the noble slaves, having the mind of a free man if not the name, as if to show that even a slave could enter into the semiotic debates of his time. But his theology is off the

26. Segal (1971, 573) discusses Egypt as a mediating symbol for the play's "exploration of the tensions between reality and appearance."

mark. If he only knew how far from automatic this plot was. Several clever hands had worked on it, and it still needed work.

The slave now celebrates Helen's vindication, addressing her as "daughter," as if he were standing in loco parentis, as is in fact the case, since the plot of the Father is never far from the surface. The theme is muted by being voiced by a slave, but even so, there is no mistaking the message. Speaking for the absent and, we might add, ghostly father, the slave congratulates Helen that she did not disgrace either him or her brothers. Now the slave remembers, like a memory that has been suppressed under the weight of shame, Helen's wedding night—himself, torch in hand, running beside the royal carriage, and inside the carriage the bride and groom, Helen and Menelaus, setting off from her father's prosperous home. With Helen of Troy erased, Helen at Sparta grows visible again.

But back to Troy again. The slave's brief memory of a happier time yields to ruminations on the foolishness of soothsayers. Kalkhas, the Greek seer at Troy, did not see the cloud or point it out to his friends as they were dying on the field; nor did Helenos, the Trojan seer. A city was destroyed in vain. So much for seers. The slave too has been pulled out of an earlier era and pressed into service in another text. It is odd to hear him critique the *Iliad* in the light of the new text, into which he has now been written. Of course Kalkhas did not see Helen's idol at Troy for the simple reason that it had not yet been invented. It would be unfair to fault Kalkhas for a flaw that was in the plot and not in his perception. In the old plot as it was given to him, his conduct was perfectly satisfactory.

Enough from the slave. He is bidden to return to the shore to explain everything to the ragged band of survivors, who are to hold themselves in readiness for a quick escape. Helen and Menelaus are alone again, and the play moves into the second act. In fact, the play is already over, though we are only halfway through. The eidolon has played its part to perfection, as a most subtle deus ex machina, floating in and out of the play to resolve the complications. The plot has been disclosed in all its mysterious windings. The impossible recognition has been accomplished; the requisite peripeteia and anagnorisis have taken place; the long-separated lovers are reunited; all has been explained and forgiven; and the cloud that came between them has faded.

But no. The plot careens now in another direction.[27] Or rather, one plot has been resolved, but another plot remains. Helen has been recuperated from Troy, but how to recuperate her from Egypt? Ecstasy gives way to deep anxiety. The happy couple have neither ship nor, in the case of Menelaus, clothes to sail in. Can the world-famous Menelaus and Helen simply slip out of the country, hidden under the cabbages in a peasant's cart? Of course not. They must sail forth from the Nile under a full panoply, as conquering heroes and honored guests, not as petty vagrants and thieves. The Egyptian story as Herodotus told it must be corrected. This correction Euripides may owe to the historian Hellanikos.[28] In any case, the point was to rewrite Herodotus, who had overvalued the piety of the Egyptians at the expense of the Greeks. An incident must be contrived to allow Menelaus to retrieve his honor, which was put in question by both Homer and Herodotus (probably by Stesichorus as well). The roles that Herodotus had assigned to the Greeks and the Egyptians are simply reversed: the honor, such as it is, is taken from the Egyptians and given back where it belongs, to the Greeks.

Also, a plan is needed to give Helen something to do, for she has been very much in want of a role since she was detached from the story seventeen years earlier. With Helen's fabled charm and cleverness no longer a threat to the plot, they could even be turned to advantage and used against the barbarian. With her charm she will

27. See Burnett (1971), who writes of the two plots in the play as "recognition" and "rescue."
28. Hellanikos, *FGrH* 4, frag. 153, tells of Menelaus and Helen in Egypt after the Trojan War. There King Thonos = Thon, in *Odyssey* 4, tries to rape Helen, and Menelaus, as an honorable man, kills him. Euripides softens the tale and has Helen and Menelaus trick the king instead of killing him. This *logos*, with its variant, is yet another to be added to the many *logoi* incorporated into the *Helen*.

win the pharaoh's ethical sister to her side; with her cleverness she will outwit the rude pharaoh and leave him the vulgar fool of the tale.

A bride contest must be staged. Helen would not be Helen without her bride competition. Menelaus may be satisfied by the idol's explanation, that Helen of Troy was a fiction, but we need more convincing. How are we in the audience, without Menelaus' privileged access to the stage, to determine whether this is truly Helen if we are not given to see her fabled beauty put to the test? But this staged bride competition, and the plot to frustrate the pharaoh's un-Hellenic lust, are a divertissement to amuse us while the plot covers its tracks, to disguise from us exactly how thin it is. To remove the scandal from the old Helen, while saving as much of her grace as would enliven the plot, was a challenge, even for a clever playwright.

With the recognition completed, the bride contest can begin. This is the old contest rewritten, much abbreviated, and given a happier ending. Theoklymenos, the barbarian king, is the real threat to the plot, and his sister Theonoe a potential threat, both of which must be disarmed. First, how to keep Theonoe, who sees everything, from informing her brother that Helen's husband has arrived? And then how to foil the barbarian, who threatens to play a second Paris and seize Helen in defiance of all international law? Helen, chaste these many years, promises to kill herself before she will suffer her honor to be violated, a commitment that receives her husband's approval. Men may violate her name, but not her body. Not to be outdone, Menelaus promises to follow suit.

But, Helen pauses, with both of them dead, how would they receive their *doxa* ("reputation," line 841)? *Doxa* is uncomfortably close to *dokēsis*; in fact, derived from the same root (*dokeō*, "to seem"), they were synonymous in philosophical parlance for "false opinion" and contrasted with *noēsis*, "true knowledge." Outside of philosophy, *doxa* was "the public estimation," a topic ever on Helen's mind, since the point of the play is to correct the public opinion that had beclouded Helen's name since Homer's time. But since Helen is the subject, *doxa* is beginning to shade into its New Testament meaning, as radiance and glory.

A double suicide would be a waste. Its glory would bloom unseen. What profit in the eidolon if the story bumbled to an end in a suicide pact in a foreign land? Without the storyteller, where would the story be? It must not fall into the wrong hands, or the radiance of the revision would be seriously diminished. Witness how easily Herodotus was misled when he allowed the Egyptians to tell the story. Someone—from the Hellenic side—must survive to tell the true story of Helen's rescue.

Menelaus rises nobly to the occasion. He will kill Helen himself at the very tomb where they stand, thus polluting sacred ground, which will certainly be a memorable act. Then he will kill himself. He promises a great *agon* (contest) for Helen's bed, hardly realizing how comic he must sound as he proudly announces a new version of Helen's bridal contest that will leave both him and Helen dead. Swelling to his full Mycenean manhood, he foresees a great spectacle that will not disgrace the Achaeans who suffered at Troy. The gods will witness the spectacle ("if they are wise," line 851). They, as the final spectators and judges, will know that Menelaus died not for some simpleton's hallucination but for Helen's very person.

Theonoe's arrival on stage puts an end to such posturing, since the required posture now is supplication. Too late to flee. Besides, there is no fleeing Theonoe's all-knowing second sight. Of course with her second sight she recognizes Menelaus at once, and she foresees grim trials in store. Her second sight also allows her to witness two goddesses at the throne of Zeus. A quarrel has broken out between them, about Helen—who else, since the two are Hera and Aphrodite? Hera, Theonoe divines, though not well disposed to Helen in the past—a point that we, in the audience had registered some time earlier—has now changed her attitude and wants Helen back in Sparta with her husband so that all Hellas may know that Aphrodite's gift to Paris was a "wedding with a pseudobride" (*pseudonumpheutoi gamoi*, line 883). Aphrodite, predictably, is opposed to such a neat solution to the story, particularly when it is at her expense. Her intention is to wreck Helen's homecoming, since she has no wish to be exposed as having bought her beauty "by a marriage that was not to be bought" (line 886).[29]

This is Homer revisited, with Euripides imitating the double determination of Homeric epic, which moves back and forth between the decisions on the human plane and the superior decisions of the gods on Mount Olympus. But these gods lack the cogency of Homer's gods. Nemesis has been removed from the story, except as a faint echo, and without nemesis the plot loses all its force. The reversal of the old roles, with Hera now playing Helen's advocate, and Aphrodite her enemy, while ingenious enough, only broadcasts its own absurdities. Who is Helen without Aphrodite? But judged by the play's own motives, the reversal of the traditional roles of the two goddesses makes sense, since the point was to subtract the libido from the text.

The quarrel between the two goddesses is an obvious fiction. Hera and Aphrodite are invoked as authorities for the fiction of a new Helen, much as Herodotus invoked Egyptian priests as the authorities for his Helen myth, though in this case the fiction is beyond argument. The real author of the plot is Euripides himself, borrowing from several predecessors, and hoping to add credibility to his plot by attributing it to the superior minds on Mount Olympus. The fiction gapes open when Theonoe informs us that though she is only a witness to the heavenly quarrel, it has been given to her to be its adjudicator. Why would two goddesses take their quarrel to Zeus, only to have him turn it over to an Egyptian princess, as if it were beyond his powers to resolve? The pieces fall into place when we remember the peculiar demands of this revision.

The real motive for the quarrel between Hera and Aphrodite, as it was vouchsafed to Theonoe's pure vision, was to revise the traditional Judgment of Paris as the necessary precondition to repealing the Judgment of Helen. But if the quarrel that Theonoe is

29. A problematic passage; see Dale 1967.

called to adjudicate is the old Judgment of Paris, where is Athena? She is Theonoe herself, as some scholars have cleverly detected, no longer one of the contestants but made the judge of the contest.[30] Hera is deeply implicated in this revisionist plot; Aphrodite less so, because the plot calls for her elimination; and Athena is mysteriously absent, until we recognize her in the Egyptian priestess, who, for all her beauty, rises above beauty contests, being, like Athena, the obedient, virgin daughter of an honorable father.

Theonoe is most conspicuously Athena when, in adjudicating the contest, she speaks as if she were Athena herself adjudicating between motherhood and fatherhood in Aeschylus' *Eumenides*. Like Athena, Theonoe is a confirmed celibate and can therefore render a decision free of human passion.[31] With all passion removed, the Judgment of Paris will easily be reversed; Hera will be declared the victor; and Sparta, with assistance from Athena sub rosa, will win the coveted trophy back from Troy at last. With Athens and Sparta now presenting a common front, Helen will be quietly removed from Aphrodite's jurisdiction, if that is the word, and placed under Hera's jurisdiction—in bed with Menelaus.

Helen and Menelaus take turns presenting their case to Theonoe, to whom the enormous power has suddenly gravitated to adjudicate the old contest among the goddesses. Helen recalls Theonoe's noble father and pleads with her to follow his example. The good pharaoh is needed still but now as a remote influence, to exert

30. Sansone 1985; Burnett (1971, 89) touches on the point more briefly. Cf. also Kannicht (1969, 1: 85), who refers to Plato *Cratylus* 407b, where "Athena" is etymologized as *a theonoa* (god's understanding); thus, being specially gifted in divine intelligence, she was called Theonoe. Euripides gives Theonoe two names, as if to call attention to Theonoe's Athena-function (lines 10–15): she was first known as Eido, "the glory of her mother, while she was a baby. But when she reached the age of marriage, they called her Theonoe, for she knows all divine affairs, both things as they are and things that will be." In short, once she reached the age of marriage, Theonoe chose Athena's path—celibacy and knowledge—and was given the name that would signify this allegiance.
31. On the power of chastity to withstand Aphrodite's seductions, cf. the *Homeric Hymn to Aphrodite* (V). Of all the gods, only three remained impervious to Aphrodite's power. All three were female, and all were consecrated virgins: Athena, Artemis, Hestia.

the subliminal father's authority from beyond the grave. There is no one, Helen continues her argument, who does not hate Helen, as the woman who betrayed her husband to live in "the golden houses of Phrygia" (line 928). But were she to return to Sparta, and the true story be known, Helen's character would be cleared, and she would be able to dower her daughter, whose unmarriageable state preys on her thoughts—the new Helen is a good Greek mother, to whom marriage is a serious business.[32]

Menelaus strikes a more manly attitude. It would disgrace Troy for him to fall to his knees and weep histrionic tears. If Theonoe is willing to save a foreigner and his lawful wife, good. But if not, it will be only one more woe for him, but Theonoe will be revealed as an evil woman. To add force to his argument, Menelaus turns to her father's tomb—the ghost of the father looming ever closer as the scene progresses—and addresses himself directly to that ever-potent presence. Invoking the very fountain of righteousness, Proteus of blessed memory, Menelaus turns back to Theonoe and threatens to pollute her reverend father's tomb with his and Helen's blood, which would be for Theonoe an immortal grief, and to her father a great reproach.

After such appeals, Theonoe's decision is a foregone conclusion. She will vote as Athena would, for the father, which is the side of justice and honor. As for Aphrodite, she carries no weight with Theonoe, since Theonoe, imitating Athena without knowing it, has made it her object to remain a virgin consecrated to her father's blessed memory. It is a nice piece of editing. The Judgment of Paris has been overturned, Aphrodite has been sent packing, the father has been reinstated (via his ghost), and the wandering Helen has been located and brought back under Athena's impartial eye (or will be, when the play is done), to be henceforth, like Athena, the perfect and obedient daughter. Her days as "The Foreign Aphrodite" are almost over.

32. Cf. the concern of the Chorus at lines 1476–78, where the women urge Helen swiftly home to her daughter, "upon whom the torches of marriage have not yet shone."

Almost, but not quite. Theonoe agrees to keep the secret from her brother Theoklymenos, but there her collaboration stops. How Helen and Menelaus will manage their escape from Egypt Theonoe leaves to their own devices, reasonably enough, since the only significant action so far has been on the part of the eidolon. Helen must prove her magic if she is to resemble the Helen we know, and Menelaus must have his moment of manhood. Theonoe retires, but though her only contribution to the conspiracy is her silence, that will be enough. In adjudicating between the goddesses, Theonoe has agreed to author the new plot, and everything else will follow of its own accord. The ghost of the father will be the presiding spirit, which will overcome the wilder spirit of his son. As the stand-in for the foreign father, Proteus, though now only a ghost of his former self, will play the part as Priam did not, to curb his son's wayward lust—Paris of the old story is finally to be given his due.

Helen and Menelaus, catching the drift, enter the plot with a right good will. Perhaps Helen can persuade someone in the palace livery stable to loan them a carriage? But how would they fare across unfamiliar, indeed barbarian, soil? And where would they go? Greece was not to be reached with a horse and carriage. Perhaps Menelaus should steal into the palace and strike the pharaoh dead? But Theonoe would draw the line at her brother's murder. And what about a ship? Menelaus' ship went down in the storm. All alternatives are rejected as impractical until Helen conceives a plan, "if a woman can speak with any cleverness" (line 1049). Would Menelaus be willing to play dead? Now is his turn to play a ghost of himself.

"Bird of evil omen," Menelaus responds, warding off the omen no doubt with a traditional Greek gesture, but if there is profit in it, Menelaus will listen. Distasteful as the thought is of playing himself as a missing corpse, necessity drives Menelaus to consent. The plan, as Helen unfolds it, is to inform Theoklymenos that a report has just arrived of Menelaus drowned at sea, the messenger being Menelaus himself, impersonating one of his own humble sailors fetched from the water by a passing fisherman. Helen will explain to Theoklymenos that the Greek custom is to hold a memorial service at sea for those who perish at sea. But the simulated burial for a simulated corpse must simulate the burial of a real corpse to the absolute final degree, or the ritual is void. Theoklymenos will be skeptical, but Helen's persuasion will overcome his resistance. It is a daring scheme, but the times are desperate, and Helen's magic is proverbial, and in this case it has the support of the ghost of the father in whose graveyard the action of the play is staged.

Theoklymenos enters and falls neatly in our oubliette, since the barbarian is no match for the Greeks, particularly when the Greeks in question are Helen and Menelaus working hand in hand to the same ends, as they were not in the old Helen story. Helen re-emerges from the palace dressed in widow's weeds, with her face lacerated to prove the lengths to which Greek womanhood will go to save its honor. Menelaus needs nothing more to play his part as the castaway, since that is exactly how he already looks.

Helen tells Theoklymenos that tragic news has just arrived—her husband drowned at sea!—thus tickling Theoklymenos into a false anticipation that Helen will now be his, forever trapped in her Egyptian tomb. In the new Helen story the barbarian must be toyed with, and definitively tantalized. Helen describes for the witless noddie the Greek custom of a mimed burial at sea for those lost at sea. Yes, it is a strange custom, but we are in the post-Herodotean age, when the most diverse ethnic customs may surprise, but no longer shock, us. Egypt had no monopoly on mystery.

Theoklymenos retains enough presence of mind to ask about "the evil thing" that was sent to Troy in Helen's place (line 1218).

"Oh," Helen replies, "you mean the cloud ghost? That was returned to the Ether" (line 1219). Helen speaks a partial truth. One cloud has been removed, but new clouds have been introduced, including now a simulated corpse, the ghost of a ghost.

With the point established that no cloud will return to interfere in the plot, the plan proceeds. Helen, now widowed and vulnerable, consents to accept the pharaoh's hand in marriage, and a grateful Theoklymenos at once grants her every wish—a bull for the sacrifice, a swift ship to carry the nonexistent remains out to sea, a full suit of armor and all the dress that befits a simulated corpse of very high station. This is Menelaus as the comic eidolon: only in the pharaoh's purple will Menelaus be able to prove himself as neither ghost nor corpse but the bloodcurdling warrior of the old Mycenean tale.

Could Helen not leave the funeral rites to the man who has brought the news? Theoklymenos asks, a little anxious at the thought of Helen taking even the briefest of sea journeys—the vagrancy theme still lingers in the air. No, Helen explains, the sad duty must fall to the dead man's nearest kin, and only them. It also strains our humor, we might add, to think of Menelaus burying his own corpse. Very well. A dutiful wife was much to be desired. Theoklymenos rubs his hands, thinking of Helen's wifely duties soon to be transferred to him. Could he himself join the funeral party and accompany Helen on her sad voyage? No, the pharaoh should not sully his hands with work that his slaves could do well enough without him.

Menelaus, entering into his part, gently chides Helen as she leaves to make the necessary preparations, reminding her of her duty to cherish the husband at hand and to relinquish the one that is gone. If Menelaus reaches Sparta safely, he adds, once the funeral ceremonies are complete, he will put an end to the rumors "if you become the woman you ought to be for your bedmate" (lines 1292–93). Menelaus no doubt enjoys speaking with a forked tongue, but a third voice speaks through him, which is the voice of the revisionists. The real motive for this plot is never far from sight. The funeral for the imaginary corpse of Menelaus was indeed make-believe. The real funeral was for the Helen who was not the bedmate she should have been. That false Helen was now to be sunk to the bottom of the sea, committed to the deep by the true Helen, who had been kept waiting in an anteroom in Egypt for seventeen years for precisely this moment.

Exeunt omnes to prepare the denouement. The Chorus, in a dithyrambic mood, now sings an extraordinary ode on the great Phrygian Mother Goddess (Cybele), to whom Demeter has been assimilated in what Dale calls "the most explicit" literary example of "the syncretism at work in fifth-century Greece."[33] Athena, Hera, Artemis, the Graces, the Muses, Aphrodite, and Helen herself are all drawn into the myth. The Greek story of Demeter's search for her lost daughter Persephone is wedded to the myth of the great Phrygian Mother Goddess, thus allowing Euripides to rewrite the old story of the Mother's sorrowful wandering into something wilder. This is Mother Nature in a corybantic frenzy, whirling in the mountain glades, spinning in the rushing rivers and in the sounding deep, shaking her rattles and uttering bloodcurdling cries, and then swinging into her Lydian chariot, with wild animals in the harness, and the two virgins accompanying her— Artemis on one side, with her bow and quiver, and Athena on the other, Gorgon-armed—all nature racing pell-mell to recover the daughter snatched from "the circle of the virgins' dance" (line 1313).

In this syncretic version of the Mother and Daughter myth, Zeus finds a different solution to console the Mother for her loss of her virgin Daughter than the arrangement familiar to us from the *Homeric Hymn to Demeter*, in which he and Hades agree to share Persephone, allowing her to spend part of the year in Hades' bleak company (as his wife), and the other part of the year as the virgin Daughter of Demeter, the Mother. His compromise in this ode is to send the Graces, the Muses, and Aphrodite to console the Great Mother and assist her in turning her wild shrieks and frenzies into graceful dance and music. Aphrodite, invited into the dance, takes up the castanets and drums, and "laughed as she received into her hands the deep-throbbing *aulos*, rejoicing in its 'din' [*alalagmos*, the women's ritual cry in the Dionysiac rites]" (lines 1349–52).

Now the Chorus addresses, or seems to address, Helen, and the

---

33. 1967, at lines 1361–68. For a full discussion of the syncretism of the ode and of the relationship of the ode to the play, see Kannicht 1969, 2: 327ff. (on lines 1301–68).

text falls to pieces, as texts are wont to do when Helen is introduced. Here, in the final strophe of the ode, where we would least
expect it, the Judgment of Helen is spelled out (lines 1353–68).
Helen, we are now told, has offended the Great Mother. But time,
alas, has been cruel to this passage, leaving us with a garbled message, and "Helen's offence is lost beyond recovery."[34] Editors
mark the passage as "locus penitus corruptus"—completely corrupt.[35]

Until this surprising disclosure, we had in our simplicity taken
the play for a palinode, after its own ironic fashion, which would
retract the guilty Helen and replace her with the blameless Helen.
Richmond Lattimore's translation of the strophe is misleading,
since its easy flow, which does not at all reflect the actual state of
the manuscript, prevents the English reader from noticing the deep
fissures in the text, and the even deeper fissures in the plot.[36] Here
is Lattimore's reconstruction:

> You had no right in this. The flames you lit   1353
> in your chambers were without sanction.
> You showed, child, no due reverence   1355
> for this goddess' sacrifice.
> You won the great mother's anger.
> The dappled dress in the deer skin
> is a great matter, . . .   1359
>
> . . . .
>
> . . .   so also the dances,   1363
> the wild hair shaken for Bromius,
> the goddess' nightlong vigils.   1365
> It is well that by daylight
> The moon obscures her.
> All your claim was your beauty.   1368

34. Dale 1967, at lines 1353ff.
35. See Alt's edition, 1964, lines 1353ff.
36. Euripides, *Helen*, in vol. 3 of *The Complete Greek Tragedies, Euripides*, ed.
David Grene and Richmond Lattimore (Chicago: University of Chicago Press,
1959).

Much indeed has been obscured here, and not only by the moon. The first sentence of the strophe begins by accusing Helen of what seems, as Dale notes, to be a sin of commission, only to end by defining it as a sin of omission. In the first case, Helen has incurred the anger of the Goddess for performing certain rites in chambers (her own chambers, is Dale's surmise, though they might be the sacred chambers of the Goddess), "which it was neither lawful nor holy" for her to perform (lines 1353ff.). The offense had to do with "fire" (line 1354). The sin of omission is that "she did not reverence the sacrifices of the Goddess" (lines 1356–57). Dale assumes that these must be two offenses, but it could be argued that they are the same offense expressed in opposite ways. In any case, the sin or sins could be summed up, in Dale's words, as "*neglect* of the Mother's ceremonies" (lines 1353ff.).[37]

The Chorus, addressing Helen as their daughter (*pais*, "child," line 1356), scolds her in a motherly fashion for disdaining the corybantic rites of the Great Mother, who at this point in the ode is one great synthesis of Cybele, Aphrodite, Persephone, Demeter, and Dionysus. There is great power, they remind Helen as if in reproach, in the deerskin trappings, the ivy twined on the hollow reed, the rattle whirled overhead, the ecstatic dance, and the night-long revelries of intoxication with the gods of wine and love.

Having thus raised their anthem in praise of the conjoined orgies of Persephone, Dionysus, Aphrodite, and Cybele (lines 1358–65), the Chorus brings us sharply out of our ecstatic state and back to the matter at hand, which is as always Helen. But once again, where Helen and her shame are concerned, the text disappears. The Chorus begins with two lines that Dale is forced to call "gibberish" (lines 1367–68—Lattimore's "It is well that by daylight/The moon obscures her"), and then brings both strophe and ode to a close with what appears to be a third charge: "You boasted of your beauty" (*morphē*, line 1368).

---

37. See the extensive discussion of the passage in both Dale 1967 and Kannicht 1969.

Perhaps the three muddled charges can be rendered down to a single charge, much as Lattimore has presented it in his translation: Helen, glorying in her own beauty, held herself aloof from the orgies of the Great Mother and took it upon herself to perform (for herself? by herself?) sacred rites that were not hers to perform. In any case, the point is established (if not triply established) that Helen is guilty of hubris against the Mother; that is the sufficient flaw to qualify Helen as a tragic protagonist.

Where Euripides found this nugget of folklore we cannot say. The motifs expressed in the Chorus's judgment of Helen are common in Greek myth. The first is the neglect of the honors due to a god; the other is simple human hubris, a human's boasts of his or her own excellence violating the ears of the jealous gods. Helen, boasting of her beauty, would be an easy addition to the story. Greek myth was rife with precedents of heroes or nymphs blasted by the deities for being too clever at their particular skills, like the beautiful Arachne, metamorphosed into a spider for challenging Athena at the loom, or Marsyas, flayed for competing with Apollo. A myth could easily be supposed in which Helen had offended "The Goddess" (but which goddess?) by boasting of her own beauty, but no one else in antiquity seems to have heard such an eccentric version of the Helen story. It sounds like an ad hoc invention; if so, it is sorely out of place.

The fulsome praise of Cybele in the ode is itself noteworthy, given the general Hellenic disapproval of her ecstasies in the classical period. But even more astonishing is the specific charge that Helen—of all people—had once been too dainty to participate in such orgies.[38] Had she performed these orgies in secret or dis-

38. On the orgiastic practices of the Cybele cult, and the general disapproval of the cult among the Greeks in the classical period, see Farnell 1921, 3: 302–3. But see also Hartog (1988, 74ff.), who argues that Cybele's "foreignness" in late fifth-century Athens was complex; she occupied a range of positions—"sometimes rejected, sometimes a marginal figure, sometimes admitted to the very center of the city" (82). But whether accepted in some circles, and despised in others, foreign she certainly was. We are nonplussed that a play purporting to restore Helen to her Greek shrine should accuse her of having offended the two deities considered most foreign—Dionysus and Cybele.

dained them altogether? Was Helen a prude, like Hippolytus or Pentheus? Of all the charges that might be leveled against Helen, this surely would appear last on anyone's list. It would be easier to indict Helen for the opposite fault, that she was too much a devotee of wine and love.

The muddied text allows many lines of thought without definitely excluding any. Perhaps Euripides borrowed from Stesichorus (frag. 223 PMG), who had charged Tyndareus with offending Aphrodite by omitting to invoke her at his sacrifices to the other gods. But the analogy falters. To punish a man's impiety by sending him promiscuous daughters is one matter. To punish a woman for her virginity by banishing her to Egypt is something else entirely.

What was the punishment? Was Helen sent to Troy to learn promiscuity, as the servitude befitting the Goddess, like the overly scrupulous Pentheus, driven to participate tragically in his mother's orgies? But no, Helen at Troy was only an eidolon. Was Helen's punishment then to be banished to Egypt, kept from the barbarian's bed yet believed by everyone to be as lusty as she was in fact chaste? Indeed, Egypt was Helen's punishment, but we have already been told that the instigator was Hera, whom no one in antiquity accused of being partial to Oriental revelries. Hera aside, there was no talk in the play, until this moment, of Helen's overweening pride (the hubris theme required in tragedy), or any suggestion that Helen had committed a sacrilege. The crime, if there was a crime, was the promiscuity of Aphrodite and of her darling Paris, which Hera put a stop to, with Theonoe's assistance.

But what is this talk of crime and punishment? The intent of the revisionists was to leave us with a new Helen, totally innocent, completely exonerated on all counts. Or so we thought until receiving this garbled message. Where we had thought to find a pure Helen we hear instead of Helen's great offense, perhaps two or three. And where we had thought to acquit Helen, we find her guilty on all charges. But Helen has been forgiven by the all-forgiving Mother. That is the final message of the strophe, though we cannot see that Helen has done anything to make amends. She is as chaste as ever, and we do not foresee Asiatic orgies in her future.

Whatever Helen's alleged offense against the Mother, the reversal of the plot is stunning. We are tempted to excuse Euripides and save his reputation by attributing the muddle to a later interpolator.[39] But whoever the author or authors of this strange digression, the passage betrays the very ambivalence that haunts Helen's name. Even in the play saturated with the intent to find Helen innocent of all charges, someone, whether Euripides or some subsequent interpolator, knew that Helen was guilty of something. How could Helen play the tragic protagonist without hamartia, hubris, and nemesis attached to her, or in this case to her name?

What was Helen's offense? Her beauty? Yes, that's it; she was too beautiful. Her beauty was too fastidious, too remote, too—je ne sais quoi. The poet or his scribe was desperate, but it was a desperate problem. Helen purified was an acceptable revision, but a Helen pure from the start was a hypothesis of another stripe. If some offense were necessary to the Helen story, almost any offense would do. The choral ode has insinuated a solution to satisfy both Helen stories. Or perhaps two separate copyists conflated their interpretations into this vexed passage, given the perennial interest in the question, Was Helen, or was she not, guilty of some offense? If between Euripides and his subsequent copyists the offense itself fell out of the text, on essentials the text is clear: item, Helen was guilty of dishonoring the Mother; item, she has been punished; item, she is now purged and forgiven.

If Helen had been falsely accused of being seduced into a Phry-

---

39. For some possible interpolations in this play, see Dale 1967, xxxiff. The whole ode has been viewed with extreme suspicion. Grube (1941, 349) calls it "the one seemingly irrelevant ode in Euripides." Some scholars regard the ode as an interpolation from another play: see Bacon 1961, 142–43; Griffith 1953, 36. Kannicht (1969, vol. 2 at lines 1361–68), acknowledging the text's dismal state and its peculiarities, reads the charge as directed less at Helen personally than as conveying a more general, symbolic warning to humanity at large. If this were true, it is still difficult to reconcile the ode in praise of the Mother's orgiastic rites with a play in which Helen is being removed from the Mother and returned to the Father.

gian bed, that was her punishment for holding herself aloof from the ecstasies of the Mother. But if she had been banished to Egypt, then exile was her punishment. She might remain immaculate if that was her pleasure, but she would be sent where she could marvel at her own beauty in peerless solitude, while an idol would sully her name at Troy. That too would be a fitting punishment for a queen who thought herself too nice for the common orgies.

Helen delivers us from sinking deeper into this morass by re-emerging from the palace to pick up the plot where we left off before we fell into our corybantic frenzy and were derailed by talk of her secret flaw. On track again, everything proceeds as it should. Theoklymenos, all but wedded already to the Greek goddess, has been tricked into being the good pharaoh, the only good pharaoh being a tricked pharaoh in this story (except for the ghostly father), a satisfying revision of the story that had put goodness on the pharaoh's side and foolishness on the Greek side.

The Phoenician ship lies ready at the pier. The bull is driven on board, and the cargo is loaded, the finest that the pharaoh's palace could provide (an important detail). We are in the *Odyssey* again; the conquering hero cannot be seen to sail into his own harbor completely empty-handed; he must have some profit for his travels. Helen boards the ship "with dainty step" (line 1528), now as light as air. The Greeks sailors, happening by, have no difficulty masquerading as a pitiable lot, the last ragged veterans of the Trojan War, whom Menelaus, feigning a soft heart, invites on board. With the Greek sailors stowed below deck, the Phoenicians bending to their oars, sails hoisted and anchors aweigh, and the pharaoh to wave bon voyage from the dock, the royal caravel sailed out from the Nile in splendor, looking like the ship of death though it was the ship of resurrection. The Chorus wafts its blessings on the ship, addressing the "The Phoenician Oar," as if it were the queen of the sea surrounded by her dolphin court, charging it, Galaneia (the Nereid who calms the waves), the Dioskouroi, and the superb but, alas, superfluous Phoenician sailors to bear their precious cargo safe to Hellenic shores.

Once beyond Egyptian waters Menelaus sacrifices the bull. Then, with "Death to the barbarian!" he turns his sword onto the hapless Phoenician sailors, who have the ill fate to stumble once again into a plot that was none of their concern. The Greek sailors, hearing themselves called "the fairest flower of Hellas" (line 1593), follow suit, to show their true Greek mettle, and in the twinkling of an eye the Phoenicians are dispatched, and the vessel is sailing under Hellenic colors.

Here are the final revisions needed in the plot. The Phoenician sailors are the lambs sacrificed for their ancestors' inadvert intrusion, when Sidon opened its harbor to the fugitive couple in Homer's story, and also for their ridicule of the Trojan affair in Herodotus. Theoklymenos is the goat made to pay for the sins of the Phrygian bed (for which, read "Paris"), but also for the too-impeccable manners of his father in the revision that left Hellas with no glory to boast of.

Theoklymenos is despoiled of his bride and much else besides, taken from his own treasury, to correct a flaw in the earlier revision. With Helen edited out of the story, and Menelaus recovering only a phantom, something was missing: the punishment that Paris deserved but failed to get if his only loss was the loss of a phantom. Compensatory damages are called for. If Helen is to be returned to the text, she must be returned with "stolen goods," to compensate for the goods that Paris stole when he stole Helen. All wrongs must be righted. The barbarian must be tricked out of a whole cargo of precious treasures, to compensate for Aphrodite and her bag of tricks.[40] Nemesis must have the final word.

Theoklymenos is enraged to discover himself duped "by a woman's wiles" (line 1621). And well he might be, though whether the woman should be blamed is another question. Little as he might suspect it, the revision would be incomplete without his rage, since he is the substitute for Paris. We should have seen Paris rage, when he discovered that he had spent his libido on a phan-

40. On Aphrodite as both the trickster and the tricked, see the *Homeric Hymn to Aphrodite* (V).

tom, but with Paris gone from the script another victim is needed, and another retrieval more to the credit of the Greeks, which will leave the barbarian to play with the phantom. Theoklymenos must serve as this unlucky foreigner. Trojans, Phrygians, Phoenicians, Egyptians—in this correction all the foreigners receive their just desserts.

Theoklymenos, frustrated "by a woman's wiles," displaces his anger onto the only woman still available as a target, his own sister Theonoe, who, as we well know, had agreed to coauthor the plot. Theoklymenos is bent on killing his sister, and there is no piety or fraternal affection in the world that would change his mind. But lo! Here the Dioskouroi fly in, with their proverbial sense of timing, with little to do but spread their wings over the plot and give it their benediction. They would have arrived earlier, they said—at least they know that tardiness is their besetting sin, particularly where their sister Helen is concerned. But their power, great as it was, was insufficient, they said, to alter destiny. Alter destiny? We bite our tongues. Still, late as they are, they are in time to play the customary gods from the machine, to tie up the loose ends and resolve whatever cannot be resolved except by such abrupt, cosmic intervention.

They persuade Theoklymenos to change his way of life, to abandon his willful temper, to abstain from murdering his sister, and to accept his destiny (as the foiled suitor in the Helen contest). Turning now to Helen, who is fast disappearing over the horizon, they waft her on her way with a favoring wind, calling themselves her "saviors" (*sōtēres*), thus echoing the Chorus, which had invoked them earlier as "the saviors of Helen" (line 1500).

They promise an equally favorable sequel to the story. Helen, rounding off her earthly life, will be delivered into heaven, called a god, and allowed to share at last in all her brothers' honors. Menelaus, rewarded at last for fortitude in the face of his great contumely, will dwell on an Island of the Blest, apparently in blessed solitude. And, to leave the mark of this revision, the island off the coast of Attica where Hermes first "defined" Helen's place by stealing her body will be henceforth named Helena, meaning "The Stolen" (lines 1670–75). Assumed immaculate into heaven, a queen enthroned between her two Sky brothers, receiving the adoration of humankind and the approval of Zeus himself, Helen will be free at last. The island named "Stolen" will be the last echo of Helen's long captivity.

Theoklymenos, bowing to necessity, agrees to reform his life and spare his sister. Composing his own palinode, he wishes the Dioskouroi farewell for Helen's sake, whose mind was the noblest, "which is not to be found in many women" (lines 1686–87). Helen's mind and body are at last reunited, and it is fitting that the barbarian be the first to voice his admiration. The Chorus comes in with the usual epilogue—the expected does not happen, and the gods contrive the unexpected—and the curtain falls with Helen purged of every last foreign influence, all Greek again, and bound for heaven.

The *Helen* is a puzzle, perhaps because we are influenced both by Aristotle's definition of the ideal tragedy and by the survival of only a small remnant of the large number of tragedies performed on the Athenian stage in the fifth century. An older generation of scholars, no matter how wide they stretched their definition of tragedy, still found the play more comic than tragic.[41] Gilbert Norwood went so far as to call it a piece of "stale confectionery."[42] A. W. Verrall, who gained a certain notoriety for arguing the most extreme case of Euripides the rationalist, went even farther here, to argue that in the *Helen* Euripides parodied himself, and that he intended the play only for a private performance.[43]

Confectionery, perhaps; but "stale" is arguable. The *Helen* is, to be sure, a hodgepodge of the old Helen stories—the tired old story of the swan and the egg; the stories of the Dioskouroi, as a constel-

41. See Segal 1971, 553–55, for an amusing recapitulation of previous scholars' assessments. Grube (1941, 352) believes himself to express the general verdict, that the play is "frankly funny." See also Griffith 1953; Burnett 1960, 1971.
42. 1954, 39.
43. 1905, 43–133.

lation, as the mariner's saviors, as Helen's saviors; the island called Helena; Helen of Troy, Helen in Egypt, Helen the ghost, Helen the daughter of two fathers, Helen the *chorēgos* of the girls' dance at Sparta, and so on. There was, we might agree, something stale about the stories endlessly repeated and endlessly rewritten, but it was not stale to place Helen herself at the center of this potpourri, again as always the spectator and the spectacle. We are surprised that no other ancient poet attempted this theme, either before or after Euripides.

More recently scholars have seen the *Helen* as a treatment of the philosophical themes current in its day.[44] The dramatic interplay of name and body, appearance and reality, with the eidolon itself as the central image, if not the principal actor, of the play—these elements and themes, taken from the debates of the philosophers, should be evidence that Euripides intended his *Helen* as a vehicle for a serious and sympathetic representation of a problem worthy to be called tragic. Yet philosophical abstractions do not make a play, as Dale reminds us. To suppose that "the *Helen* gains in profundity, or qualifies as 'tragic' in our sense, because it concerns the interplay between illusion and reality," Dale argues, "is to allow oneself to be mesmerized by abstract nouns."[45] What makes the *Helen* a drama, and not an abstract argument, is Helen herself, who has been stationed in the penumbral dusk of Seeming. Helen's laments, echoed by the Chorus, whose laments are even lovelier than hers, that she is a woman divorced from her name yet blamed for everything attributed to her name, are persuasive and tragic. Who was more alienated than Helen? What theme could be more compelling than the problem of her alienation?

Dale, acknowledging the comedy and romance of the *Helen*, strikes a balance in assessing the play as "tragedy." The play was, Dale reminds us, a "tragedy" for Euripides and his audience, "and

44. Solmsen 1934; Burnett 1960, calls it "a comedy of ideas." In her 1971 study, she gives us a lively treatment of the comic aspects of the play.
45. 1967, xvi. For the *Helen*'s use of the philosophical terms of its day, see Solmsen 1934; Burnett 1960; Kannicht 1969, 1: 62–68; Segal 1971.

that concept is a hospitable one."[46] Her point is well taken that Athenian tragedy, despite Aristotle's prescription, is better charac- terized as taking figures "from the national heritage," and treating them with "fundamental seriousness." "Within these limits," Dale goes on to explain, "the tragedy may be grave, terrible, exciting, witty, inventive; . . . but there must *be* issues at stake, and some- thing must emerge, however darkly, fitfully, or enigmatically, about the dealing of the gods with men."[47] Certainly we could say of Euripides' *Helen* that a theme is treated with fundamental seri- ousness and something emerges, however darkly, though less per- haps about the gods than about humans living in the shadow of their own signifiers.

Reference to the national heritage is a more useful way to ap- proach the *Helen* than the labels that refer to later developments in European theater—romance, comedy, romantic comedy, trag- icomedy, and so on. The *Helen* has all these forms within it. It stands as the final pillar of Athenian tragedy, when tragedy itself had exhausted the national themes. Or rather, the philosophical debates had rendered the magnificent, golden beings on Olympus foolish idols, and when the gods fell, the national heritage went with them. When Mount Olympus had become comic opera, comedy was the best form in which to view the existential human condition. New Comedy was Athenian tragedy's inevitable step- child.

The *Helen* is a significant representative of the last phase of Athenian tragedy. But it wobbles, since it is, at the same time, the first New Comedy.[48] It has all the characters and situations of New Comedy, which were simply conventions borrowed from tragedy and turned to comic effect. The storm at sea; the long-lost lovers discovering each other after unbelievable vicissitudes; the recogni- tion scene, with its secret token being in this case a phantom, than which nothing could offer more comic possibilities; the lusting

46. 1967, ix.
47. 1967, ix.
48. On the *Helen* as the link between fifth-century tragedy and the New Comedy of Menander and Plautus, see Kannicht 1969, 1: 83.

prince; the virgin princess; the concierge, who is kinder than she seems; the clever wife with the heart of gold and the patience of Penelope; the confused and cowering husband; the strutting barbarian, despoiled in the end; a daring scheme, a hair-raising escape, virtue, honor, lust, the breezy gods on the machine, and clouds and clouds of magic everywhere—comedy could not ask for more.

When Strauss, after *Ariadne auf Naxos*, turned to Hofmannsthal for another theme from classical antiquity suitable for comic opera, Hofmannsthal gave him the libretto for *Die ägyptische Helena*.[49] Strauss thought that his gifts lay in the direction of operetta, but as he worked on Hofmannsthal's libretto he confessed that it had become a more serious vehicle. The story of the Egyptian Helen had overtones of tragedy, which interfered with its being comic opera. Yet it could not be a tragedy either, since the point of the story was to remove the tragedy and produce a romance in its place. In the end Strauss called *Die ägyptische Helena* a light opera. Euripides faced the same dilemma. If light opera had existed in his day, that is what his *Helen* would have been. Perhaps Euripides too hoped that the seriousness of his intentions would be discovered in his music, in the play's odes and arias, which are pure gold. Gorgeous music can cover the thinnest plot.

Yes, the story of Helen and her eidolon was a serious theme, worthy of the ancient tragic stage, as Dale has defined it. Who was more a national treasure than Helen (whether her body or her name), and what motive more laudable than to rescue the lovely Helen from her disgrace? To do so, Euripides placed Helen at the center of the philosophical debates of his time, as the one person most nearly conscious of the plot to separate her body from her name. She at least knows, whatever else she may not know, that she is not her name, sign, icon, or image. But she is powerless to make this distinction clear to anyone else, even, as it turns out, to her own husband. This theme Euripides endowed with insight, pathos, beauty, and compassion.[50]

49. See Hofmannsthal's essay (1928) on the opera.
50. Segal (1971) has drawn our attention to many of the beauties of the play. On Helen as alienated from herself, see Kannicht 1969, 1: 60: "Erst Euripides hat

If the full extent of the tragedy escaped him, Euripides deserves recognition for perceiving the problem. The hymn to the Great Mother is a masterpiece of dithyrambic exaltation, but for the confusion in the final strophe. The choral prayer to the sleek Phoenician ship surrounded by playful dolphins; to Galaneia and the mighty Dioskouroi, riding across the heavens, to waft their queen swiftly and safely into her own harbor, is surely the loveliest lullaby ever sung to the unhappy Helen. The choral odes of the *Helen*, taken in themselves, form a palinode in the fullest and most beautiful sense, celebrating a woman tragically wronged, and comforting her in her solitary confinement.

Helen herself is at many points a character endowed with credibility. Her story of herself seized by Hermes when she was picking flowers for Athena is a heartrending image of a young woman's fate. Her arias are lyric masterpieces. The *kommos* sung between Helen and the Chorus (at lines 164–250) brings to mind the old stories of Helen as *chorēgos* of the girls' dance at Sparta.[51] Since Helen has been displaced to a sepulcher in Egypt, the mood here cannot be joyous and carefree, as it would have been in Sparta, but must be one of sorrow and lamentation. Yet few passages in ancient Greek lyric can match this dance, in which Helen leads the dirge for the woman separated from her name, and all but forgotten. At moments, when Helen speaks of her fate, we hear the voice of the woman herself, who regards her own alienation with bewilderment, disbelief, anger, and even terror. "Was I born to be a monster?" she asks. This is not an abstraction speaking but a wom-

---

Helena und Eidolon in innere Beziehung zueinander gesetzt" ("Euripides was the first to bring Helen and the eidolon into an inner connection with each other"). Cf. also Lattimore (1959, 485), who writes that the "dominant theme is paradox, illusion, surprise, all to be summed up in the relation of Helen to that other self, the idol who is not, but in some way is, Helen herself."

51. On Helen as *chorēgos* of the girls' dance at Sparta, see Aristophanes *Lysistrata* 1308; Theocritus *Idyll* 18; Calame 1977, 2: 121ff. In the *Helen* the Chorus alludes to this traditional function when they urge Helen to rejoin the dances of the daughters of Leukippos, whether by the Eurotas River or at Athena's temple, and the night-long festive celebrations in honor of Hyakinthos.

an who knows that her fate is a kind of monstrosity, the monstrosity of beauty.

If, to do the impossible, we could separate the plot from the play, Euripides' *Helen* would be a sustained lyric poem of extraordinary power, portraying a Helen as tragic as we could ask. When Helen remembers herself as the innocent bride whom Hermes seized and set down "in this unprosperous land" (line 247), the rape of Persephone is the obvious model. The analogy between the two rapes is apt.[52] Helen is more truly tragic than she knows. Like Persephone, Helen has been forcibly seized from her home and, if not raped, then sent to a land that might as well be, and in fact is, the land of the dead, so that, with Helen as good as dead, the men might be safely left to fight for her good name at Troy.[53]

Here, in a nutshell, was the problem. The revision, said to have been blessed by Helen herself, called for Helen to be removed from Troy so that she could be separated from the shame that was her legacy from Homer. However noble the motive, a cloud was introduced so small that it passed even Euripides' scrutiny. If Helen at Troy was only imaginary, where was the real Helen? Sparta being out of the question, Helen was sent to Egypt. It was a good compromise. But to post Helen to the margin was eventually revealed as an inadequate measure, given Helen's wayward character, which was the reason for the revision. To contain her waywardness, Helen was first nullified at Troy. Well and good. But then she must be nullified in Sparta, since we cannot think of Helen playing "Helen" at home while her dull-witted husband was fighting for her good name abroad. So far so good. But, finally, she must be nullified in Egypt. Helen cannot be playing "Helen" any-

52. On Helen as Persephone, see Wolff 1973, 63.
53. Grube 1941, 349: "There may be some relevance in the general idea of imprisonment [in the Great Mother ode], that of Persephone in the underworld and of Helen in Egypt— . . . but this is insufficient." The relevance is much greater than Grube assumed, but also greater than Euripides was able or willing to articulate, since he, as one of Helen's revisionists, was also one of her jailers. The rape of Aphrodite, to which the *Homeric Hymn to Aphrodite* (V) refers, should be included here, as another example of the archetype.

where, even in Egypt, while her reputation still hangs in the balance.

The eidolon nullifies Helen at Troy—the first cloud. Then, at Sparta, another cloud is introduced, and Helen is softly nullified a second time. At this point the pharaoh is kind enough to join the conspiracy and complete the circle by nullifying Helen a third time, in Egypt. The ghost of the Egyptian pharaoh is the third cloud in the plot. Farthest from the revisionists' minds was the intention to leave Helen to herself, alive and well, even if only on the margin, while they worked so assiduously to erase her shame. In short, Euripides discovered that the story of the *Palinode* included no plot, except the plot to write Helen out of the plot. Intuiting the problem, perhaps, Euripides scared up a plot to write Helen back into the text, but his inventiveness only exposed the conspiracy, which required Helen's complete and absolute absence from the story.[54]

What could Helen do in Egypt? Nothing. "I am dead in effect, if not in fact," Helen says (line 286). Never were words more truly spoken. Helen could have memories of herself as a girl in Sparta; she had a future to look forward to, sunny and cloudless; but what she was not allowed was a present, since that exact slot was occupied by her eidolon. While her imaginary self was alive and well at Troy, it would be unseemly for Helen to set up in people's minds a bewildering oscillation between her and her lustier Trojan twin. The phantom at Troy being an imitation of the original Helen, Helen in Egypt could be nothing more than phantom twice removed from the original. With such a protagonist, what could the plot be but a phantom plot?

But what is a Helen story with all Helen's vital signs registering zero? The new Helen must be the exact replica of the old Helen,

---

54. Wolff (1973, 61) notes the "chameleon-like" tone of the play. I attribute this quality to Euripides' attempt to create, on one hand, a plot where none existed, and, on the other hand, to accommodate all the Helen plots in a single, cohesive plot. The chameleonlike changes are, in fact, an attractive feature of the play, though we must, in all honesty, acknowledge the reason for them, which was to reconstruct Helen of Troy into another Helen altogether.

her identical twin, except in one respect. The new Helen must be beautiful—that goes without saying; she must be graceful, considerate, clever, sad, even tragic. To this Helen, Euripides has given his great skills as a playwright, lyric poet, and psychologist. This Helen is completely credible. But she is circumscribed by one taboo: she must not, whether by her own will or under any other kind of compulsion, enter the odious foreign bed. To make the taboo credible, Helen herself consents to it. Helen in Egypt is a woman whose chastity was originally enforced by Proteus, but now that he is gone Helen has internalized the taboo, and the Helen we see has consecrated herself to virginity.

But a Helen with so much beauty blooming unseen and untried is a story that will not hold. A woman for whose beauty whole empires are destroyed but who is kept out of sight and out of mind for seventeen years, confined to silence and idleness, and never allowed a passing thought, much less a passing fancy, can be at best the ghost of a ghost. The Helen that Euripides has struggled to bring alive on the stage can never be the real Helen, whether as woman or as goddess, if to be real is to be endowed with thoughts, motives, and acts. The little deceit she plays on Theoklymenos, in pretending that her husband is dead when she herself is the corpse, is the best Euripides can do to overcome the flaw in the revision, which laid out as its first rule that Helen, to be rehabilitated, could do as she liked, provided she did not act. Should she by chance see the revision for what it was, and decide to vacate her place on the margin, the balance so delicately achieved by her ghost would be thrown into confusion, and pandemonium would ensue.

The gods in this play act with the perfidy that we might expect of Euripidean gods. The universe of this play is not simply irrational in the random sense of the Atomists but rational through and through—what could be more rational than the attempt to rewrite the Helen story? But reason here has been made to serve several dark motives, albeit such motives have been displaced onto the gods. There are the requisite passages in which the human actors denounce the perfidy of the gods and contrast it with the greater piety, honor, and dignity of the human race. The slave with the noble mind, who reports the vanishing of the phantom, expresses his deep contempt for all forms of divination, since the gods not only obscure their motives but actively conspire to delude us with fantasies, which have little to do with us but everything to do with their own petty escapades on their celestial heights. It is not an edifying picture—the gods on their side acting out their perversities, and the humans at the mercy of those perversions, helpless to prevent or foresee them. And yet, the noble slave concludes, "it is ours to sacrifice to the gods and ask their blessing, but let us put away divination." The gods in the *Helen* are inflated with any fault we might want to impute to them, but human nobility is to accept our servile state, while cleaving to the path of righteousness even when, or because, righteousness is unknown in heaven.

The gods who govern our universe may be as inscrutable and vicious as they are portrayed in the *Helen*, or as comic. And the only proper attitude for us may be an existential dignity in the face of benefactors who know next to nothing of human dignity and care less. But the *Helen* is not the vehicle to drive this philosophy home, since we know why each of the gods was introduced into the plot, for what motive, and by whom. Theonoe's noble speech, in which she adjudicates between Aphrodite and Hera, is so much stardust thrown in our eyes.[55]

If Hera in the *Helen* is, as Charles Segal finds her, spiteful and savage, that is a sly trick on the poet's part to have us believe we are still in Homer's world, where Hera is a wild animal licking her lips, ready to devour Priam and his city raw, to satisfy her honor.[56] But the Hera of the *Helen* is as newly minted as Helen herself, for precisely her role in this plot. Homer's Hera might be blamed on the tradition, but the Hera of this play has no such excuse, since the

55. The nobility of her speech has been often commented on. See Kannicht 1969, 1: 71–77; Matthiessen 1969; Burnett 1971, 89–96; Dimock 1977; and Sansone 1985, for a more skeptical position. I too find it a noble human document, but it is a speech that belongs in another play, where it would seem less obviously manufactured to conceal the fissures in the plot.

56. 1971, 565. For the voracious Hera of the *Iliad*, consult MacCary 1982, 172ff.

play is a deliberate rewriting of the whole epic tradition. If Hera is cast as the principal instigator of the plot, we are not fooled. She is but the author's instrument. The author, we well know, is Euripides; his is the power to rewrite destiny. The obstruction to Aphrodite's will comes not from Hera but from Euripides, borrowing Hera's, alas, much-faded credibility to varnish over his own dark motives. "Hera's jealousy is well understood and painted in the most terrible colors"; so Walter Burkert describes the traditional portrait of Hera in archaic Greek literature.[57] Who better to scapegoat for this plot to seize Helen from her foreign bed than the ruthless defender of the marriage bed?

So with the other intrusions of the divine into the *Helen*. They are, in varying degrees, the hocus-pocus with which we happily conspire, to keep our eyes amused while the play busies itself with other concerns. Having read Herodotus, we can almost predict that Hermes will be needed sooner or later, or another celestial being with his dexterity, to correct an error in Herodotus. From the *Homeric Hymn to Aphrodite* (V), we learn that Hermes had a traditional role as the god who seized brides-to-be from the chorus of Artemis. Ergo, when a cloud is needed to smuggle Helen out of Sparta, Hermes would be a logical choice.

We could also have almost predicted, with the advantage of hindsight to be sure, exactly when the Dioskouroi would appear on the scene. Appear they certainly will, since they must be given their honor as "the saviors of Helen." But with the *Iliad* never far from our reach, we know that the Dioskouroi will be detained not by some factitious destiny standing in their path but because this is both a simulation and a correction of the *Iliad*, where their absence from the battlefield was taken by Helen to be another instance in her catalogue of shame.

When the Dioskouroi talk of being delayed by destiny, that is all it is—talk—since we know the intention of the *Helen* was to rewrite destiny. Destiny in the *Helen* is not what it was in the *Iliad*.

57. 1985, 129.

Theonoe rewrites Helen's destiny with hardly a moment's hesitation. The Dioskouroi could have done as much themselves without her help. Mighty sons of Zeus, surely the Twins could have settled the question of their sister's honor without the comic spectacle of the *Helen*, where several deities are conscripted to collaborate on the project. But to summon the Dioskouroi at the beginning of the story would be gauche indeed; it would show that we had not read Homer, without whom there would be no Helen in Egypt. A more satisfactory solution was to implicate Hera as the prime mover, whose anger at Aphrodite had dominated the *Iliad*, and leave the final benedictions to the blameless Dioskouroi.

Space must be cleared too for Menelaus, for he too has his honor to think of. He must be given room to exercise himself in his new role, as the once-cuckolded husband now uncuckolded. Helen too must exercise her part, to turn her Hellenic magic and beauty *sans pareil* against the foreigner. The ghost of the father must have his say from deep within his hallowed sepulcher. The Phoenician mariners must plunge to a watery death. Then the Dioskouroi, who have been waiting on their machines for their cue that the *Iliad* has been completely revised, can descend like storm winds, just in time to recuperate their own honor, which Homer had called in question.

And, of course, Helen's honor too. Leaving Theoklymenos with his libido feeling the empty air, the Dioskouroi welcome Helen, now rehabilitated, to share in their celestial privileges. First they waft their sister, now an icon of spun gold, back to her human devotees in Sparta. But they promise also to raise her to the skies, where they will shortly present her at the court of her heavenly father as the loveliest of sisters and daughters.

We know that Helen was guilty of no offense against the Great Mother, but fault there had to be, or why was rehabilitation needed? When the revisionists displaced Helen's flaw onto her ghost, a gap yawned open that the ghost was invented to conceal: there was no flaw. And so someone added a new flaw, without which Helen's rehabilitation would scarcely seem credible. The flaw? Helen's beauty. But it could not be so baldly stated—how could beauty be a flaw? A more poetic solution was suggested: Helen, priding herself on her beauty, had alienated herself from—of all people—the Mother. Helen was thus made the mother of her own alienation, though thanks to the interventions of other mothers (Hera, Athena, Theonoe) she was forgiven and made whole again.

We are bewildered by all this talk of hubris and nemesis, tempered by mercy. Have we walked in on the wrong play? Homer's Helen surely had not committed any offense against the Phrygian Mother. And the only offense we could impute to this new Helen in Egypt is abstinence from un-Hellenic orgies. Again the revisionists have been at work with their decoys and blinds. Helen was removed to Egypt precisely because it was thought that Troy was dangerously close to Phrygian influence—by the fifth century "Phygrian" was synonymous with "Trojan."[58] Helen's offense, if there was one, was not that she abstained from the nightlong revelries of the Mother but that she had violated the law of the Father. This was the plot that had to be worked out before the celestial Twins could arrive to welcome their sister back into the Hellenic pantheon as an icon washed clean of Phrygian influences.

So with the other elements of the play. Helen spends the whole of the play clutching the tomb of Proteus because that is where Herodotus put her until Menelaus came to fetch her, but also because the ghost of the father is the final authority in the play. She is sent home in a Phoenician ship because she is the Greek goddess mistaken for "The Foreign Aphrodite," being returned to her Hel-

---

58. Throughout the *Helen*, Phrygia and Troy are synonymous: see lines 39, 42, 109; also Helen's reference to "the golden houses of the Phrygians" (line 928), which, she is proud to say, she did not enter. Cf. Taplin 1992, 110, on the fifth-century view of Troy as "the alien East." Significant in this connection is the *Homeric Hymn to Aphrodite* (V), where Aphrodite, masquerading before Anchises as a Phrygian woman of noble birth, explicitly associates Phrygia with tricks and lust. Note also Farnell 1921, 3: 302–3, on the opposition to the cult of the Phrygian Cybele in fifth-century Greece.

lenic roots. Proteus must be dead because a space must open just wide enough for his son to play the lusty barbarian prince. Theoklymenos must be foiled but then invited to close the play by calling Helen the wisest of women, since even the barbarian must make his palinode. Theonoe must be a virgin so that, standing in for Athena, she can declare the intention of the revisionists to write Aphrodite—wild Nature herself—out of the script and produce a new Helen, virginal, obedient, and dependent on the law of the Father, as her double at Troy so conspicuously was not.

Perhaps Euripides did not at first intend the *Helen* to be a comedy, or did not dream that it would appear so comic to us. The beauty of the choral lyrics, the reflections on the human tragedy of misperception, the sympathetic portrait of Helen as a woman conscious that she is powerless to recuperate her own honor—these aspects of the play should be sufficient to dissuade us from reading it as farce or sentimental romance. Nothing in the play, whether in the dialogue or in the choral odes, specifically invites us to behold the events as a comedy, while Comedy in contrast, whether Old or New, loses no opportunity for winks and nudges. If Euripides intended the *Helen* to be taken for comedy, it could be only because he took the very idea of revising the Helen myth to be nonsensical. In that case, we would have to imagine that he submitted the play as a tragedy while expecting the audience to recognize it as a comedy and to enjoy its parody of the tragic stage. Verrall's hypothesis, that Euripides wrote the play for a private performance, to amuse his more sophisticated friends, is not as implausible as it sounds if the alternative is to believe that Euripides submitted his *Helen* as a comedy in the tragic competition.

The difficulty lay in the plot itself. There was something inevitably comic in the notion of the real Helen languishing in Egypt while her phantom kept her name alive in Troy.[59] But the comedy hints at the deeper problem: with Helen removed from the story, there was no story. The Helen story, in contrast to the various

---

59. Burnett (1971, 79) notes "a general air of lassitude" in the tempo of the play. I attribute this atmosphere, in part at least, to the structural problems inherent in a tragic play without a protagonist.

Helen cults, was "Helen of Troy." "Helen in Egypt" was not a story but a substitute for a story. Euripides papered over the problem, but his cardboard characters could not conceal that they were at best simulating a plot, with a simulated protagonist, since everyone knew where the real Helen was.[60] Homer was not easily corrected by the simple expedient of sending Helen to Egypt.

Gorgias offered a more credible solution, to leave Helen in Troy, fully responsible for her actions, and then to argue for her acquittal on the grounds that she was justified in choosing Paris, even if her choice entailed the Trojan War.[61] But to sequester Helen in Egypt behind a *cordon sanitaire* was no solution, and naming an island "Stolen" was insufficient compensation for her exclusion from the plot. Even Penelope, on whom this new Helen was modeled, was more real. By comparison, Penelope had real dangers to face, a real son to raise, and real decisions to make. The eidolon was a comic solution to the problem, and comedy was the inevitable result.

Theonoe makes only one appearance in the play, but it is significant. Some would argue that it is the most significant scene in the play, and Theonoe the most significant, if not the only significant, character in the whole play.[62] She is the honorable daughter of the honorable father; the virgin princess, uncontaminated by even a passing lustful thought; the prophet, seer, and judge of the play. Her entrance is appropriately marked.

The eidolon has just evaporated into the Ether, thus clearing up the mystery of Helen's identity. Helen and Menelaus, truly united, are now plotting their escape, which requires Theonoe's consent, when the doors of the palace open, and Theonoe emerges, accompanied by two women, whom she commands to sweep the air and ground with "sulphur and flame" to purge the stage of any possible contamination (lines 865–67).

Once again, where lucidity is to be desired in the Helen story,

60. Cf. Loráux 1985, 57: "Il est vrai que les bonnes épouses ne sont pas tragiques" ("It is true that good wives are not tragic").
61. Gorgias *Encomium on Helen*.
62. On Theonoe's role, see Kannicht 1969, 1: 71–77; Sansone 1985; Burnett 1971, 89–97; Dimock 1977; Matthiessen 1969.

the text falls to pieces. R. Kannicht estimates that some twenty scholars have tried their hand at "healing" the first three verses of Theonoe's speech, in which she commands the first servant to clear the air.[63] The servant is carrying a *thumiatērion*, the thurible to hold the fumigating incense. So much is clear. But now, as the servant censes the air, a cloud descends. We cannot be sure whether sulphur is included in the incense; whether she is to bring the thurible from the inner rooms of the palace or to sweep contamination from the farthest recesses of the Ether (line 866). A phrase, inserted as if it were a predicate—"holy ordinance"—further interferes in the construction, and scholars have pulled it in every possible direction. What is being predicated of what? Dale and Kannicht adopt quite different readings for the three verses, and neither is comfortable with the result. Lattimore even detected an idol lurking in the fog, which he has the servant bringing out of the palace:

> *Theonoe.*   Carry torches, let them shine, and bring
>   the image, gift of the solemn sky, from its inward room
>   so we may take and breathe the purity of this air.

Lattimore's reading seems improbable; surely we would hear something more of this idol if its role were to purge the stage of idols. But if Lattimore has discovered one idol too many in the play, the mistake is understandable.

The general sense of the three vexed verses is clear. The servant is to perform a catharsis, for which scholars can adduce parallels from both Greek and Egyptian cult. More puzzling is the need for the catharsis. What unhallowed foot has trod upon the stage before Theonoe's entrance? Who has polluted the air? We feel the influence of Herodotus again. If the palace doubles as the sanctuary of the heroized Proteus, Theonoe must double as the pharaoh's sister and as the priestess at the sanctuary of the heroized father, where Helen's metamorphosis is to be effected. Service at such a shrine might well include ritual lustrations of the temple grounds. In this

63. 1969, vol. 2, at lines 865–67; also Dale 1967 ad loc. for a different reading.

case, what might pass for a routine ceremony receives extra emphasis, since the honored ghost of the father is soon to manifest his latent power. With Theonoe as the priestess, her two assistants are acolytes, if we like, in this imagined cult. Incensing the air with a little Egyptian pomp adds sacramental mystery to this august moment when, thanks to Theonoe's credentials as the perfect seer, Helen is about to be metamorphosed from the fallen woman into the peerless goddess.

At the more mundane level, Theonoe is simply setting the stage for a seance—she commands the acolyte to purge the stage, as required "by solemn ordinance," so that she may receive "the pure breath [*pneuma*] of heaven" (line 867).[64] Moments later she receives what is not visible to impure human sight—a vision of the quarrel in heaven between the two goddesses, which Theonoe, empowered by her virginity, will also resolve.

The air certainly needs clearing, but what needs to be cleared away is, finally, the eidolon. Though the eidolon has now vanished from the earth of its own accord, it leaves lingering traces of its influence, if only in heaven. While the eidolon no longer serves Hera's purpose, since it has succeeded in its mission to outwit Aphrodite, it now serves Aphrodite's purpose to keep the eidolon alive and well lest people discover that Aphrodite was cozened by a ghost. Aphrodite's scheme is to put the phantom to use now in Sparta, to impersonate Helen while Helen herself remains immobilized in Egypt as, in effect, another ghost of herself. This is the plot that needs to be seen, purged, and finally dissolved by Theonoe's magic.

We smile at the abracadabra that Theonoe waves over the stage to exorcise Helen's ghost, because ghosts with their uncanny ways are easy targets of fun—even the ghost of Hamlet's father provokes Hamlet to humor, though his message is deadly. But if we laugh at Euripides' *Helen*, with all its absurd ruses to make us believe in the new Helen, that is because the ghost in the play is more tenacious

---

64. The sacred *pneuma* that Theonoe prepares to receive is one of the clearest anticipations in pagan Greek literature of the *Pneuma* of the Christians.

than we care to admit, and we will happily join Euripides to jolly it off the stage. Call it a cloud, and all that is needed is a little Egyptian hugger-mugger, and the cloud will steal from the scene like a dream melting at the break of day. Our good humor will be the fresh air and sunshine to fumigate the room and sweep the horrified ghost back to its dismal charnel house.

But ghosts are a serious business, even if they lapse easily into comic devices. Phantoms, Nicolas Abraham notes, are inventions of the living, "meant to objectify, even if under the guise of individual or collective hallucination, the gap that the concealment of some part of a loved one's life produced in us. . . . Consequently what haunts are not the dead but the gaps left within us by the secrets of others."[65] The ghost of Hamlet's father was, on one hand, the gap left in Hamlet's consciousness by his father's disappearance; on the other hand, it was the ghostly reification of a secret passed from father to son, the secret of the father's dishonor. The secret so took control of Hamlet's mind that Hamlet, confused as people are by ghosts, assumed it as his own secret loss and shame and went to his death both to protect the secret and to correct it.

What was the secret which Helen first divulged to Stesichorus by sending him the vision of her phantom double? Why were several other poets needed to correct the vision, or to clarify it? Did Euripides think he had deciphered the secret, and had he finally found the remedy? When we have had our fun over Seeming and Being, the name and the body, and the lighthearted scenes that such shadows engender, we should still praise Euripides for seeing that to solve Helen's riddle we should turn to Helen herself. That was an advance on Herodotus, who looked to the Egyptians for the answer. For that much alone, the *Helen* deserves to be called a palinode; even, perhaps, a great palinode, since humor stretched to the point of vaudeville was the only approach available in Euripides' time to a problem of such complexity as Helen's eidolon.

65. 1987, 287. Abraham bases his argument on his clinical practice.

"Would that I might be rubbed away, like a statue, and given a more disgraceful body"—for a moment the cloud parts, and Helen speaks for herself, a woman weary of a beauty that was an idol to others but for herself a disgrace (lines 262–63). Her wish is fraught with irony, since she is indeed a statue, but, unlike other statues, she cannot be rubbed away.[66] Even marble statues could be rubbed away by time or by the reverent hands of many devotees, but Helen saw herself as an idol frozen for eternity in the same perfect condition. A beauty that could be worn away in time would be a blessed relief. But her voice is quickly drowned in the noise of the ghost thumping about in the cellar, the clouds scuttling across the stage, and the fancy scrims flapping in the breeze, pretending to be real scenes in the life of a real woman. Almost smothered beneath this farrago was the Helen who revealed to Stesichorus that she had been transformed into a ghost. Helen's secret was the eidolon itself, which stole her body away and left her speechless. Displacing Helen's body to the far corners of the earth, while not the solution, at least revealed the problem. Even in Egypt Helen was still a statue for others to sculpt. The sculptors may have grown more sophisticated than the old mythographers; no doubt they thought themselves more humane. But Helen, for all their polishing, was as much an idol as she ever was.

66. For "statue," Helen uses the word *agalma*, the term for a cult idol; see LSJ. Menelaus uses the same word in reference to the eidolon at Troy, which he explains as an *agalma* of cloud (line 705). Dale (1967, at lines 262ff.) prefers to take *agalma* to mean "painting," since the verb (*exaleiphō*) "must mean obliterate, not wipe clean." But the simple verb (*aleiphō*) means "to anoint, to rub, to polish," and is used specifically of statues at Artemidorus Daldianus 2.33 (see LSJ); *exaleiphō* is thus "to rub away, rub out."

Glossary of Greek Terms

aethlos.	Competition.
agalma.	Statue.
aidōs.	Respect, reverence.
aiskhros.	Shameful, disgraceful, ugly (masc. sing. adj.).
anagnorisis.	Recognition, revelation, as in a tragedy.
Argeione.	Woman of Argos; i.e., Helen.
aristos.	Best (masc. sing. adj.).
blasphēmeō.	To speak profanely of sacred matters.
catharsis.	Purification.
chorēgos.	Leader of the dance.
daimon.	Spirit, deity.
Dioskouroi.	The sons of Zeus; i.e., Castor and Pollux.
dokēsis.	Appearance, opinion, phantom, reputation.
doxa.	Reputation, glory.
eidolon.	Ghost, phantom, image.
epistēmē.	Knowledge.
eros.	Desire.
etumos.	True.
hamartia.	Tragic flaw (as defined by Aristotle).
hubris.	Insolent pride, arrogance.
kallistos.	Most beautiful (masc. sing. adj.).
kalos.	Beautiful (masc. sing. adj.).
katēgoria.	Accusation.
khoros.	Dance, dance floor, chorus.
kleos.	Reputation, fame, glory.

kouros (korē, fem.).	Young shoot, youth.
kourotrophos.	Nurse of the young.
logos.	Word, story, argument.
mētis.	Cunning intelligence.
mythologia.	The telling of sacred stories.
nemesis.	Retribution.
noos (nous).	Mind, perception, plan, intention.
numpha.	Bride.
ololugai.	Loud cries, often made by women invoking a god.
onoma.	Name.
ouranos.	Sky.
paideia.	Education.
palinode.	Song resung, recantation.
paradeigma.	Pattern, model, precedent, paradigm.
peripeteia.	Reversal of situation, as in a tragedy.
pharmakon.	Medicine, drug.
pneuma.	Breath.
priamel.	A series leading to a climactic term.
puer aeternus.	Eternal boy.
sēma.	Sign.
sēmantōr.	Sign giver.
sōma.	Body.
sōtēres.	Saviors (masc. pl., used of the Dioskouroi).
ta onta.	What is; Being.
temenos.	Sacred precinct.
xeinos.	Stranger, guest, friend.

Bibliography

Abraham, Nicolas. 1987. "Notes on the Phantom: A Complement to Freud's Metapsychology." *Critical Inquiry* 13: 287–92.

Adkins, A. W. H. 1960. *Merit and Responsibility*. Oxford: Clarendon Press.

Alt, Karin, ed. 1964. Euripides, *Helena*. Leipzig: Teubner.

Anderson, W. S. 1958. "Calypso and Elysium." *Classical Journal* 54: 2–11.

Austin, Norman. 1966. "The Function of Digressions in the *Iliad*." *Greek, Roman and Byzantine Studies* 7: 295–312.

———. 1975. *Archery at the Dark of the Moon*. Berkeley and Los Angeles: University of California Press.

———. 1990. *Meaning and Being in Myth*. University Park and London: Pennsylvania State University Press.

Backès, Jean-Louis. 1984. *Le mythe d'Hélène*. Paris: Editions Adosa.

Bacon, Helen H. 1961. *Barbarians in Greek Tragedy*. New Haven: Yale University Press.

Barnard, Mary, trans. 1958. *Sappho: A New Translation*. Berkeley: University of California Press.

Barnstone, Willis. 1988. *Sappho and the Greek Lyric Poets*. New York: Schocken.

Bassi, Karen. 1993. "Helen and the Discourse of Denial in Stesichorus' Palinode." *Arethusa* 26: 51–75.

Beazley, John D. 1989. *Greek Vases: Lectures by J. D. Beazley*. Edited by D. C. Kurtz. Oxford: Clarendon Press.

Benardete, Seth. 1969. *Herodotean Inquiries*. The Hague: Martinus Nijhoff.

Bergren, Ann. 1979. "Helen's Web: Time and Tableau in the *Iliad*." *Helios* 7: 19–34.

——. 1981. "Helen's Good 'Drug,' *Odyssey* iv. 1–305." In *Contemporary Literary Hermeneutics and Interpretation of Classical Texts*, edited by Stephan Kresice. Ottawa: University of Ottawa Press.

——. 1983. "Language and the Female in Early Greek Thought." *Arethusa* 16: 69–95.

——. 1989. "The *Homeric Hymn to Aphrodite*: Tradition and Rhetoric, Praise and Blame." *Classical Antiquity* 8: 1–41.

Beye, Charles R. 1966. *The* Iliad, *the* Odyssey, *and the Epic Tradition*. Garden City, N. Y.: Anchor Books.

Boedeker, Deborah D. 1974. *Aphrodite's Entry into Greek Epic*. Leiden: E. J. Brill.

——. 1987. "The Two Faces of Demaratus." *Arethusa* 20: 185–201.

Bowra, C. M. 1934. "Stesichorus in the Peloponnese." *Classical Quarterly* 28: 115–19.

——. 1961. *Greek Lyric Poetry from Alcman to Simonides*. 2d ed. Oxford: Clarendon Press.

——. 1970. "The Two Palinodes of Stesichorus." In *On Greek Margins*, 87–98. Oxford: Clarendon Press.

Bundy, E. L. 1962. *Studia Pindarica*. University of California Publications in Classical Philology 18. Berkeley and Los Angeles: University of California Press (reissued as *Studia Pindarica* [Berkeley and Los Angeles: University of California Press, 1986]).

Burkert, Walter. 1965. "Demaratos, Astrabakos und Herakles." *Museum Helveticum* 22: 166–77.

——. 1985. *Greek Religion*. Translated by J. Raffan. Cambridge and London: Harvard University Press.

Burnett, Anne Pippin. 1960. "Euripides' *Helen*: A Comedy of Ideas." *Classical Philology* 55: 151–63.

——. 1971. *Catastrophe Survived: Euripides' Plays of Mixed Reversal*. Oxford: Clarendon Press.

——. 1983. *Three Archaic Poets: Archilochus, Alcaeus, Sappho*. Cambridge: Harvard University Press.

——. 1987. "The Scrutiny of Song: Pindar, Politics, and Poetry." *Critical Inquiry* 13: 434–49.

——. 1988. "Jocasta in the West: The Lille Stesichorus." *Classical Antiquity* 7: 107–54.

Cairns, Douglas L. 1993. *Aidōs: The Psychology and Ethics of Honour and Shame in Ancient Greek Literature*. Oxford: Clarendon Press.

Calame, Claude. 1977. *Les choeurs de jeune filles en Grèce archaïque*. 2 vols. Rome: Edizioni dell' Ateneo & Bizzari.

———. 1981. "Hélène: Son culte et l'initiation tribale féminine en Grèce." In *Dictionnaire des mythologies.* Paris: Flammarion.

Campbell, D. A., ed. and trans. 1988. *Anacreon.* Vol. 2. Loeb Classical Library. Cambridge: Harvard University Press.

Cingano, E. 1982. "Quante testimonianze sulle palinodie di Stesichoro?" *Quaderni Urbinati* 12: 21–33.

Clader, Linda Lee. 1976. *Helen: The Evolution from Divine to Heroic in Greek Epic Tradition.* Leiden: E. J. Brill.

Cook, A. B. 1925. *Zeus.* 3 vols. Cambridge: Cambridge University Press.

Dale, A. M., ed. 1967. Euripides, *Helen.*

Davies, Malcolm, ed. 1991. *Poetarum melicorum Graecorum fragmenta.* Vol. 1. Oxford: Clarendon Press.

DeJean, Joan. 1987. "Fictions of Sappho." *Critical Inquiry* 13: 787–805.

Detienne, Marcel, and J.-P. Vernant. 1978. *Cunning Intelligence in Greek Culture and Society.* Translated by J. Lloyd. Atlantic Highlands, N.J.: Humanities Press.

Dewald, Carolyn, and John Marincola. 1987. "A Selective Introduction to Herodotean Studies." *Arethusa* 20: 9–40.

Diels, Hermann. 1887. "Herodot und Hekataios." *Hermes* 22: 411–44.

Dimock, George E., Jr. 1977. *"God, or Not God, or Between the Two?"—Euripides'* Helen. (Northampton, Mass.: Smith College.

Dodds, E. R. 1951. *The Greeks and the Irrational.* Berkeley: University of California Press.

Doherty, Lilian. 1994. *Siren Songs: Gender, Audiences, and Narrators in the Odyssey.* Ann Arbor: University of Michigan. Forthcoming.

Donlan, Walter. 1982. "Reciprocities in Homer." *Classical World* 75: 137–75.

Dover, Sir Kenneth J. 1978. *Greek Homosexuality.* Cambridge: Harvard University Press.

———. 1984. "Classical Greek Attitudes to Sexual Behavior." In *Women in the Ancient World: The Arethusa Papers,* edited by J. Peradotto and J. P. Sullivan, 143–57. Albany, N. Y.: State University of New York.

duBois, Page. 1984. "Sappho and Helen." In *Women in the Ancient World: The Arethusa Papers,* edited by J. Peradotto and J. P. Sullivan, 95–105. Albany, N.Y.: State University of New York.

Edmonds, J. M. 1931. *Greek Elegy and Iambus.* Loeb Classical Library. Vol. 2. Cambridge: Harvard University Press.

Edwards, Anthony T. 1985. *Odysseus against Achilles.* Beiträge zur classischen Philologie, vol. 171, 15–41. Königstein/Ts: Hain.

Edwards, Mark W. 1980. "The Structure of Homeric Catalogues." *Transactions of the American Philological Association* 110: 81–105.

———. 1987. *Homer: Poet of the* Iliad. Baltimore and London: Johns Hopkins University Press.

Farnell, L. R. 1921. *Greek Hero Cults and Ideas of Immortality.* 5 vols. Oxford: Clarendon Press.

Fehling, Detlev. 1989. *Herodotus and His "Sources."* Translated by J. G. Howie. Leeds: Francis Cairns Publications (= *Die Quellenangaben bei Herodot* [Berlin and New York: W. de Gruyter, 1971]).

Foley, Helene P., ed. 1981. *Reflections of Women in Antiquity.* New York, London, and Paris: Gordon & Breach.

Ford, Andrew. 1992. *Homer: The Poetry of the Past.* Ithaca, N.Y.: Cornell University Press.

Fornara, C. W. 1971. *Herodotus: An Interpretive Essay.* Oxford: Clarendon Press.

Frazer, James G. 1935. *The Golden Bough: A Study in Comparative Religion.* 12 vols. 3d ed. London and New York: MacMillan.

Gentili, Bruno. 1988. *Poetry and Its Public in Ancient Greece.* Translated by A. T. Cole. Baltimore: Johns Hopkins University Press.

Ghali-Kahil, Lilly B. 1955. *Les enlèvements et le retour d'Hélène dans les textes et documents figurés.* 2 vols. Travaux et Mémoires, fasc. 10. Paris: Ecole Française d'Athènes.

Grenfell, B. P., and A. S. Hunt, eds. 1914. *Oxyrhynchus Papyri.* Vol. 10. London: Egypt Exploration Fund. (*P. Oxy.* 10)

Griffith, John G. 1953. "Some Thoughts on the 'Helena' of Euripides." *Journal of Hellenic Studies* 73: 36–41.

Grube, G. M. A. 1941. *The Drama of Euripides.* London: Methuen.

H. D. 1961. *Helen in Egypt.* New York: Grove Press.

Hallett, Judith P. 1979. "Sappho and Her Social Context." *Signs* 4: 447–64.

Hampe, Roland. 1951. "Paris oder Menelaus." *Museum Helveticum* 8: 144–46.

Hartog, François. 1988. *The Mirror of Herodotus: The Representation of the Other in the Writing of History.* Berkeley and Los Angeles: University of California Press.

Havelock, Eric. 1963. *Preface to Plato.* Oxford: Oxford University Press.

Hofmannsthal, Hugo von. 1928. "Die ägyptische Helena." In *Gesammelte Werke.* Vol. 4, *Prosa,* edited by H. Steiner. Frankfurt: S. Fischer, 1955.

How, W. W., and J. Wells. 1957. *A Commentary on Herodotus.* Oxford: Clarendon Press.

Immerwahr, Henry. 1966. *Form and Thought in Herodotus.* Philological Monographs 23. Cleveland: Western Reserve University.

Kannicht, R., ed. 1969. Euripides, *Helena.* 2 vols. Heidelberg: Winter.

Kennedy, George A. 1986. "Helen's Web Unraveled." *Arethusa* 19: 5–14.

Kirk, G. S., and J. E. Raven. 1957. *The Presocratic Philosophers.* Cambridge: Cambridge University Press. (KR)

Koniaris, G. 1967. "On Sappho, Fr. 16 (L.P.)." *Hermes* 95: 257–69.

Lacan, Jacques. 1978. *The Four Fundamental Concepts of Psychoanalysis.* Translated by A. Sheridan. New York: W. W. Norton.

Lattimore, Richmond, trans. 1959. Euripides, *Helen.* In vol. 3 of *The Complete Greek Tragedies, Euripides,* edited by David Grene and Richmond Lattimore. Chicago: University of Chicago Press (see the introduction to the *Helen,* pp. 483–86).

Lefkowitz, Mary. 1981. *The Lives of the Greek Poets.* London: Duckworth.

Levi-Strauss, Claude. 1975. *La voie des masques.* Geneva: Skira.

Liebermann, W. 1980. "Überlegungen zu Sapphos 'Höchstwert.'" *Antike und Abendland* 26: 51–74.

Lindsay, Jack. 1974. *Helen of Troy: Woman and Goddess.* London: Constable.

Lloyd, Alan B. 1988. *Herodotus Book II.* Vol. 3, *Commentary on 99–182.* Leiden: E. J. Brill.

Lobel, E., and Denys Page, eds. 1955. *Poetarum Lesbiorum fragmenta.* Oxford: Clarendon Press. (LP)

Long, A. A. 1970. "Morals and Values in Homer." *Journal of Hellenic Studies* 90: 121–39.

Loraux, Nicole. 1985. *Façons tragiques de tuer une femme.* Paris: Hachette.

———. 1986. *The Invention of Athens: The Funeral Oration in the Classical City.* Translated by A. Sheridan. Cambridge and London: Harvard University Press.

MacCary, W. Thomas. 1982. *Childlike Achilles.* New York: Columbia University Press.

Matthiessen, K. 1969. "Zur Theonoeszene der euripidischen Helena." *Hermes* 96: 685–704.

Merkelbach, R., and M. L. West, eds. 1967. *Fragmenta Hesiodea.* Oxford: Clarendon Press. (MW)

Morgan, Kathleen. 1991. "*Odyssey* 23.218–24: Adultery, Shame, and Marriage." *American Journal of Philology* 112: 1–3.

Mueller, Martin. 1984. *The Iliad.* London: George Allen and Unwin.

Mullen, William. 1982. *Choreia: Pindar and Dance.* Princeton: Princeton University Press.

Murnaghan, Sheila. 1987. *Disguise and Recognition in the Odyssey*. Princeton: Princeton University Press.

Nagy, Gregory. 1979. *The Best of the Achaeans*. Baltimore: Johns Hopkins University Press.

———. 1983. "On the Death of Sarpedon." In *Approaches to Homer*, edited by C. A. Rubino and C. W. Shelmerdine, 189–217. Austin: University of Texas Press.

———. 1990a. *Greek Mythology and Poetics*. Ithaca, N.Y.: Cornell University Press.

———. 1990b. *Pindar's Homer: The Lyric Possession of an Epic Past*. Baltimore and London: Johns Hopkins University Press.

———. 1993. "Alcaeus in Sacred Space." Forthcoming.

Neumann, Erich. 1963. *The Great Mother: An Analysis of the Archetype*. Translated by R. Manheim. 2d ed. Bollingen Series 47. Princeton: Princeton University Press.

Norwood, Gilbert. 1954. *Essays on Euripidean Drama*. Berkeley and Los Angeles: University of California Press.

Olson, S. Douglas. 1989. "The Stories of Helen and Menelaus (*Odyssey* 4.240–89) and the Return of Odysseus." *American Journal of Philology* 110: 387–94.

Ong, Walter. 1982. *Orality and Literacy: The Technologizing of the Word*. London and New York: Methuen.

Örtel, F. 1970. *Herodots ägyptischer Logos und die Glaubwürdigkeit Herodots*. Bonn: Habelt.

Page, Denys L. 1955. *Sappho and Alcaeus*. Oxford: Clarendon Press.

———. 1959. *History and the Homeric Iliad*. Berkeley and Los Angeles: University of California Press.

———, ed. 1962. *Poetae melici Graeci*. Oxford: Clarendon Press. (PMG)

———, ed. 1963. *Oxyrhynchus Papyri*. Vol. 29. London: Egypt Exploration Society. (*P Oxy. 29*)

Paglia, Camille. 1990. *Sexual Personae: Art and Decadence from Nefertiti to Emily Dickinson*. London and New Haven: Yale University Press.

Pavlock, Barbara. 1990. *Eros, Imitation, and the Epic Tradition*. Ithaca, N.Y.: Cornell University Press.

Pellegrino, Carlo, ed. 1975. Petronius, *Satyricon*. Rome: Edizioni dell' Ateneo.

Podlecki, A. J. 1971. "Stesichoreia." *Athenaeum* 49: 313–27.

Poulsen, Birte. 1991. "The Dioscuri and Ruler Ideology." *Symbolae Osloenses* 66: 119–46.

Powell, J. U. 1915. "Notes on Recent Discoveries." *Classical Quarterly* 9: 142–43.

Pucci, Pietro. 1987. *Odysseus Polutropos*. Ithaca, N.Y.: Cornell University Press.

Race, W. 1982. *The Classical Priamel from Homer to Boethius*. Mnemosyne Supplement 74. Leiden: E. J. Brill.

Raphals, Lisa. 1992. *Knowing Words: Wisdom and Cunning in the Classical Traditions of China and Greece*. Ithaca, N.Y.: Cornell University Press.

Redfield, James M. 1975. *Nature and Culture in the* Iliad: *The Tragedy of Hector*. Chicago: University of Chicago Press.

Rissman, Leah. 1983. *Love as War: Homeric Allusion in the Poetry of Sappho*. Königstein: Hain.

Roscher, W. H. 1884–90. *Ausführliches Lexicon der griechischen und römischen Mythologie*. 6 vols. Leipzig: Teubner.

Rubin, Gayle. 1975. "The Traffic in Women: Notes Toward a Political Economy of Sex." In *Toward an Anthropology of Women*, edited by Rayna Reiter, 157–210. New York: Monthly Review Press.

Sansone, David. 1985. "Theonoe and Theoclymenus." *Symbolae Osloenses* 60: 17–36.

Schein, Seth. 1984. *The Mortal Hero: An Introduction to Homer's* Iliad. Berkeley, Los Angeles, and London: University of California Press.

Schubart, Wilhelm. 1938. "Bemerkungen zu Sappho." *Hermes* 73: 297–306.

Sedgwick, Eve K. 1985. *Between Men: English Literature and Male Homosocial Desire*. New York: Columbia University Press.

Segal, Charles. 1971. "The Two Worlds of Euripides' *Helen*." *Transactions of the American Philological Association* 102: 553–614.

Segal, Robert A. 1991. "Adonis: A Greek Eternal Child." In *Myth and the Polis*, edited by Dora C. Pozzi and John M. Wickersham, 64–85. Ithaca, N.Y.: Cornell University Press.

Skutsch, Otto. 1987. "Helen, Her Name and Nature." *Journal of Hellenic Studies* 107: 188–93.

Slatkin, Laura. 1991. *The Power of Thetis: Allusion and Interpretation in the* Iliad. Berkeley, Los Angeles, and Oxford: University of California Press.

Solmsen, Friedrich. 1934. "*Onoma* and *pragma* in Euripides' *Helen*." *Classical Review* 48: 188–90.

Stanford, W. B., ed. 1965. Homer, *Odyssey*. 2 vols. 2d ed. London: Macmillan.

————. 1969. "The Lily Voice of the Cicadas (*Iliad* 3.152)." *Phoenix* 23: 3–8.

Stewart, Andrew. 1983. "Stesichorus and the François Vase." In *Ancient Greek Art and Iconography*, edited by W. G. Moon, 53–74. Madison, Wis.: University of Wisconsin Press.

Stigers, Eva S. 1979. "Romantic Sensuality, Poetic Sense: A Response to Hallett on Sappho." *Signs* 4: 465–71.

————. 1981. "Sappho's Private World." In *Reflections of Women in Antiquity*, edited by Helene Foley, 45–61. New York, London, and Paris: Gordon & Breach.

Suter, Ann. 1993. "Paris and Dionysos: *Iambos* in the *Iliad*." *Arethusa* 26: 1–18.

Suzuki, Mihoko. 1989. *Metamorphoses of Helen: Authority, Difference, and the Epic*. Ithaca, N.Y.: Cornell University Press.

Svenbro, Jesper. 1988. *Phrasikleia: Anthropologie de la lecture en Grèce ancienne*. Paris: Editions La Découverte.

Taplin, Oliver. 1992. *Homeric Soundings: The Shaping of the* Iliad. Oxford: Clarendon Press.

Theander, Carl. 1934. "Studia Sapphica." *Eranos* 32: 57–85.

Vandiver, Elizabeth. 1991. *Heroes in Herodotus: The Interaction of Myth and History*. Frankfurt, Bern, New York, and Paris: Peter Lang.

Van Groningen, B. A. 1953. *In the Grip of the Past*. Leiden: E. J. Brill.

Van Nortwick, Thomas. 1979. "Penelope and Nausicaa." *Transactions of the American Philological Association* 109: 269–76.

Verrall, A. W. 1895. *Euripides the Rationalist*. Cambridge: Cambridge University Press.

————. 1905. *Essays on Four Plays of Euripides:* Andromache, Helen, Heracles, Orestes. Cambridge: Cambridge University Press (see pp. 43–133, on the *Helen*).

Voigt, Eva-Maria, ed. 1971. *Sappho et Alcaeus: Fragmenta*. Amsterdam: Athenaeum.

Von Fritz, Kurt. 1967. *Die griechische Geschichtsschreibung*. Berlin: de Gruyter.

Walcott, Derek. 1990. *Omeros*. New York: Farrar, Straus, Giroux.

West, M. L. 1969. "Stesichorus Redivivus." *Zeitschrift für Papyrologie und Epigraphik* 4: 135–49.

————. 1970. "Burning Sappho." *Maia* 22: 307–30.

————. 1971a. *Iambi et elegi Graeci*. 2 vols. Oxford: Clarendon Press. (IEG)

————. 1971b. "Stesichorus." *Classical Quarterly* n.s. 21: 302–14.

————. 1985. *The Hesiodic Catalogue of Women*. Oxford: Clarendon Press.

Whitman, Cedric. 1958. *Homer and the Heroic Tradition*. Cambridge: Harvard University Press.

Wilamowitz-Moellendorff, Ulrich von. 1913. *Sappho und Simonides*. Berlin: Weidmann.

———. 1971. "Neue lesbische Lyrik." In *Kleine Schriften*, 1: 384–414. Berlin: Akademie-Verlag (= *Neue Jahrbücher für das klassische Altertum* 33 [1914] 225–47).

Winkler, John J. 1981. "Gardens of Nymphs: Public and Private in Sappho's Lyrics." In *Reflections of Women in Antiquity*, edited by Helene Foley, 63–89. New York, London, and Paris: Gordon & Breach.

———. 1990. *Constraints of Desire*. London: Routledge.

Wohl, Victoria Josselyn. 1993. "Standing by the Stathmos: Sexual Ideology in the *Odyssey*." *Arethusa* 26: 19–50.

Wolff, Christian. 1973. "On Euripides' *Helen*." *Harvard Studies in Classical Philology* 77: 61–84.

Woodbury, Leonard. 1967. "Helen and the Palinode." *Phoenix* 21: 157–76.

Zeitlin, Froma. 1981. "Travesties of Gender and Genre in Aristophanes' *Thesmophoriazusae*." In *Reflections of Women in Antiquity*, edited by Helene Foley, 169–217. New York, London, and Paris: Gordon & Breach.

Index

217

MYTH AND POETICS

A series edited by

GREGORY NAGY